Spirituality in the Flesh

Spirituality in the Flesh

Bodily Sources of Religious Experience

ROBERT C. FULLER

OXFORD

UNIVERSITY PRESS

2008

OXFORD
UNIVERSITY PRESS

Oxford University Press, Inc., publishes works that further
Oxford University's objective of excellence
in research, scholarship, and education.

Oxford   New York
Auckland   Cape Town   Dar es Salaam   Hong Kong   Karachi
Kuala Lumpur   Madrid   Melbourne   Mexico City   Nairobi
New Delhi   Shanghai   Taipei   Toronto

With offices in
Argentina   Austria   Brazil   Chile   Czech Republic   France   Greece
Guatemala   Hungary   Italy   Japan   Poland   Portugal   Singapore
South Korea   Switzerland   Thailand   Turkey   Ukraine   Vietnam

Published by Oxford University Press, Inc.
198 Madison Avenue, New York, New York 10016

www.oup.com

Oxford is a registered trademark of Oxford University Press

Library of Congress Cataloging-in-Publication Data
Fuller, Robert C., 1952–
Spirituality in the flesh : bodily sources of religious experience / Robert C. Fuller.
    p. cm.
Includes bibliographical references and index.
ISBN 978-0-19-536917-5
1. Body, Human—Religious aspects.   I. Title.
BL604.B64F85 2008
204'.2—dc22   2007044265

9 8 7 6 5 4 3 2 1
Printed in the United States of America
on acid-free paper

Acknowledgments

This book illustrates some very new approaches to the psychological study of religion. I had the good fortune of studying this field some thirty years ago at the University of Chicago under the able direction of Don Browning. At that time, the field revolved primarily around theories emanating from personality theory (e.g., Freud, Jung, Erikson, self psychology, object relations theory). Over the next two decades other scholarly projects prevented me from keeping abreast of new theoretical trends within academic psychology. Thus, when Don asked me to speak at a conference honoring his prodigious career as a scholar, I decided to emulate his professional energy by renewing my competence in psychological theory.

I am fortunate to have excellent colleagues in Bradley University's Department of Psychology. Derek Montgomery has patiently tutored me in the theoretical debates that currently animate both cognitive and developmental psychology. Dave Schmitt, meanwhile, has sparked considerable interest in recent work being done in such fields as evolutionary psychology, attachment theory, and cognitive science. I am most appreciative of their guidance.

Other colleagues have proven steady friends. Claire Etaugh, a developmental psychologist and my dean of many years, can be counted on for support and encouragement. Kevin Stein, Doug Crowe, Kevin Teeven, Chuck Stoner, Sam Fan, Craig Dahlquist, and Dave Pardieck come quickly to mind among those who have made Bradley University my academic family for the past three decades.

And not to be omitted is Bradley's assistant vice president for university relations, my wife, Kathy, who is for me a radiant example of "spirited living in the flesh."

A final acknowledgment of gratitude is reserved for Cynthia Read of Oxford University Press. Her intellect and editorial duties have combined to make her one of the most astute interpreters of religion in the world. To have her support and counsel—as I have for five books now—is a privilege indeed.

Contents

Spirituality in the Flesh

I

Introduction

The Body as Adaptive Agent

Few subjects are as puzzling as religion. All of us have a basic understanding of what religion is, yet no one has been able to define the word in a way that accounts for all of its various manifestations. Is religion principally about belief in gods, concern with the afterlife, or procuring visionary experiences? Consensus is hard to come by. After all, most of the features that seem to capture the essence of Western monotheistic religions are often entirely absent in Asian religions, such as early Buddhism or Chinese Daoism. Even more difficult than defining religion is the attempt to evaluate its overall value to human welfare. For example, does religion typically foster good will among humans, or does it inherently lead to pernicious violence? The academic study of religion emerged to address these types of questions. Yet the field of religious studies is still searching for critical terms that might illuminate distinctive elements of religion or stipulate criteria for evaluating religion's overall value for human well-being.

Most scholars who have undertaken the theoretical challenges posed by religion have backgrounds in the humanities. Literary theorists, philosophers, and historians have traditionally been at the forefront of efforts to achieve clearer understandings of religion. They have used their academic training to generate core concepts that can be used to interpret this complex phenomenon. Thus, for example, humanists have argued that we can best understand religion by organizing our inquiry around such core concepts as myth, sacred texts, belief, moral codes, or mysticism. Humanities-based studies of religion therefore typically focus on such issues as the literary genre to which sacred texts belong, the epistemological status of a creed, or the rhetorical strategies employed in descriptions of religious experience.

About a century ago, the social sciences emerged as exciting new academic disciplines. One of their first projects was to provide new, and ostensibly superior, explanations of human religiosity. Psychologists, sociologists, and even economists proposed new critical terms that grew out of empirical data lacking in traditional humanistic scholarship. They offered fresh insights into religion by explaining its connections with new critical categories such as the oedipal complex, archetypes of the unconscious, consumer choice theory, and protest strategies employed by marginalized people. All of these critical terms have illuminated important—and previously underappreciated—factors that explain why humans become religious and how religion functions in their lives.

Some of the most exciting inquiries into religion today, however, emanate from the natural sciences. Natural scientists have proposed entirely new sets of critical terms for understanding the origin and function of religion in human life. The highly regarded biologist Edward O. Wilson was at the forefront of this trend when, almost thirty years ago, he pronounced that "we have come to the crucial stage in the history of biology when religion itself is subject to the explanations of the natural sciences."[1] Wilson argues that religion—like all cultural phenomena—can be profitably explained by the principle of natural selection acting on the genetically evolving material structure of the human brain. Wilson notes that cultural anthropologists estimate that humans have produced as many as one hundred thousand different religions so far in our evolutionary history. Wilson reasons that although their mythological, doctrinal, and ritual content varies, these religions have performed very similar biological functions. All in some way confer genetic advantage on their adherents. That is, religions emerge and function in ways that enhance the welfare of the practitioners. According to Wilson, religion is "above all the process by which individuals are persuaded to subordinate their immediate self-interests to the interests of the group."[2]

Guiding Wilson's and most other biologists' interpretation of religion is the fact that humans are neither stronger nor faster than many of the species with whom they have competed throughout evolutionary history. Traits that foster group cooperation were consequently critical to humanity's biological survival. In considering how religion performs this important biological function, we might note that there is considerable debate among researchers as to whether religion should itself be considered an evolutionary adaptation or a by-product of more general adaptations that make cooperation possible. On balance, the latter appears to be the case. There are, after all, many ways other than religion to foster group loyalty or legitimate tribal morality. The important point is that natural selection favored brains and nervous systems that dispose us to subordinate self-interest to the interests of the group, and these biological dispositions are often dominant features of religiosity.[3]

Since Wilson first made these bold claims a number of natural scientists have proposed new core concepts for defining and assessing religion. Some evolutionary biologists, for example, point out that religion is implicated in what is called "the selfish gene"—genetically encoded strategies for ensuring the reproductive success of one's own kinship group. Other biologists have proposed the existence of a specific "god gene" that inclines us toward religious faith. They argue that religious belief has survival value since it provides humans with a sense of purpose and the courage to overcome hardship. Theories such as these draw upon a great deal of research in neurobiology. It seems that the human brain might very well be organized in such a way as to incline us toward belief in a higher power. Moreover, certain alterations in brain chemistry trigger the very mystical experiences that many believe are at the heart of most religious traditions. It also seems probable that certain emotions predispose us to various kinds of religious thought or feeling. Insofar as emotions are biologically based, they are yet another tool with which our genes shape us to think and behave in religious ways. In sum, the natural sciences are now proposing a host of very new critical terms, such as the "selfish gene," the "neurochemistry of religious experience," and the "motivational function of discrete emotions." These interpretive categories rest on impressive empirical data that bestow a heightened prestige on their descriptions and evaluations. They have, however, been largely ignored by those themselves not trained in the natural sciences—creating the impression that most scholars in the humanities have as yet failed to recognize how they help us understand human religiosity in the widest possible context.

The Body and Critical Theory

This book explores the exciting new perspectives that are now possible through truly interdisciplinary analyses of religion. It does so by developing critical terms or categories that are all in some fundamental way connected with the human body. That is, all of these concepts have something to do with our shared biological nature. All human thought and feeling—including religious thought and feeling—are grounded in biological processes. Religion thus has a biological substrate. To be sure, biology does not fully determine the role that religion has in our lives. But this should not prevent us from being curious about the many ways our biological nature does shape our religious propensities.

Each of the following chapters examines a different way that our biological natures prompt particular expressions of religiosity. The biological sciences will furnish the initial starting point for each of these explorations—thereby grounding these explorations in certain empirically based knowledge about our bodily tendencies. The fact that these explorations begin with biological concepts is not meant to suggest that the natural sciences are on any more solid epistemological ground than the social sciences or the humanities. Indeed, knowledge about the body is constructed in particular historical and cultural contexts. Modern sciences are laden with their own ontological and epistemological biases. This is, in fact, one of the reasons that most scientists who study religion overlook those aspects of spirituality that don't conform to their theoretical assumptions. Recognizing this fact is itself a first step toward interdisciplinary conversation and toward overcoming the kinds of reductionism so often found in scientific analyses of religion. We will avail ourselves of current biological knowledge about the body, but do so while realizing that all such knowledge is open to differences of opinion, critique, or reinterpretation. This is why any effort to understand the biological contexts of religious experience and belief must also draw upon history, cultural theory, and philosophy.

I am by no means the first to suggest that we interpret religion in terms that are fundamentally connected with the human body. Just a few years ago, the respected philosopher of religion Mark Taylor edited a volume exploring the most promising critical terms for understanding religion in the modern world. In the volume's second essay, William LaFleur proposes the "body" as a core concept for interpreting religion across academic disciplines. LaFleur notes that "research into psychedelics, the brain, and the chemical components of health and happiness has been impressive. . . . The leverage on our minds exerted by our DNA and what has been called the 'selfish' gene cannot be denied. Studies that reject or ignore such data now seem out-of-date."[4] LaFleur went so far as to suggest that twenty years ago mysticism would have been widely considered a core term in religious study and the body was given no attention whatsoever. LaFleur states that the situation now seems to be reversed. He didn't mean that mysticism is no longer a prime topic of religious investigation. His point was that we now ask new questions about mysticism and structure our investigations into mysticism around new critical terms. Among these terms are concepts drawn from the study of the body's biological functions—its genetic predispositions, its neurochemical processes, and its emotional programs.

My goal, then, is to explore some of the ways that our biological nature shapes human spirituality. In doing this, I hope to explicate what might be called "spirituality in the flesh." That is, I am exploring the intriguing thesis that many aspects of religion can be understood in terms of the body's efforts to reconstitute reality as part of its ongoing adaptation to the environment. The title has been chosen to acknowledge continuity with the basic thesis presented by George Lakoff and Mark Johnson in their *Philosophy in the Flesh*. Lakoff's and Johnson's intention was to draw attention to the embodied nature of all human thought. Their position was really not new, restating the essential position of Neo-Darwinism and the philosophical tradition of American pragmatism. What they succeeded in doing, however, was making a strong case in support of their view that all human thought is "shaped crucially by the peculiarities of our human bodies, by the remarkable details of the neural structure of our brains, and by the specifics of our everyday functioning in the world."[5] It follows that "what we understand the world to be like is determined by many things: our sensory organs, our ability to move and to manipulate objects, the detailed structure of our brain, our culture, and our interactions in the environment, at the very least."[6]

Drawing attention to the "leverage" that the body has on religious thought and experience by no means ignores the role of culture in constructing human experience. Indeed, Edward O. Wilson warns that biological explanations of human behavior can never be complete since, in humans, "genes have given away most of their sovereignty" to culture.[7] Human experience is never fully biological. There are philosophical, cultural, and historical determinants of all human experience—especially religious experience. Understanding spirituality in the flesh, then, is not about reducing human thought and experience to biology. It is, however, about mapping the anthropological roots of humanity's spiritual impulses. It seeks to explain religion from below (i.e., in terms of the biological properties of human beings) rather than from above (i.e., divine revelation). We have a great deal of new data that explicates some of the ways our bodies prompt us to adopt religious postures toward life. Studies that reject or ignore such data, as LaFleur suggests, now run the risk of seeming out of date.

My efforts to understand spirituality in the flesh will no doubt prove controversial. This is somewhat puzzling to me since we live in an age that has witnessed the mapping of the human genome. Every day I overhear conversations in which educated persons acknowledge the role that heredity plays in human life. Almost no one doubts that genetic factors play a crucial role in determining our likeliness of contracting certain diseases, our life expectancy, our sexuality, our predisposition to antisocial behavior, and so on. Yet scholars of religion—those in the humanities and even many in the social sciences—seem peculiarly uninterested in examining the biological forces that affect human spirituality. A principal reason for this is that most humanists (and many social scientists) today adhere to an outlook known as postmodernism. Postmodernists are skeptical of claims concerning the existence of either universal truths or universal characteristics of human nature. They instead embrace a position known as "constructivism." Constructivism holds that all truths and all claims about human nature are constructed by specific kinds of cultural discourse (and are thus culturally relative). Constructivism has had such a strong hold on academic inquiry in recent years that the study of religion has become outdated and insulated.

Religious studies scholars traditionally prided themselves in belonging to the most interdisciplinary of all academic disciplines. In truth, however, recent allegiance to constructivism has abetted disciplinary insularity to the point where few religious studies scholars even try to keep abreast of recent research in the natural and social sciences. It would appear that it is time to quit ignoring this new information and to, instead, begin building bridges that make interdisciplinary exchange possible. Such an approach promises to take us well beyond postmodernist discourse about how religions "construct" discourse about the body to an informed consideration of how the body influences the construction of religion.

There is a need for studies that overcome this isolationism and create meaningful connections between the humanities and sciences. It is a promising sign that many studies of religion over the past few decades have focused on the body or have sought to explicate the embodied nature of religion. Perhaps the best of these is Ariel Glucklich's study (which will be cited more fully in chapter 5) of the relationship between religion and bodily pain. He aptly notes that studying the relationship between bodily experience and religious thought takes us to a "fuzzy area where culture meets biology. This is the place where sensation becomes representation, and conversely consciousness is experienced somatically in the body."[8] The key to such inquiry, Glucklich points out, is to realize that "embodied experience . . . [is] a mix of biological facts and cultural consciousness."[9]

Unfortunately, however, few scholars in the humanities have as yet incorporated scientific interpretations of the "biological facts" of experience into their analyses of human experience. Most continue to view the body in wholly postmodern ways and thus see it as consisting of culturally constructed rather than biological factors. For example, most humanities scholars who study the body consider it to be a condensed site for the contestation of power or the engraving of ideology (e.g., the labeling and diagnosis of the female body by male medical authorities, or the characterization of the appearance, smell, or sensory faculties of African-American slaves by white slave owners). Studies of the relationship between the body and religion make scant use of biological facts and instead focus almost solely on cultural consciousness. It is thus easy to understand why Daniel Dennett has come to the conclusion that religious fundamentalism is not the most frustrating barrier to a truly academic understanding of religion; postmodernism is. In Dennett's experience, "anyone who tries to bring an evolutionary perspective to bear on any item of human culture, not just religion, can expect rebuffs ranging from howls of outrage to haughty dismissal from the literary, historical, and cultural experts in the humanities and social sciences."[10]

Selecting the body as a critical term for the study of religion shows how much is omitted by those who adhere to either strong versions of constructivism (or, for that matter, by those who adhere to strong versions of what might be called "biologism"). It is helpful to repeat Lakoff's and Johnson's observation that "what we understand the world to be like is determined by many things: our sensory organs, our ability to move and to manipulate objects, the detailed structure of our brain, our culture, and our interactions in the environment, at the very least."[11] Studies that ignore the full range of what we know about such matters of the flesh—cultural or biological—will increasingly risk having their analyses deemed irrelevant by their colleagues across the academy.

Humanity's Biological History

Human beings did not arrive on this planet in a historical or biological vacuum. We are the products of a grand evolutionary history that has spawned the vast web of life existing on earth today. This historical process has been marked by ceaseless change and transformation. New species come into existence. Some become extinct. Most modify over time. Biological existence is a dynamic process, creating and improvising as it goes along.

It was Charles Darwin who first educed the fundamental laws that have shaped this long historical process. As a young man, Darwin read the writings of the British economist Thomas Malthus. Malthus had developed the rather pessimistic thesis that because the human population was growing at an exponential rate, we would eventually outstrip available food supplies. He saw no way of avoiding widespread famine unless population growth was curbed by war, disease, or "moral restraint." Darwin was intrigued by Malthus's argument because he had observed that most populations of animals and plants are in fact fairly stable. It became obvious to him that in any species many more individuals are born than ultimately survive. He reasoned that the survivors must possess some characteristics that permit them to make use of the limited resources at their disposal, while other members of the species, lacking these same characteristics, simply die. Darwin further concluded that the survivors then pass on these survival-oriented characteristics to their offspring. In the meantime, those organisms that lack these characteristics will have fewer or even no offspring. If this process repeats itself for just a few generations, the entire species will gradually be transformed.

Darwin's genius was revealed in his uncannily precise explanation of how this competition between organisms drives the evolutionary process:

> Owing to this struggle, *variations*, however slight and from whatever cause proceeding, if they be in any degree profitable to the individuals of a species, in their infinitely complex relations to other organic beings and to their physical conditions of life, will tend to the preservation of such individuals, and will generally be inherited by the offspring. The offspring, also, will thus have a better chance of surviving, for, of the many individuals of any species which are periodically born, but a small number can survive. I have called this principle, by which each slight variation, if useful, is preserved, by the term *natural selection*, in order to mark its relation to man's power of selection.[12]

Darwin's contribution to biological science, then, was his delineation of the two principal factors that influence the change and development of living things: variation and natural selection. Unfortunately, Darwin lived a few decades too early to be able to understand just why and how variations occur. He knew that variations occur, but could only guess at "from whatever cause proceeding." It was the Austrian botanist Gregor Mendel who later pioneered the modern science that explains how variations arise in the genetic code that transmits life. The scientific study of genetics has completed the Darwinian revolution in our understanding of nature's ceaseless transformations. We now know that accidental alterations sometimes occur when a DNA sequence is being replicated. The most common type of alteration is called a "point mutation" that happens during replication when one or more nucleotides are substituted for others in the original sequence, or when one or more nucleotides are added or deleted from that original sequence. This spontaneous variation in the genetic code is commonly called a "mutation." Mutations occur wholly randomly. They are completely a matter of chance. It is also important to understand that mutations are essentially a disordering process and occur wholly irrespective of whether they are harmful or beneficial to the organism that inherits these altered genetic codes.

Some changes in the genetic code may be so slight that they neither impair nor improve the organism's ability to function within its environment. These changes will then be passed to subsequent generations and impart additional variety among members of that species. In many other instances, changes in the genetic code can lead to serious malformation of the organism inheriting the changed DNA and thus impair both its ability to function within its environment and its ability to produce offspring. These genetic mutations will then disappear with the individual organism in which they appeared. Occasionally, however, a newly risen mutation may alter the organism's development in such a way as to enhance its ability to adapt successfully to the environment. As Theodosius Dobzhansky and his coauthors point out, "The probability of such an event is greater when organisms colonize a new habitat, or when environmental changes present a population with new challenges. In these cases the adaptation of the population is less than optimal and there is greater opportunity for new mutations to be adaptive."[13] Natural selection is thus the process whereby originally random and accidental genetic changes are either "selected for" or "selected against" by the larger environment. Darwin wrote that "natural selection is daily and hourly scrutinizing, throughout the world, the slightest variations, rejecting those that are bad, preserving and adding up all that are good; silently and insensibly working, whenever and wherever opportunity offers, at the improvement of each organic being in relation to its organic and inorganic conditions of life."[14] Natural selection screens out genetic codes that impair an organism's ability to compete successfully for limited resources. Alternatively, natural selection favors genetic codes that promote the adaptation of a species to its environment. What is often called "Darwinian fitness" refers to an organism's ability to survive and even flourish by taking maximum advantage of the resources within its environment.

From the standpoint of natural selection, biological fitness is measured by a species' ability to survive and successfully generate offspring. Biological fitness is a quality that is specific to each species. Thus, for example, a cockroach is every bit as "fit" as a human in terms of adaptation to the environmental challenges it must surmount en route to successfully generating offspring. For this reason, some species have existed with the same genetic structure for over eighty million years. Natural selection, or the "survival of the fittest" as it is sometimes called, does not necessarily require continuing change in every species. What natural selection does require is that every species possess biological structures that ensure survival and procreation.

The "struggle for survival" needn't entail combative struggles in the sense of one species or individual doing battle with another (although it might include this). This struggle is instead about a species' ability to accomplish such things as making efficient use of available food, caring for its young, eliminating intragroup discord, and controlling the destructive consequences of unrestrained aggression. It follows that natural selection should be thought of not only in a negative way (i.e., eliminating inferior gene groups) but also in terms of its positive function of favoring genetic codes that enhance a species' ongoing adaptation to its environment. In this sense, natural selection might be considered creative. For even though mutations are themselves "blind" in the sense of being chance alterations with no foresight of their consequences, natural selection represents the cumulative trend of changes tending toward species' improved relations with the surrounding world.

It is important to highlight the fact that evolutionary change occurs in the genetic code existing within populations and not in the acquired behaviors exhibited by individuals. Characteristics and traits acquired during an organism's lifetime have no influence upon the genetic code that will be transmitted to offspring. As Dobzhansky and his coauthors have put it, "From the evolutionary point of view the individual is ephemeral; only populations persist over time. The continuity drives from the mechanism of biological heredity."[15] There is yet another important way of understanding the role of individual organisms in biological evolution. Individual organisms are ephemeral from a biological point of view. It is DNA that lasts over time. Edward O. Wilson put this in stark terms when he drew attention to the fact that "the organism is only DNA's way of making more DNA."[16] Our genetic codes construct individual organisms that are programmed to survive and to reproduce. Individual organisms are genetically encoded to perform very specific biological functions that are designed to perpetuate these genetic codes to the next generation.

Religion, as we shall see, emerged part and parcel with our evolutionary-adaptive heritage. Our neural structure evolved in ways that enable us to reconstitute reality in ways more likely to lead to our overall biological well-being. Religion is an effective variation of some of the mechanisms through which DNA has learned to make more DNA.

The Human Brain: Rendering the World Actable

The genetic variations that drive biological evolution occur in random, capricious ways. Thus, there is no overall goal or purpose to evolution per se. Natural selection does not in any way direct evolution toward any particular organism or toward any particular properties.[17] G. G. Simpson explains, "Evolution is not invariably accompanied by progress, nor does it really seem to be characterized by progress as an essential feature."[18] Yet even though there is no direction to evolution as a whole, each species has emerged through a succession of mutations that have enabled it to thrive in its own ecological niche. Only in this limited sense of focusing on just one particular species can we speak of evolutionary progress. Simpson writes, "To humans, evolutionary change in the direction of humans is progress, of this particular sort. It is not progress in a general or objective sense and does not warrant choice of the line of humanity's ancestry as the central line of evolution as a whole."[19] Biologist G. Ledyard Stebbins, for example, sees in the evolution of the human species a tendency toward increased complexity of organization.[20] Francisco Ayala puts this a bit differently when he argues that human evolution displays a general tendency toward enhanced abilities to gather and process information about the environment.[21] Both of these hypotheses concerning the direction of human evolution point to the gradual emergence of humanity's unprecedentedly large cerebral cortex that has made possible both increased complexity of organization and increased ability to process information about the environment.

Humanity's cerebral cortex permits greater flexibility in responding to the environment than can be discerned in any other species. To be sure, humans have inherited a massive array of genetically encoded behavioral tendencies. We have more, not less, emotions and instincts than other animals. Yet what is biologically unique to us is that our proportionately large cerebral cortex makes it possible to override instinctual responses to environmental stimuli and to substitute others instead. In short, we have some measure of cognitive control over our behavior. We can think hypothetically; we can envision two or more possible behavioral strategies and select among them that which seems most likely to serve our interests. To this extent, the human brain is "plastic" or malleable. Because our brains are not exclusively controlled by the information encoded in our genes, they require extrasomatic sources of information. Konrad Lorenz explains that humanity's "whole system of innate activities and reactions is phylogenetically so constructed, so 'calculated' by evolution, as to need to be complemented by cultural tradition."[22] Culture supplements our genetic codes in ways that make possible levels of complex organization and systems for gathering or processing information that far exceed their strictly biological foundations.

What makes human behavior so distinct from that of other species is what Edward O. Wilson describes as the fact that in humans, "genes have given away most of their sovereignty" to the patterning that culture provides the organism.[23] The significance of this fact can hardly be overstated. Culture adds a new dimension to the evolutionary process. Nothing in the previous history of life on this planet even remotely compares to human culture in terms of its rapid ability to invent new forms of life (mutations) and immediately test them for their capacity to enhance life (natural selection). Whereas acquired characteristics are irrelevant to biological evolution, "the new evolution peculiar to humans operates directly by the inheritance of acquired characters, of knowledge, and learned activities which arise in and are continuously a part of an organismic-environmental system, that of social organization."[24] This is, again, why any effort to interpret religion on a strictly biological basis is impossible. The continuum connecting genetic and environmental factors that influence human behavior is a particularly subtle one, making distinctions difficult to come by. But the subtlety of the topic needn't prevent us from being curious about the biological roots of our religious tendencies and pushing our investigation as far as possible.

From a biological point of view, the human brain coordinates the central nervous system and thereby controls our continuing interactions with the surrounding world. MIT psychologist Steven Pinker summarizes this view by explaining that the mind is "a naturally selected computer." Genes build the brain to ensure their own survival. This evolutionary perspective thus provides what might be called a functional view of the human brain. That is, it focuses on what the mind does rather than on what it is (the typical interest of philosophy). Pinker explains, "The mind is what the brain does . . . the mind is organized into modules . . . their operation was shaped by natural selection to solve the problem of the hunting and gathering lives led by our ancestors."[25] This functionalist approach to the human brain has been a persisting tradition in American psychology.[26] The goal of functionalism is to understand the mind in its full evolutionary and biological context. Natural selection gradually shaped brains that coordinate adaptive behavior. Most of this activity is unconscious in the sense that is performed without an individual's awareness. For this reason George Lakoff and Mark Johnson refer to most of the brain's adaptive functions as "the cognitive unconscious."[27] We breathe, digest food, fight off infections, and execute habitual behaviors with no deliberate mental effort. Every act of perception involves selective attention, the labeling of sensory data, and cognitive categorization that all occur without conscious awareness. Every human possesses a host of cognitive structures that automatically and unconsciously enrich conception by shaping sensory stimuli into patterns that make inference and expectation possible. We typically don't become conscious of such mental activities unless we encounter situations that are sufficiently novel or complex that neither instinct nor acquired habit is able to guide us automatically toward the correct adaptive behavior. It is in these situations that we become aware of our brain's role in both constructing and selecting between hypothetical strategies. Yet whether conscious or unconscious, the biological purpose of mental activity is to guide behavior in ways that maximally adapt us to our surroundings.

William James suggested that the functionalist understanding of the human brain is most easily grasped in terms of the metaphor of a "reflex arc." By this James meant that we might conceptualize our brains in terms of three interacting structures: sensation, reflection, and action. It should be noted, however, that functionalists such as William James and John Dewey were seeking to overcome the dualistic tendencies of Western thought that traditionally make ontological distinctions between self and world, thought and action, soul and body. Their use of the notion of a reflex arc was intended to explain three modes of function within a single, seamless process rather than three distinct entities.[28] With this in mind, we can appreciate the clarity of James's explanation:

> The structural unit of the nervous system is in fact a triad, neither of whose elements has any independent existence. The sensory impression exists only for the sake of awaking the central process of reflection, and the central process of reflection exists only for the sake of calling forth the final act. All action is thus re-action upon the outer world; and the middle stage of consideration or contemplation or thinking is only a place of transit, the bottom of a loop, both whose ends have their point of application in the outer world.[29]

The mind, then, is the "middle loop" that coordinates the acting organism's attempts to gather information, process this information, and act in a strategic way. From an evolutionary-adaptive perspective, all mental operations are ultimately in the service of this quest to survive and reproduce. We should be careful, however, not to misinterpret the mind's middle loop as merely reactive. The human brain is not just an organ that passively reacts to sensory information. We are beings that not only seek survival but seek to increase or enhance the range of our subjective satisfactions. The purpose of all activities in the middle loop of the brain is to make the world actable, but actable for more than just physical survival. James pointed out that we shape and reconstitute images of the world in order to satisfy a wide range of peculiarly human interests. We reconstitute the world in ways that are likely to satisfy what James called "the social affections, all the various forms of play, the thrilling intimations of art, the delights of philosophic contemplation, the rest of religious emotion, the joy of moral self-approbation, [and] the charm of fancy and wit."[30] The human brain is thus not a passive organ. It actively seeks out and configures images of the world in such a way as to make likely the satisfaction of a very wide range of objective and subjective interests. Religion is, as we shall see, an important ingredient of this middle loop in the brain. Humans frequently reconstitute images of the world in religious ways, hoping to thereby make the world more actable and more amenable to human interests.

We are now in a position to understand what Lakoff and Johnson meant when they proposed that "evolution has provided us with adapted bodies and brains that allow us to accommodate to, and even transform, our surroundings."[31] Our brains continuously create and re-create images of the world that seem capable of guiding our actions. These images of the world often have religious qualities or characteristics. As we interpret and structure experience in the middle loop of our brain's activity, we frequently constitute the world in religious ways as a strategy for satisfying a wide variety of objective and subjective interests. A truly interdisciplinary spirituality in the flesh must therefore understand the widest context in which all human thought and feeling occur. This will require, among other things, that we pay attention to just how religion originates and functions within this middle loop of human experience.

Brain-Born Religion

Religion arises and functions in bodies that evolution has shaped in ways that enable us to accommodate to, and even transform, our surroundings. An important step toward understanding how the adapted features of our brains create religious ideas has recently been taken in the field of cognitive science.[32] The basic premise of cognitive science is that our brains consist of a complex array of innate cognitive processes (often referred to as "mental modules"). Each mental module is designed to solve the kinds of adaptive problems faced by our evolutionary ancestors. Human cognition is thus shaped by biologically grounded processes designed to resolve such recurring problems as detecting causal agents, identifying food sources, selecting mates, forming alliances, or discerning kinship.

Perhaps the most critical problem that our brains have been designed to solve is that of detecting agents in the immediate environment. Quickly identifying agents is crucial to survival. Natural selection therefore favored brains containing intricate mechanisms for detecting causal forces or agents in the environment. It also seems that our brains are wired to imbue suspected causal agents with sentience and intentionality. We assume agents are alive and operate according to conscious motives. From the standpoint of biological fitness, it is far better for organisms to identify intentional agents operating in their environment, even when in fact there are none, than to risk ignoring potential danger or opportunity. As Scott Atran explains, "Cognitive schema for recognizing and interpreting animate agents may be a crucial part of our evolutionary heritage, which primes us to anticipate intention in the unseen causes of uncertain situations that carry the risk of danger or the promise of opportunity, such as predators, protectors, and prey."[33]

These insights into human cognition go a long way in explaining belief in the existence of gods or similar supernatural beings as a nearly universal human trait. We are hardwired to anticipate intention in the unseen causes of uncertain situations. In ambiguous situations that lack obvious physical agents, our brains spontaneously construct hypothetical, imaginative candidates (particularly those candidates already believed in by others). In Atran's view, humans are "cognitively susceptible to invoke supernatural agents whenever emotionally eruptive events arise... with no apparent CONTROLLING FORCE."[34] Once constructed, religious ideas have cognitive properties that make them especially appealing. After all, religious ideas are created by the same mental modules that generate other kinds of human thought. They alleviate anxiety by making us believe we now understand and can to some extent even control our surroundings. And, unlike other kinds of conceptions about situations that carry the risk of danger or the promise of opportunity, religious ideas are almost impossible to disconfirm in the light of ongoing experience. And, importantly, religious ideas are sufficiently novel to capture the imagination in ways that facilitate communication and retention. Thus, of all types of ideas, religious ideas are uniquely prone to endure, be transmitted, and be remembered.

Our innate cognitive tendency to identify animate agents plays a significant role in the formation of the kinds of imaginative beliefs we find in fantasy, folklore, and religion. The capacity to detect agency is itself adaptive and advantageous. Natural selection favored brains with this capacity to ensure physical survival. In all likelihood, however, the construction of imaginative beliefs such as those found in religion would appear to be a by-product or biologically unintended consequence of this capacity. The mental modules for detecting agency and discerning will or intentionality make imaginative beliefs possible, but this was not the biological function these modules were designed to perform. It follows that even though religion often serves important functions, it can not itself be considered an evolutionary adaptation. Todd Tremlin summarizes this point by explaining that "religious thought is a by-product of similar, seemingly more 'natural' forms of thinking. The cognitivist approach to religion is not that humans evolved to think religiously or that religious thought is somehow adaptive, but that religious thought rests on normal mental structures and processes designed for different though functionally related purposes."[35]

Religious thoughts and ideas thus enter the middle loop of human experience the same way all ideas enter. They are imaginative or hypothetical constructs built from our innate mental capacities to make inferences, detect causal agency, discern intentions, and derive practical solutions to everyday problems. Cognitive scientists argue that what distinguishes an idea as religious is belief in some form of "superhuman agency" that violates our ordinary expectations about how things work in the real world. Religion, then, is a very specific variation of our natural and ordinary capacity for agency detection. From the perspective of cognitive science, religion is unique from other mental functions in that it revolves around conceptions of superhuman (rather than human or worldly) entities and agency. Most cognitive scientists go so far as to suggest that belief in superhuman agents is the only substantive universal found in all religious ideas—thereby providing a formal criterion for distinguishing between religious and nonreligious thoughts.[36]

Cognitive science is surely on the right track in its attempt to understand religion in terms of the cognitive processes that underlie all forms of human cognition—religious or otherwise. It is also on the right track in appreciating the need to distinguish between religious and nonreligious forms of embodied experience. Yet much more needs to be known. Most researchers in the field of cognitive science have linked religious thought with only a handful of mental modules (e.g., agency detection and the attribution of sentience or intentionality) that orient humans to the surrounding world. The result is that cognitive science defines religion almost exclusively in terms of god-ideas. While this helps us understand the cognitive structures that make religious belief possible, it tells us very little about what motivates us to deem religious ideas as either relevant or practical.[37] One objective of this book, therefore, is to demonstrate that there are other bodily processes that stimulate humanity to construct experience in distinctively religious ways. Altered neurochemistry, sexuality, pain, and the so-called social emotions are additional examples of brain-born activities that motivate humans to create, modify, commit to, or reject religious constructions of experience. Paying attention to this wider range of brain-born activities will hopefully supplement what cognitive science has learned about how humans are able to create religious conceptions. A broader spirituality in the flesh can help us understand not just how, but also why, we continually revise these conceptions in ways dictated by their pragmatic consequences and by their congruence with socially generated belief systems.

As mentioned earlier, the ability to construct the world in religious ways is probably not an evolutionary adaptation per se. The many bodily capacities that help us solve adaptive problems can operate effectively without assuming any specifically religious form. To this extent, religion needs to be understood as an unintended by-product of the adaptive modules that were selected by evolution, owing to their ability to meet pressing issues of biological survival. Yet, it turns out, brain-born ideas that take a religious form are especially suited to a variety of human needs and interests that are part of the (biologically evolved) human condition. The ability of religious thought to meet these needs and interests (e.g., interest in novelty, the social affections, playfulness, aesthetic delight, theodicy, security, attachment, etc.) explains why individuals continue to invent such ideas, why cultures select them, and why these ideas survive through historical change. There may, in fact, be certain needs, interests, and motivations that can only be met in religious ways.[38] Once we move beyond *how* humans are able to think religiously and also consider *why* they are continuously motivated to do so, it becomes clear that religion performs powerful biological functions. Even though personal spirituality has no evolutionary function in and of itself, it persists in human history owing to its striking ability to satisfy a wide range of motivations that are critical to humanity's sense of fulfillment and well-being.

Studying the biological sources of religion requires at least a preliminary definition of religion. Our assumption is that human beings are inherently motivated to generate brain-born constructions of experience that will satisfy bodily needs and resolve adaptive problems. It is thus imperative that we have at least some general way to distinguish between a religious and nonreligious construction of experience. This is one of the major advantages of cognitive theories of religion. By showing how religious thought is produced by innate mental modules designed for agency detection and for attribution of sentience/intentionality, cognitive science has focused on "supernatural agency" as the distinctive feature of human thought. This study of spirituality in the flesh, however, is interested in the role of many other bodily activities that also influence the middle loop of experience. It is important, therefore, that we slightly expand the definition of religion to include any brain-born construction of a "more-than-worldly" aspect of experience (regardless of whether belief in person-like agents are entailed in this brain-born construction). This is what William James intended when he suggested that religion is distinguished by the belief that there is a "more" to experience than can be constructed on the basis of information from the physical senses alone. In its adaptive pursuits, the body is sometimes motivated to construct the world in religious ways. According to James, a religious construction of experience is distinct from nonreligious constructions insofar as it includes belief (1) that the visible world is part of a more spiritual universe from which it draws its chief significance and (2) that union or harmonious relation with that higher universe is our true end.[39] For James, religious thought arises in the middle-loop of brain activity as the body seeks to accommodate to, and even transform, its surroundings. Bodily processes (e.g., emotions, pain, sexuality) exert leverage on how images of the world are continually reconstituted in the hope of thereby rendering the world more actable and more amenable to human interests. A religious construction of experience differs from a nonreligious construction in that it acknowledges (even if only hypothetically) the existence of something more than is envisioned in a purely materialistic conception of the world and that this "more" bears a causal relationship to our ongoing pursuit of bodily well-being. James points out that it is this "more" that gives a religious conception of the world "*a natural constitution* different at some point from that which a materialistic world would have. It must be such that different events can be expected in it, different conduct must be required."[40] Spirituality, in turn, might be understood as the "different conduct" required to achieve the kind of harmonious relation with this "more" that will bring a sense of fulfillment or well-being. There are, as we shall see, a variety of ways that such spirituality arises from the flesh. Altered brain chemistry, pain, sexuality, and various discrete emotions are among the many bodily sources of humanity's spiritual quests.

Spirituality in the Flesh: An Agenda

There is no single way to interpret spirituality in a broadly biological context. Nor is there only one philosophical platform from which we might view the scope and significance of such interpretive efforts. Indeed, many scholars in the humanities today advocate what might be called a "strong version" of constructivism (i.e., the view that all human thought and knowledge is constructed through specific social and cultural activities). Strong versions of constructivism assert that human nature is shaped by social—not biological—contexts. Strong constructivist positions deny the existence of universal or biologically based characteristics that comprise "human nature." Moreover, this position is highly suspicious of all knowledge claims (especially those of modern science) since it believes that all human thought is radically determined by historical and social forces. Scholars who hold strong versions of constructivism tend to be the least interdisciplinary members of the academic community. Not only are constructivists the least interested in mutually informing discussions with other academic disciplines, they are also quick to insist upon the misguided nature of every form of academic inquiry save their own. Clearly the chapters that follow are least likely to be amenable to this philosophical outlook.

Exploring spirituality in the flesh is, however, of great potential interest to those persons who adhere to either weak or moderate versions of constructivism. Volney Gay has observed that "adherents of the weak version of constructivism tend to be moderate supporters of evolutionary psychology. They hold that cultures [direct and restrain genetic predispositions], but these are secondary restraints on an underlying and unvarying biochemical reality."[41] Emile Durkheim, Max Weber, Sigmund Freud, Claude Levi-Strauss, and Talcott Parsons would all be examples of scholars who held that humans share certain biological commonalities but that cultures nonetheless regulate both the manner and degree to which these biological tendencies are expressed. Adherents of the moderate version of constructivism are less likely to draw on biology than adherents of the weak version, but still recognize some biological sources of human nature. Leaning closer to constructivism, they suggest that "we are more than our genes, more than our inherited constraints; there is something sui generis and potentially free within human capacities."[42] This position goes so far as to argue for the social creation of many phenomena (e.g., emotions) that are often considered biologically based. Moderate constructivism is held by a significant minority of social scientists and has proved helpful in generating interdisciplinary exchange and more nuanced understandings of the human condition. This book leans toward the weak version of constructivism (and hence toward a "moderate biologism"). I reject both strong versions of constructivism and strong versions of biologism. I therefore intend to emphasize the biochemical determinants of human thought and behavior while acknowledging that thought and behavior are subsequently reconfigured by cultural factors. It is important to note, however, that all the following explorations could just as easily be reworked from alternative philosophical platforms.

There are, then, any number of possible lines of inquiry we might pursue in an effort to place human spirituality in the context of the flesh. We might begin, for example, by looking at the role that emotions have in shaping our religious sensibilities. The modern study of emotions is itself a disparate field with many separate schools of thought. Yet there is an emerging consensus in the natural and social sciences that emotions constitute the primary motivational system in human beings. There is, furthermore, consensus that we should move beyond thinking about emotion as a general category and instead identify the motivational functions of separate or discrete emotions.

Recent scholarship on the leverage that discrete emotions exert on such mental operations as attention, apperception, memory, and goal selection has tremendous implications for understanding how certain religious sensibilities shape our stance toward life. A great deal is now known about the motivational effect of several discrete emotions, including the emotion of fear. Fear tends to produce tunnel vision by focusing attention on the source of the threat and restricting cue utilization. Such keen attention to the threatening agent or situation can be adaptive in guiding self-protective behavior. Yet fear becomes maladaptive when it channels attention so narrowly that the organism remains in a perpetual state of defensive anxiety. I hope to show the value of such recent research on the emotions by bringing it to bear upon the interpretation of certain facets of one particular religious phenomenon: North American Protestant apocalypticism. Appreciation of the biological context in which fear motivates human perception and cognition helps explain why North American Protestant apocalypticism is so frequently characterized by tribalism, boundary posturing, and excessive concern for demonizing enemies real or imagined.

A very different emotion, the emotion of wonder, helps us see other possibilities for understanding the role of emotions in shaping different kinds of religious sensibilities. Wonder arises in response to the perception of something novel or unexpected, particularly perceptions of exceptionally vivid instances of beauty or vitality. Recent research in such diverse disciplines as evolutionary psychology, developmental psychology, philosophy, and cultural history show how wonder directs attention away from particular entities in the immediate environment and toward ever-more-general categories of causation (i.e., it predisposes persons to consider more-than-physical notions of causal agency). And, too, wonder can be considered a "social emotion" insofar as it lures people beyond their narrow pursuit of self-interest and enables them to see others as part of their own circle of concern. The discrete emotion of wonder can be shown to be responsible for shaping very distinct kinds of personal spirituality. The specific motivational functions of wonder illuminate the distinctive features of the "nature spirituality" advocated by such seminal American writers as John Muir and Rachel Carson.

Evolution has produced adapted bodies and adapted brains through which we experience the world. The neural structure of our brains ensures efficient adaptation to our physical and social environments. These same neural structures also regulate the chemical components of health and happiness. Dean Hamer, Andrew Newburg, Eugene d'Aquili, and others have conducted extensive research into the "chemistry of consciousness" and believe they have found solid evidence indicating that some aspects of our propensity toward religion are hardwired in our neurochemistry. We know, furthermore, that consciousness is affected in powerful ways by even simple changes in the brain's chemistry—not the least of which are changes that induce mystical states of awareness. Any study of the history of "alternative spirituality" throughout American history must acknowledge the pivotal role of chemically altered states of consciousness. We can, therefore, extend our agenda concerning the biological context of religion to include a closer look at the leverage that altered neurochemistry has played in the innovative spirituality found in such disparate episodes of American religious history as Native American peyotism and the 1960s counterculture's religious experimentalism.

From the bird's-eye view of biological evolution, individual human beings are just DNA's way of making more DNA. It is possible, therefore, to study religion as a technique that human organisms use to propagate their genes. Religion, after all, frequently functions in ways that serve territorial and tribal interests. Many biologically based studies of religion have emphasized the role that religion plays in building group loyalty and heightening distinctions between in-group and out-group membership. In this way, religion helps minimize intragroup discord while sanctioning aggression toward outsiders. There is, however, another facet of our genetic makeup that has been less seriously studied in regard to religion: our sexuality. Sexual drive, though biologically based, expresses itself in many cultural forms. Religion is surely one of them. And although many scholars discuss the cultural connections between religion and gender, few examine the biological expressions of sexuality in religion. The value of such an approach to various forms of religious expression can be explored by examining two enduring strains of American piety: (1) the sexually charged conversion experiences often occurring in evangelical Protestantism, and (2) the hundred-year heritage of tantric-like sexual practices in American alternative religion.

Yet another theoretical agenda generated by a broadly biological approach to religion stems from the fact that the body and its afflictions register cultural dysfunction. More specifically, our bodily ailments are often the source of radical efforts toward cultural and theological reconstruction. For this reason, throughout American history there has been a thin line separating alternative medicine and alternative religion. A close examination of specific kinds of bodily affliction and the theological metaphors used to assuage opens up yet another perspective from which we can view the biological foundations of innovative attempts to reconstruct reality in religious ways (e.g., Christian Science, New Age healing systems, Seventh-Day Adventism).

Metaphor structures a great deal of human thought and knowledge. Most metaphors originate in the patterns of our bodily movement, the contours of our spatial and temporal orientation, and our efforts to manipulate objects in our immediate environment. It is not surprising, then, that "embodied categories of thought" influence both why and how we think about religious topics (e.g., the body of Christ, being touched by Jesus, opening our hearts to God, the lifting of burdens, sins of the flesh, finding balance, aligning our astral and physical bodies, etc). Examining how bodily metaphors influence religious thinking invites us to consider a final theoretical agenda: a move from examining spirituality *in* the flesh to celebrating a spirituality *of* the flesh. It is certainly possible to view our flesh as itself sacred. In this view, the normal distinctions between description and norm no longer hold. Indeed, it is quite possible that empirical descriptions of how the body *does* seek to reconstitute reality in religious ways might furnish new approaches to understanding how we *should* think about the sacred character of our worldly embodiment.

The chapters that follow are intended to be suggestive, not exhaustive. My principal thesis is that the body itself provides several critical terms or categories that can guide us toward truly interdisciplinary understandings of religion. I am content with identifying a few of these terms and categories and showing how they might be used to understand various themes in American religious life. I have certainly not tried to contribute new substantive information about these themes or episodes in American religion (although in many cases, I have done so in previous publications). My goal is to sketch out a distinctive approach to both historiography and interpretive method in the field of religious studies. I selected these historical themes and episodes for their illustrative value only. As a long-time scholar of American religion, I thought it wise to select examples from ranges of material I know well. And while my review of these themes and episodes is not intended to contribute new substantive information, it is meant to demonstrate how a broadly biological account of the body generates critical terms and categories that provide important insight into how and why humans reconstitute their world in religious ways. The success of this project is to be measured by whether it convinces readers that a "spirituality in the flesh" is at least one viable path to an interdisciplinary understanding of religion.

2

Religion and Natural Selection

Fear, Anger, and Religious Territorialism

Our biological ancestors faced any number of challenges. These challenges came in a variety of forms. Some were largely biochemical in nature: organisms must efficiently metabolize food and fight off infections or parasites. Other survival problems have to do with self-defense and self-preservation: organisms must make appropriate responses to predators and prey. Still other survival problems are more properly social in nature: organisms must make appropriate responses to caregivers and must behave in ways that minimize intragroup discord and maximize group harmony.

Persistent environmental challenges have the long-term effect of favoring organisms whose genetic codes ensure proper adaptive behavior. Evolutionary theorists refer to such persistent environmental challenges as "evolutionarily recurrent situations," by which they mean "a cluster of repeated probabilistic relationships among events, conditions, actions, and choice consequences that endured over a sufficient stretch of evolutionary time to have had selective consequences on the design of the mind."[1] Thus, owing to natural selection, persistent environmental challenges have had a great deal to do with how our brain and nervous system operate.

Two very different features of our genetic makeup illustrate how natural selection designed us to meet persistent environmental challenges: our predisposition to territorialism and our emotional systems. Both territorialism and certain emotional systems motivate humans in ways that promote biological survival. And, importantly, both are recurring sources of certain kinds of religious thoughts and ideas. The historical record indicates that specific kinds of religiosity elicit loyalty and endure over time precisely owing to the efficiency with which they symbolize, channel, and even evoke these powerful bodily forces.

From Territorialism to Tribalism

Hunting, gathering, mating, raising young, and forming social units all occur in physical space. Survival depends on continued access to the various resources contained within certain kinds of physical boundaries. It is thus not surprising that most animals, including almost all vertebrates, have inherited DNA that regulates their behavior in relation to physical space. Foremost among these genetic tendencies is territoriality—the predisposition to identify and defend a very specific territory. The biological meaning of a territory is "an area occupied more or less exclusively by an animal or group of animals by means of repulsion through overt defense or advertisement."[2] Territoriality has taken different forms along different evolutionary lines. Some species defend their territory through aggressive behaviors, such as when dragonflies attack intruders by darting at them. Other species use vocal signaling to advertise the boundaries of their territory to potential intruders, while still others use odors by depositing a demarcating line of urine or some other scent. Thus, the techniques of repulsing would-be predators "can be as explicit as a precipitous all-out attack or as subtle as the deposit of a chemical secretion at a scent post."[3]

Territoriality functions to ensure adequate spacing between individuals and groups. In humans, however, this space is not simply physical. Humans also bond together in groups whose boundaries are often defined in cultural rather than geographical ways. Villages, tribes, clans, kinship groups, clubs, and political organizations are all examples of groups with well-defined cultural boundaries. Humans advertise and defend these cultural boundaries in ways that bear striking resemblance to the aggressive characteristics observed in dragonflies or wolves. Humanity's genetic makeup is, however, in some respects inadequate for the complex relationships that civilization requires. As a consequence, our biology interacts with culture to produce a variant of territorialism that biologist Garrett Hardin defines as "tribalism":

> Any group of people that perceives itself as a distinct group and
> which is so perceived by the outside world, may be called a tribe. The
> group might be a race, as ordinarily defined, but it need not be; it

can just as well be a religious sect, a political group, or an occupa-
tional group. The essential characteristic of a tribe is that it should
follow a double standard of morality—one kind of behavior for in-
group relations, another for out-group.[4]

Territoriality and tribalism are hardwired into humanity's genes. We have
evolved as cultural beings, and many cultures have proven successful at
"overriding" these genetic programs and channeling human behavior toward
peaceful coexistence. But it would be foolish to overlook the fact that certain
identifiable propensities for behavior are in the wiring. Our cultural mode of
existence remains tethered to our biological natures. Lionel Tiger and Robin
Fox have cautioned that our cerebral cortex struggles with a heritage it did not
ask for. Even though we find ourselves functioning in a highly sophisticated
civilization, we have the same basic wiring favored by natural selection early
in our evolutionary history. "We have to make the imaginative and unset-
tling leap into understanding that agricultural and industrial civilizations have
put nothing into the basic wiring of the human animal. We are wired for
hunting—for the emotions, the excitements, the curiosities, the regularities,
the fears, and the social relationships that were needed to survive in the
hunting way of life."[5]

One final implication of humanity's tribalistic tendencies deserves attention. Natural selection favored the survival of humans who can live effectively
in social groups. Michael Ruse observes that "we are not particularly mobile
nor particularly agile. We are neither too large to threaten nor too small to be
overlooked. Thus, we need each other to survive and reproduce, and others
need us."[6] Our large cerebral cortex and our cultural mode of exist co-evolved.
As Konrad Lorenz further explains, the whole structure of our brain and
nervous system "has been so constructed, so calculated by evolution, as to need
to be complemented by cultural tradition."[7]

But if cultural traditions are to succeed in patterning human behavior,
they must first successfully establish tendencies toward loyalty and conformity.
Human survival—both now and throughout our evolutionary history—has
required such loyalty to cultural tradition. We should therefore be alert to the
biological foundations of the cultural mechanisms through which individuals
are induced to surrender their personal interests for the welfare of their group
or tribe. Although natural selection did not shape our brains to be religious
per se, it did shape our brains in ways that predispose us toward cooperation,
loyalty, and conformity. Religion surely springs from these deep biological
tendencies.

Emotions and Adaptation: The Motivational Function of Fear

Among the most prominent biological systems shaped by natural selection are our emotions. Seen from an evolutionary-adaptive perspective, emotions are part of a circular feedback system that connects persons with their environment.[8] We continually scan our environments (often unconsciously) in order to identify potential harms or potential benefits. Certain kinds of sensory information trigger emotional programs whose purpose is to mobilize the organism for an appropriate response. This is particularly the case when we encounter unexpected or uncertain sensory information that can't easily be understood on the basis of our previous experiences.

One of the foremost authorities on emotion, psychologist Carroll Izard, explains that because emotions mobilize us for action, they "constitute the primary motivational system for human beings."[9] Emotions arouse the neural programs that direct behavior. Research shows that emotions not only activate, but also coordinate, such vital activities as setting goals, gathering information, establishing selective attention, retrieving goal-specific memory, regulating physiological processes, communicating intent, and shifting energy levels.[10] The overall effect of these activities is the restructuring of both perception and cognition. Emotions prompt us to scan our environment while selectively attending to data that appear relevant to our survival or other mobilized interests. Emotions also send out distinct instructions to our organ systems, muscle groups, and various metabolic processes—thereby readying us for specific kinds of action. And, too, emotions produce species-typical gestures or expressions (e.g., facial expressions, drooping the shoulders, raising hair) that communicate our behavioral intentions to others. Such emotionally driven communication contributes to a species' survival and to the achievement of both individual and communal goals.

If we wish to understand in greater detail how emotions affect human religiosity, we need to move past thinking of emotion as a general category and instead isolate the motivational influences of distinct emotions. Joseph LeDoux explained this well when he pointed out that there is no one emotional region of the brain. Instead, "the various classes of emotions are mediated by separate neural systems that have evolved for different reasons."[11] Distinct emotions have distinct biological functions. Thus, "if we are interested in understanding the various phenomena that we use the term 'emotion' to refer to, we have to focus on specific classes of emotions."[12]

Identifying specific emotions remains a difficult task. Emotions are, after all, among the most slippery and variable human attributes. It is difficult to distinguish between those emotions present at birth (primary emotions) and those that develop later either as permutations of those original emotions or due to cultural influence (secondary emotions). There is, however, strong consensus in the fields of biology and psychology that humans possess several clearly identifiable basic or primary emotions (and that even secondary or "blended" emotions have identifiable biological substrates).[13] Thus, for example, in a recent survey of sixteen highly regarded theories of emotion, all sixteen listed both fear and anger as paradigmatic examples of primary emotions.[14] Identifying emotions such as fear and anger as "primary" indicates wide consensus that these distinct emotions are universal, genetically encoded, and are associated with neural activities that are evolutionarily ancient and thus the least amenable to cultural influence, learning, or volitional control.

A word of caution needs to be interjected into any discussion of discrete emotions. Aaron Ben-Ze'ev calls attention to what he terms "subtlety of emotions."[15] One implication of this subtlety is that the feeling states we label emotions (as well as their nature, causes, and consequences) are far too variable and complex to be neatly categorized. The very concept of an emotion is what Ben-Ze'ev calls a "prototypical category" based on a preponderance of empirical characteristics. He argues that various feeling states are to be considered emotions to their degree of similarity to the most typical case. The same applies to the argument for distinct emotions. The existence of distinct emotions is not an all-or-nothing affair; it is, rather, a matter of the degree of similarity to the most typical case. The point here is that no claim is being made that recent studies of the emotions have at last put us on some stable, solid ground that is inherently more factual than carefully reasoned conclusions within the humanities. We need to resist premature foreclosure on any one definition of emotion in general, let alone distinct emotions, until we get much closer to understanding the precise "mix" of biological and cultural factors that make emotions so subtle and variable.

Caution is needed, too, in distinguishing between several words that are closely related to the concept of emotion. Words such as "feeling," "mood," and "temperament" are all commonly used to refer to emotion. Some of the confusion surrounding the use of these affective terms stems from the fact that most theories of emotion have been erected on a very narrow basis. Indeed, theoretical discussions of emotion typically concentrate almost solely on a few primary emotions (e.g., fear or anger) that are most clearly linked to short-term occurrent reactions.[16] We might note, therefore, that emotions vary widely in relation to their temporal effect and we should consequently distinguish between such terms as "emotional experience," "mood," and "disposition."[17]

There is some consensus that the terms "emotion" and "emotional experience" are best restricted to feeling states aroused by an immediate stimulus and that last a few seconds or, at most, a few minutes. Yet emotional experiences—especially to the extent they are as much a part of cultural consciousness as they are biological activity—can also exert identifiable influences on motivation, perception, and cognition over days or weeks (moods) and even years (temperament or personality traits). We must, therefore, keep in mind that emotions vary widely from one another. We should also keep in mind that although many emotions first appear in immediate stimulus-response situations, these emotional experiences are often the experiential template from which longer-lasting moods, cognitive styles, and habitual tendencies gradually develop.

With these cautions in mind, we can begin to appreciate the evolutionary-adaptive functions of emotions such as fear and anger. Fear mobilizes avoidance behaviors in response to something perceived as threatening. From an evolutionary point of view, it was necessary for organisms to have genetic programs that mobilize them to avoid dangerous situations. While we use the word fear to represent pronounced episodes of this avoidance emotion, it is closely associated with the more enduring mood or personality trait we refer to as anxiety. According to psychologist Robert Plutchik, fear often gives rise to a longer-lasting "appraisal and coping style that focuses on threats and loss of status in a hostile and competitive world."[18] Fear, then, mobilizes our physiology and cognition in a number of ways. It causes a shift in our perception and attention, redirecting our information-gathering programs to detect the causal agency responsible for the perceived threat in the environment.[19] Fear alters our goals and motivational weightings, making safety a far higher priority than the pursuit of satisfactions that do not bear upon immediate survival. It redirects memory to retrieve similar threatening patterns or successful escape strategies form our past. Fear also leads to communication patterns that alert others to danger and, in some cases, that mobilize others to strengthen their communal bond through loyalty and solidarity. In sum, fear organizes our perceptual and cognitive processes in what psychologists Carroll Izard and Brian Ackerman have found to be clearly identifiable ways:

> Fear tends to produce "tunnel vision" by focusing attention on the source of the threat and restricting cue utilization. Keen attention to the threatening agent or situation can be adaptive in guiding self-protective behavior. Such restrictions on attentional processes in unrealistic or unwarranted fear are maladaptive.[20]

The motivational function unique to fear is that of mobilizing cognitive and behavioral programs that will help us to escape from dangerous situations.

In humans, one of these behaviors is continuing apprehensiveness or antici-
pation of recurring threat. This threat, furthermore, may be cultural or psychological as well as physical. Carroll Izard explains that "threats to one's self-
concept, one's integrity, or one's psychological well-being can elicit fear, and
such threats are rarely eliminated by physically running away."[21] We must
protect our self-concept from threats that are more psychological or cultural in
nature, but we do so not by physical avoidance so much as by protecting our
cultural territory through trying to fortify existing cultural boundaries. This
requires heightened loyalty and conformity on the part of the threatened
group. And, as we have just noted, it calls forth modes of cultural discourse and
communication characterized by tunnel vision, restricted cue utilization, and
keen attention to the threatening agent. For social units, as for individuals, if
the narrowing of perception and cognition motivated by fear is unrealistic or
unwarranted, this fear-driven mode of cultural discourse is likely to be maladaptive.

To summarize, fear originates in an alarm system shaped by evolution to
protect us from impending danger. This system is designed to discover threat,
and it results in mobilizing us to a fight or flight response pattern.[22] Yet even
though fear has certain adaptive qualities, it can nonetheless become maladaptive when it causes us to become overly fixated on a threatening agent that
does not in fact pose danger.

The threatening agents that arouse fear understandably often become the
targets of anger or hatred. Anger is adaptive to the extent that it mobilizes and
sustains energy at high levels. At the level of physiology, anger "directs increased blood flow away from the viscera and toward the muscles of action. No
other emotion can equal the consistency and vigor of anger in increasing and
sustaining extremely high levels of motor activity."[23]

Fear-induced anger also serves psychological and cultural functions. Anger protects self-esteem. Anger redirects aggression away from ourselves (such
as might happen if guilt or shame prevailed). In this way, anger "blunts feelings of personal insecurity and prevents feelings of helplessness from reaching
levels of conscious awareness."[24] Anger, if properly directed, can also contribute to communal solidarity. It mobilizes energy against a common enemy,
reinforcing the need for conformity and loyalty to the group. This is what Eric
Hoffer had in mind when he observed that fanatic devotion to a cause requires
the presence of anger and hate. As Hoffer observed, you can sustain zealous
devotion and loyalty without a god. But you cannot sustain such long-term
fanaticism without a devil.[25] The kind of person that Hoffer described as a
"true believer" is thus someone in whom both fear and anger might be expected to be exerting powerful motivation.

Many expressions of anger alert us also to the cultural components of emotions. For example, anger is frequently elicited by perceived violations of a culture's moral order.[26] The perception of an unjustifiable transgression of a person's sense of "ought" frequently generates fear or hatred as strongly as when his or her physical well-being is in jeopardy. Anger, then, is frequently mobilized in instances of seeming transgressions of moral, ritual, or cultural tradition. Such reactions appear to be universal, suggesting that we are biologically wired for emotions that ensure our cultural bonds. The wide variation in how such episodes of anger are evoked or expressed, however, reminds us that the meaning of this emotion is generated by very particular social frameworks.

Emotion, Fear, and the Explanation of Religion

Sigmund Freud explored the relationship between fear and religiosity about eighty years ago in *The Future of an Illusion*. Freud observed that nature threatens us on a daily basis. Floods, earthquakes, disease, and death all mock our efforts at human control. We are helpless in the face of nature's fickle ways. This helplessness elicits powerful feelings of fear and dependency. So long as we continue to understand nature in impersonal forms, we remain helpless. Yet, Freud points out that humans try to gain some control over their personal fates by generating belief in the existence of gods or spirits residing just behind the natural world. Freud calls this the "humanization of nature." Belief in the existence of heavenly beings suggests that we are not wholly powerless. We can apply the same methods against these powerful superbeings in the sky that we employ in our own everyday life; we can attempt to influence them by appeasing them, bribing them, or in other ways beseeching them to come to our aid. "And thus," Freud concludes, "a store of ideas is created, born from man's need to make his helplessness tolerable."[27] In Western civilization this store of ideas gradually gave rise to belief in a Heavenly Father who can be worshipped and prayed to in order to relieve us of our ever-present fears and anxieties.

Freud's interest in depicting the emotional sources of religious belief was motivated by his own aversion to religious ways of thinking. Freud, a humanist, was a steadfast champion of the kind of rationality he associated with science. He proclaimed that religious thinking was driven by emotion, not reason. Religion is thus an illusion; we hold religious beliefs only because we wish them to be true, not because we have real reason or evidence for them to be true. In sharp contrast to the illusions of religion, "science has given us evidence by its numerous and important successes that it is no illusion."[28]

Freud admitted that there are many questions to which science as yet has no answers. But he reaffirmed that "scientific work" is the only reliable path to human progress. Science, because it is governed by reason rather than emotion, can be trusted to yield dependable knowledge about the world.

Freud's attempt to link fearful emotions with the rise of religious belief needs to be radically updated in light of the last several decades of emotion research. Freud tended to have a fairly simplistic conception of emotion, equating it with sentimentality, subjective feeling, or a kind of solipsistic outlook that lacks firm connection with the world outside the self. As a result, his discussions of emotion and religion frequently created a forced dichotomy between the role of the heart versus the head, sentiment versus rational calculation, subjective personal need versus objective facts about the world. Modern emotion research shows us, however, that such a sharp contrast between emotion and reason is unfounded. Cognition is necessarily entailed in the arousal of emotions. We continually evaluate (often without conscious awareness) the potential harms and benefits existing in the surrounding environment. Emotions are particularly likely to arise in the face of unexpected or uncertain perceptions. Discrepancies between expectations built on past experiences and signals from the present environment create uncertainty, thereby triggering the brain's inherited emotion programs designed to mobilize the organism for appropriate response.

Not only is cognition involved in the arousal of emotions, but emotions mobilize and coordinate a host of perceptual, cognitive, and behavioral subprograms (e.g., attention, inferences, learning, memory, goal choice, motivational priorities, communication of intention) geared to serve the organism's interests. Emotions constitute the primary motivational system for human beings and thus exert a profound influence on both cognition and behavior. This is why philosopher Robert Solomon has tried to erase the myth that there is an inherent antithesis between emotion and reason. "Every emotion," he writes, "is a strategy, a purposive attempt to structure our world in such a way as to maximize our sense of personal dignity and self-esteem."[29] Solomon has perhaps overly emphasized the distinctively psychological issues of dignity and self-esteem as opposed to other organismic needs and interests. But his point is well taken. Emotions are adaptive strategies. In humans, emotions seek to maximize subjective measures of well-being and self-worth.

The important point here is that human beings bring vital needs and interests to their evaluation of, and response to, the surrounding environment. There is no such thing as emotion-free cognition.[30] It is not really a question of *whether* emotions influence our thinking, but rather a matter of *which* emotions most strongly mobilize the subprograms that collectively constitute cognition. Emotions, after all, vary a great deal from one another. They represent very different appraisals of opportunities for gain and loss in relation to one's surroundings. Distinct emotions bring distinct strategies to bear in the organization of perception, cognition, and behavior.

To the extent that fear is involved in the mobilization of thoughts or forms of communication, we might expect to discern one or more of the prototypical characteristics distinctly associated with this emotion. We might, for example, expect fear-driven forms of thought or communication to be especially preoccupied with boundary-setting and boundary-defense. We would also expect to see cognitive styles marked by appraisal and coping functions that focus on threats and loss of status in a hostile and competitive world. Fear-driven cognition is characterized by tunnel-vision, focusing attention on continuing threats to one's self esteem as well as restricted cue utilization (i.e., persistent efforts to detect a restricted set of environmental cues that would fit readily with heightened expectation of threat). Fear and anxiety similarly encourage communication patterns that alert others to danger, strengthen group members' loyalty to communal defense, and sustain high levels of vigor in warding off sources of threat.

Fear, then, suggests itself as a critical category that can help elucidate themes or episodes in humanity's religious life. Considered as a discrete emotion, fear is characterized by "prototypical characteristics" that can enrich understandings of both the origin and function of specific displays of religious thought or behavior. These prototypical characteristics are, moreover, not only helpful in describing aspects of religiosity, but they can also inform our efforts to evaluate or assess religion. That is, critical categories that arise in a fully interdisciplinary account of "religion in the flesh" help us make informed judgments concerning how likely specific instances of religion are to guide humans to productive relationships with their natural and social environments.

Emotion and the Apocalyptic Imagination

Religion is never so enthralling as when there is complete confidence that the end of human history is near. The complacency of religion-as-usual is replaced with fervent expectation of an imminent manifestation of God, leading to the glorious exaltation of the faithful. Additional enthusiasm comes from knowing that all one's doubters and enemies will soon face stern justice, leading to eternal suffering and damnation. The many variations of such end-times belief are referred to as apocalypticism (from the Greek *apokalypsis*, which means "an unveiling or uncovering of truths that are ordinarily hidden"). Adherents of

apocalyptic faith have the certainty of possessing truths hidden from unbe-
lievers. In the case of Christian apocalypticism, these truths come from the
most enigmatic sections of the Bible, specifically the Jewish book of Daniel,
the Christian book of Revelation, and isolated passages strewn across any
number of other sacred texts.[31] These texts are thought to contain special
revelations that provide "inside information" concerning God's timetable and
game plan for his final confrontation with Satan. They are filled with highly
cryptic, indeed downright confounding, references to dragons, beasts, false
prophets, angels, and other supernatural entities, all of whom have precise
roles in a carefully orchestrated sequence of cataclysmic events through which
God will vindicate the faithful and wreak havoc upon their enemies.

The apocalyptic worldview is wholly alien to the scientific spirit of the
secularist outlook we associate with educated persons living in highly advanced
economies such as Japan, the United States, and Western European countries.
Apocalyptic belief, for example, presupposes a literal interpretation of ancient
biblical writings and postulates an overtly supernaturalist vision of reality in
which angelic beings are expected to intervene in worldly events. All of this
flies in the face of modern intellectual trends. Adherents of apocalyptic faith
deliberately choose a countervailing outlook on the world. Their faith is rooted
in the conviction that (1) the world is sharply divided into the forces of good and
those of evil, and (2) the conflict between these two forces is about to be joined
by supernatural forces who will intervene decisively on behalf of the righteous,
assuring them that they will be victorious and will inherit a purified earth.
Such beliefs, we shall see, defy modern secularism at least partially because
they are grounded in biological motivations. Our selection of religious beliefs is
guided by the "mental modules" that natural selection has bequeathed us for
addressing the challenges posed by our natural and social environments. The
tenacious hold that apocalyptic beliefs continue to have on modern persons,
then, must be understood at least partially owing to bodily (rather than purely
cultural) motivations.

Given the oppositional character of apocalyptic belief, it is not surprising
that both historical and sociological studies indicate that the classic apocalyptic texts were originally "intended for a group in crisis with the purpose of
exhortation and or consolation by means of divine authority."[32] Apocalyptic
writing is a patterned response to severe persecution, a threat to group welfare,
a decline in religious enthusiasm, or a growing awareness of the discrepancy
between the group's way of life and current sociopolitical realities. Its purpose is to show that people can and must endure such crises, secure in the
knowledge that their tribulations are part of God's plan for the final triumph
over evil. The promised day of the Lord is at hand, regardless of how bleak the

prospects of victory may seem. Apocalypticism is thus a message of consolation and exhortation. It conveys its message in language that is neither descriptive nor denotative but, rather, poetic.[33] It is the art of apocalyptic writing
to use symbols and imagery that convey a particular sense or feeling about the
world—a feeling of anxiety or impending threat. Its purpose is to evoke these
deep-seated emotions and mobilize them in ways that motivate strengthened
loyalty to the group and redoubled anger directed toward those sinister agents
deemed responsible for such unwarranted persecution.

It is in this context that we can best appreciate the early origins of Judeo-
Christian apocalypticism. Just who authored the book of Daniel is unknown to
us.[34] We know only that he lived in Judea in the second century BCE during a
protracted struggle between the Jews and the king of Syria, Antiochus IV.
Antiochus, it seems, had plundered the temple in Jerusalem in order to steal
anything of value that might help finance a military campaign against Egypt.
Conflict between Antiochus and the local Jewish community continued to
escalate until violence erupted, and Antiochus, in turn, intensified his efforts
to subdue all opposition. Because Jews were consequently under siege by an
overpowering enemy, their spirits began to falter. It was at this juncture, in
about 165 BCE, that an unknown author produced an apocalyptic masterpiece
that to this day evokes the deeply seated emotions of fear and anger, directing
them toward such defensive maneuvers as strengthened group loyalty and
tribalistic posturing.

The book of Daniel skillfully evokes the apocalyptic outlook. The story's
hero, Daniel, is the recipient of a mysterious vision that explains how the events
besetting the faithful community had not occurred by accident but, rather, are
integral parts of a divine plan foreordained by God. Antiochus was merely a
puppet under the control of an ancient cosmic enemy. The faithful people of
God were not facing a mere worldly adversary, but were instead facing a conspiracy unleashed by the forces of darkness. Yet, hope was still warranted. The
tribulations Antioch heaped on them were necessary parts of God's majestic
plan. The moment was near when God would act decisively to turn the tables
and vanquish their enemies.

The imagery in Daniel's vision is highly evocative. Images of frightful
supernatural agency abound, alerting audiences to the dangerous presence of
sinister intentions. Daniel relates how "four great beasts came up out of the
sea." The first was like a lion and had eagle's wings. The second was like a bear,
and the third was like a leopard with four wings on his back. The fourth was by
far the most dreadful. It was exceedingly strong, had great iron teeth, and—
most terrifying of all—had ten horns. While beholding these horns, Daniel saw
yet another tiny horn with eyes and a mouth. This tiny horn, a thinly veiled

allusion to Antiochus IV, continued to grow and uproot other horns that got in his way: "This horn made war with the saints, and prevailed over them."[35]

But even as evil reached its zenith, the ultimate triumph of good was assured. Daniel learned that a mysterious figure of awesome power, "the Ancient of Days," would appear and destroy the beasts. Then from the clouds of heaven there would come one like a "son of man" to whom would be given dominion over a kingdom that shall not be destroyed. Thus, despite the terrible persecutions that Jews were suffering at the hands of the four beasts (i.e., the four worldly kingdoms whose policies threatened the people of Yahweh), the book of Daniel was able to promise that "the saints of the Most High shall receive the kingdom, and possess the kingdom for ever, for ever and ever."[36]

Apocalyptic thought captured the imaginations of certain segments of ancient Jewish society. It was particularly appealing to those who, like the Qumran community that produced the Dead Sea Scrolls, withdrew from mainstream culture and instead decided to live in seclusion so as to adhere to strict rules of holiness in an otherwise unholy world. It especially appealed to a Jewish and Palestinian man named John, of whom little is known except the book of Revelation he composed around the year 95 CE. John was a convert to a radical sect of Judaism—Christianity. If anyone in history has possessed an intuitive grasp of how the emotions of fear and anger can be evoked in ways to redouble group loyalty, it is this mysterious author of the final book of the Christian Bible.

Christians of the late first century found themselves a beleaguered group.[37] Their public status was dismal. They were in continual conflict with the majority of Jews, who found most of their theological innovations irritating. Christians also found themselves in conflict with the Romans and were openly anarchical. They withdrew from public life, secure in the knowledge that next week or next month the King of Kings would return to reverse the current socioeconomic order: the first would become last, and the last would become first. Christians were, moreover, social pariahs. For the most part they were poor and socially disenfranchised. Their low socioeconomic status caused them to resent the fact that so many Jews and Gentiles among them openly cooperated with the Roman system—and profited both economically and socially from such cooperation. From the Christian point of view, such worldly riches would prove tragically ephemeral, fating those with ill-gained wealth to eternal damnation at the time of final judgment. Christians, on the other hand, would receive their eternal reward if they could hold out and sustain their exclusivist, world-renouncing stance toward life just a little longer. One among them, John, sensed the doubts and wavering commitments, and he was able to portray the contemporary situation in a mythic, apocalyptic framework. His aim was to show that the conflicts and tensions felt by his fellow Christians had cosmic significance. At stake in each person's decision to remain faithful was nothing less than his or her eternal destiny. John was also shrewd enough to realize that nothing so unites a community as having a common enemy. His book, known as the Apocalypse or the Revelation to John, vividly depicted just such an enemy—Satan's ally—the Antichrist, which John described with the mytho-poetic imagery of Daniel's beast.

Anyone who has tried to read John's Revelation can sympathize with George Bernard Shaw's remark that it is "a curious record of the visions of a drug addict."[38] There is such a profusion of images and such an apparent lack of structure that even the most conscientious reader cannot help but be be-wildered. The narrative jumbles together a serious of inchoate images, such as seven messages, seven seals, seven trumpets, seven bowls, and seven un-numbered visions until the reader is lost in hopeless confusion. With repeated readings, however, it becomes clear that there is a pattern running through each series of John's visions. The cyclical or repetitive pattern is characteristic of apocalyptic language and is an indication that the book's message is the overall flow of the events rather than the particular details of any one story or image. Each sequence of events recapitulates a threefold pattern of (1) persecution, (2) punishment of the persecutors, and (3) salvation of the faithful accompanied by the triumph of the lamb over the beast.[39] Revelation is therefore a variant on the many "combat myths" in which order (God) triumphs over the dragon of chaos. Adela Yarboro Collins points out that a Jew hearing about a dragon or a beast in the first century CE. would immediately place that image in a political context.[40] The dragons and beasts that appear in Revelation represent not only the great deceiver, Satan, but also a long line of national enemies that had advanced Satan's cause by thwarting the purposes of God's chosen people. Revelation is thus a staunchly tribalistic text. It draws clear boundaries separating the chosen people from the threatening cultures that engulf them. It warns of the dangers of crossing over that boundary and promises great reward for those who remain steadfast in their tribal loyalty. Its purpose is to reinforce resistance to Rome and to inspire willingness for martyrdom.

John's narrative constructs ferocious images that vividly depict the fear and anxiety of early Christians who found themselves threatened by social, political, and economic forces over which they had no control. These Chris-tians, already familiar with the threatening beast of Daniel's narrative, detected the causal agency of a beastly supernatural agent everywhere about them. John alerts his audience to the presence of a giant "beast rising out of the sea, with ten horns and seven heads with ten diadems upon its horns and a blasphe-mous name upon its head."[41] John informs his audience that that humanity's only hope rests in the superior supernatural agency of God who possesses the power to vanquish all competing powers. Humans' only hope rests in the angelic armies of God who, we are told, will soon intervene to rescue His loyal followers.

John intended his work to be read aloud before an assembly of Christians and to help them see themselves in this mythic context. His use of expressive and evocative language helped elicit from his audience the emotional charge they needed both to alleviate their existential anxieties and to endure as a cohesive social group. His apocalypse plays on the audience's fears and anxieties, projecting them onto a cosmic screen on which victory is assured. Adela Yarbro Collins notes that through its use of evocative symbols and artful plots,

> The Apocalypse made feelings which were probably latent, vague, complex, and ambiguous explicit, conscious, and simple. Complex relationships were simplified by the use of a dualistic framework. The Jews who reject and denounce Christians are followers of Satan. Those who do not have God's seal bear the mark of the beast and are doomed to destruction.[42]

The symbol of the Antichrist, the beast from the sea, gave John and his audience a mythic image with which to label the causal agency responsible for their fears and anxieties. Apocalyptic symbolism helped explain and make bearable the tension between what was (i.e., the powerlessness of Christians in the world defined by the social elite) and what should be (i.e., the triumph of Christianity over all its enemies). This otherwise obscure first-century writer managed to generate a system of symbols which has proven effective for channeling a very particular set of human emotions for nearly two thousand years.

The enduring power of apocalyptic rhetoric in western religious communities thus rests—at least in part—in its ability first to evoke specific emotions and then to channel these emotions in ways that both alleviate the existential anxieties connected with these emotions and strengthen communal bonds. The repetitive nature of the plot and the frightful imagery of beasts and dragons gradually construct—and intensify—an experience of imminent threat among those in the listening audience. Collins explains that the rhetorical strategy of Revelation is to "intensify the fear of the hearers."[43]

> There is a certain analogy between Aristotle's explanation of the function of Greek tragedy and the function of Revelation. In each case certain emotions are aroused and then a catharsis of these emotions is achieved. Tragedy manipulates the emotions of fear and pity; Revelation, primarily fear and resentment.[44]

The vivid images of beasts and dragons were designed to evoke terror and exacerbate resentment of those outside the gathered community who are nonetheless economically prosperous. Once such primary emotional responses are evoked, they are then connected with very specific cultural and theological meanings. Thus, "fear, the sense of powerlessness, and aggressive feelings are not minimized, but heightened. They are placed in a cosmic framework, projected onto the screen of the heavenly world."[45]

Understanding the apocalyptic imagination, then, requires sensitivity to biological as well as cultural factors. The connection that Revelation makes between fear and anger (toward Christianity's worldly enemies) is, therefore, at least partially due to the fact that the emotion of fear typically mobilizes anger and aggressiveness directed toward threatening agents. Revelation, by linking emotional experiences of fear, anger, and resentment with culturally elaborated eschatological hopes, forged lasting communal and theological bonds among early Christians. And, insofar as this emotional experience is triggered by those who read or hear apocalyptic narratives even to this day, it stands to reason that the longer-lasting moods and temperaments associated with apocalyptic faith are at least partially rooted in emotional episodes of fear.

Fear, Anger, and Apocalyptic Faith

There is, as we have noted, no such thing as emotion-free cognition. Nor is there such a thing as emotion-free religion. It is not really a question of whether emotions influence our religious thought and actions, but rather a matter of which emotions most strongly affect our perceptual, cognitive, and behavioral systems. The previous section reviewed the fairly accepted historical argument that interest in apocalyptic thought is greatest among those who feel threatened, persecuted, or in danger of being left behind by prevailing cultural trends. Such historical and cultural explanations must, however, be supplemented with biological explanations of the sources of distinct styles of religious thought or behavior. We have already noted that apocalyptic literature is rife with imagery designed to elicit short-term emotional episodes of fear, anger, and resentment. To this extent, then, we should expect that apocalyptic religiosity rests—at least in part—on emotional programs that would be prototypically characterized by heightened interest in boundary setting and boundary defense. We would expect that religious beliefs mobilized by fear and anxiety would be characterized by a form of tunnel vision, focusing inordinately on perceived threats to one's self-esteem. We would also expect to see cognitive styles marked by restricted cue utilization: apprehensive scanning of the environment for particular cues that signal threat or loss of status in a hostile world. And finally, we might also expect to see a preponderance of religious hatred, a venting of anger in order to direct attention outward and thereby prevent feelings of helplessness from reaching levels of conscious awareness.

These are, as we shall see, the most salient characteristics of the American apocalyptic tradition from colonial times to recent cultural response to the Left Behind series of prophecy novels.[46] The Puritan tradition that dominated co-lonial religious thought was well acquainted with apocalyptic imagery. Many early colonists believed they were called upon to perform God's errand into the wilderness and were thus prone to interpreting the obstacles in their path as the working of the feared Antichrist. As the Reverend Increase Mather argued in 1682, "A dying Beast will bite cruelly . . . since he is going out of the world, we may expect he will give a cruel bite at the Church of God."[47] And bite he did. The very first of these bites came in the form of the Native Americans, whom the colonists had originally intended to convert to the true faith of Christianity. Yet right from the start it became abundantly clear that interests of the Native Americans and the European settlers were inalterably opposed. Just weeks of arriving on the shores of Plymouth, the Pilgrims had been forced, out of ne-cessity, to raid Indian storage bins for corn and native crafts. Violent skirmishes broke out periodically, leading up the Pequot War of 1637 in which the Puritans killed more than five hundred native men, women, and children in a single battle. The Native Americans posed a continuing threat to the safety and the religious mission of the colonists. It was reassuring to learn from Increase Mather's son, Cotton Mather, that many of those Native Americans they were forced to kill were in fact "Daemons, in the Shape of Armed Indians."[48] Apocalyptic theology redirected fear and anxiety into a concrete plan of action: exterminating Satan's agents who were scheming to undermine the estab-lishment of a Kingdom of God on earth.

The eighteenth and nineteenth centuries witnessed any number of similar scenarios in which the evocation of fear served the short-term interests of apocalyptically oriented Protestant groups. Deism, Masonry, intemperance, and Catholic immigrants all sufficiently threatened those entrusted with God's errand to generate new rounds of apocalyptic name calling. Imbuing worldly adversaries with demonic qualities made it possible for clergy to remind the faithful of their theological and social boundaries. It was, however, the rise of modernism that posed the most dangerous threat to Protestantism's hopes of presiding over a Christian America. By the last two decades of the nineteenth century it had become clear that the natural sciences had displaced theology as the intellectual nucleus of Western culture. The acceptance of Darwin's account of biological evolution by virtually every important American scientist dealt a deathblow to the educated citizenry's ability to believe in the literal truth of the Bible. Continued immigration, industrialization, and urbanization further eroded Protestantism's aspirations for cultural hegemony. By the dawn of the twentieth century, intellectual secularism and social pluralism combined to redefine religious conservatives as cultural outsiders.

For the past one hundred years, apocalyptic literature has voiced the "over and againstness" felt by many conservative religious groups. Apocalyptic literature, by linking bodily experiences of fear, anger, and resentment with culturally elaborated eschatological hopes, has rallied popular audiences into ardent defense of their tribe. As historians R. Scott Appleby and Martin Marty observe, sermons and books that sustain the emotions of fear and resentment central to the apocalyptic imagination imbue "boundary-setting and purity-preserving activities with an apocalyptic urgency, and foster a crisis mentality that serves both to intensify missionary efforts and to justify extremism."[49]

An example of how emotional episodes of fear mobilize specific kinds of theological commitments can be found in readers' responses to the recent evangelical prophecy books known as the Left Behind series, written by Tim LaHaye and Jerry Jenkins. Like the book of Revelation, these best-selling books weave evocative images and artful plotting in ways that first elicit and then gradually intensify fear in many readers. According to Glenn Shuck, the underlying premise of the Left Behind series is that recent economic and technological changes in American culture threaten evangelicals' identity.[50] Shuck points out that by reinterpreting these threats as Satan's deceptive machinations, these prophecy novels provide readers a new set of strategies for relating to the wider culture.

Amy Johnson Frykholm's extensive interviews with persons who had read one or more volumes in the Left Behind series further illustrates Shuck's thesis about the role of threat or fear in motivating readers to reconfigure their worlds. Much like Adela Yarboro Collins discovered about the communities to whom the book of Daniel and the book of Revelation were addressed, Frykholm found that many of those drawn to the Left Behind series revealed noticeable levels of "fear and longing."[51] Frykholm was particularly struck by one interviewee who confessed that as a working-class woman, her economic status was increasingly jeopardized by the fact that she had no training in computer-based technology. The Left Behind series brought this otherwise latent threat to the surface, mobilizing fear-driven changes in thought and feeling. Frykholm suggests that "this fear of technology, and the association between technology and the supreme worldly power of the Antichrist is, in part, a class-based fear."[52] Frykholm's interviews thus confirmed Glenn Shuck's contention that this series' widespread appeal must be viewed against the backdrop of recent economic and technological changes that threaten evangelicals' identity. Insofar as imagery of sinister supernatural adversaries raises these threats to the surface of awareness, it can trigger emotional episodes of fear that motivate commitment to religious strategies characterized by fear-driven restricted cue utilization, narrowed attention, and concern for boundary posturing.

Frykholm cautions us to remember that "the interpretive communities of readers, in Stanley Fish's terms, are frequently plural and not always in agreement about the meaning of the text."[53] We need to exercise caution, being careful not to suggest that all Christians drawn to apocalyptic themes can be understood in terms of the same interpretive categories. Frykholm nonetheless proposes that the Left Behind series was so successful in provoking strong commitment to evangelical beliefs largely because its portrait of end-time prophecies "conjures doubt, particularly self-doubt."[54] Feelings of doubt and vulnerability (Frykholm observes that sales of the Left Behind books reportedly increased 60 percent after the September 11, 2001, attacks on New York City) further enable apocalyptic literature to extend emotional episodes of fear into longer-lasting theological moods and motivations predicated on a continuing perception of imminent threat.

Assessing Fear-Driven Religiosity

The premise of this investigation is that there is no such thing as emotion-free religiosity. Our brains and nervous systems are wired in such a way that we always bring vital needs and interests to our evaluation of, and response to, the surrounding environment. There is no such thing as emotion-free cognition—religious or otherwise.

Fear and anger are not the only emotions present in those who hold strongly to apocalyptic belief systems. Humans are a mixture of emotions. All of these emotions play some role in shaping our overall religious sensibility. It is important, then, that we be careful not to assume that all persons who embrace apocalyptic theology do so out of fear or anxiety. Interest in eschatology (end-times) has many roots, including the sheer delight of speculating about the future. But it seems fair to conclude that fear and anxiety play a more prominent role in apocalypticism than they do in many other forms of religiosity (such as will be explored in the next chapter). It also seems fair for scholars to examine how these distinct emotions affect the role of religion in a person's life.

Many scholars have ventured into the precarious territory of evaluating the psychological and sociological effects of an apocalyptic approach to life. One of the best known is Norman Cohn, who maintains that apocalyptic thinking is essentially a paranoid response to economic depravation, political persecution, and other threats to personal well-being. Cohn argues that any attempt to explain apocalyptic fantasies

> cannot afford to ignore the psychic content of the fantasies which have inspired them. All these fantasies are precisely such as are commonly found in individual cases of paranoia. The megalomaniac view of oneself as the elect, wholly good, abominably persecuted yet assured of ultimate triumph; the attribution of gigantic and demonic powers to the adversary; the refusal to accept the ineluctable limitations and imperfections of human existence, such as transience, dissension, conflict, fallibility whether intellectual or moral; the obsession with inerrable prophecies—these attitudes are symptoms which together constitute the unmistakable syndrome of paranoia. But a paranoiac delusion does not cease to be so because it is shared by so many individuals, nor yet because those individuals have real and ample grounds for regarding themselves as victims of oppression.[55]

Michael Barkun offers another version of this scholarly tendency to view apocalyptic thinking as a "coping" mechanism prevalent among the educationally and economically deprived. In his *Disaster and the Millennium*, Barkun contends that natural and human disasters predispose people to an apocalyptic view of the world. He analyzes the historical settings in which apocalyptic movements have arisen in diverse cultures and historical eras and concludes that disasters serve to predispose individuals to millenarian conversion.[56] Yet another variation on this theme is David Aberle's theory of "relative deprivation." Aberle defines relative deprivation as "a negative discrepancy between legitimate expectation and actuality" and argues that apocalyptic belief tends to prevail among people who experience such discrepancy in their pursuit of possessions, status, behavior, or worth.[57] Charles Strozier offers an interesting psychological analysis of American apocalypticism when he suggests that preoccupation with end-times imagery "has roots in trauma in the self." The first part of Strozier's analysis focuses on how psychological trauma gives rise to magical fantasies about a cosmic battle between the forces of good and evil. But the second part of his assessment is even more intriguing. He argues that apocalyptic fantasies tragically lead people even further away from satisfactory relationships with the surrounding world. The dualistic categories of apocalyptic thinking mirror the brokenness within the self and thus further "isolate the fundamentalist individual from complex social interaction."[58] Because apocalyptic thinking denigrates the present moment and shifts the source of agency away from the self to God, it "tends to undermine personal efficacy and a commitment to human purpose."[59]

Each of these analyses of apocalyptic theories confirms my principal thesis that apocalyptic religiosity is rooted in the body's most powerful motivational systems—in this case, the discrete emotions of fear and anger. Historical and cultural studies of apocalypticism, however, have notoriously failed in identifying specific environmental sources of fear (e.g., economic deprivation, political persecution, natural disaster). Standard historical accounts of apocalypticism have consequently had even more difficulty explaining why such differing environmental events elicit the specific characteristics of apocalyptic thought. Although a spirituality in the flesh cannot alone answer the many perplexing questions raised by the persistence of apocalyptic theology, it can take a first step in this direction by better calibrating our understanding of the "mix" between biological and cultural factors that together comprise embodied experience.

A self-conscious commitment to understanding the embodied nature of readers' responses to apocalyptic imagery can supplement existing historical and cultural analyses in at least three ways. First, research on discrete emotions helps us appreciate the evolutionary-adaptive reasons why humans are motivated to adopt an apocalyptic orientation to life. Fear-driven cognition alerts organisms to potential danger and therefore mobilizes individuals and communities into more strident boundary-posturing and boundary-defending behavior. These motivational impulses are understandable reactions to environmental threats and, from the community's own perspective, can give rise to potentially adaptive behaviors—at least in the short run.

Second, recent research on the emotions alerts us to what happens in the middle loop of human experience. We now have a great deal of information about how a distinct emotion such as fear exerts distinctive influences on perception, cognition, memory retrieval, restricted cue utilization (i.e., search for "signs of the times" or "marks of the beast"), preoccupation with suspected sources of threat, and alarmist communication patterns that alert others to strengthen communal bonds. By abandoning strong versions of constructivism and availing ourselves of what is now known about the neural structure of our brains and the specifics of our everyday functioning in the world, we are in a better position to understand audience response to apocalyptic imagery (and possibly why some members of an audience might be more prone to specific kinds of emotional episodes than others). A spirituality in the flesh alerts us to the motivational functions performed by emotional episodes and thus enables us to identify the prototypical characteristics of the longer-lasting moods or dispositions they might generate.

Third, a broadly biological approach to religion also generates criteria that can be used to evaluate the relative merits of fear-driven religiosity for the organism's overall well-being. Many scholars in the field of religious studies are so acutely aware of the limitations of their own culturally constructed world views that they are understandably reluctant to make judgments of any kind. The result is scholarship that is frequently of the blandest sort. We are left with descriptive narratives in which every cause is just, every group noble, every belief as valuable as any other belief. Scholarship of this sort might help us know the past or present, but it does little to help us consider more life-affirming possibilities for the future.

By expanding the study of religion to include interpretive categories built upon a broad interdisciplinary basis, scholars of religion can avail themselves of the kinds of criteria that biologists or psychologists might use to evaluate the long-term adaptive consequences of any specific mode of thought or behavior. That is, a spirituality in the flesh opens up the possibility of interpreting the value of religion in a functionalist context. As a theoretical orientation in both the natural and social sciences, functionalism focuses not on what specific mental activities are but, rather, on what they do. Functionalism assesses various actions or ideas in terms of how effectively they facilitate organisms' adaptation to the social, economic, and moral worlds they inhabit. The value of a particular perceptual or cognitive style is thus determined by the degree to which it enables organisms to function effectively and healthfully in the larger natural and social environments.

Humanities disciplines are especially alert to the fact that embodied lives develop over time and through community. They are, therefore, particularly sensitive to the ethical dimension of attempts to specify measures of "health," "adaptation," or "fitness." Religious studies, for example, is a discipline that is in a special position not just to borrow from but also to enrich and complicate what other disciplines have taught us about functional assessments of organisms' behaviors. Humans are somewhat unique in that they bring vital interests to their interactions with the world, often seeking to adapt themselves to an ideal environment that it not currently "out there" in any simple or straightforward sense. As the biologically trained physician, psychologist, and philosopher William James put it, we should not shrink from the task of making informed judgments concerning which forms of religious life most clearly aim "for the richer universe, for the good which seems most organizable, most fit to enter into complex combinations, most apt to become a member of a more inclusive whole."[60]

A rich understanding of the biological, psychological, social, and cultural substrates of discrete emotions helps put scholars in a better position to make nuanced functional assessments of complex phenomena such as apocalyptic religiosity. It is important, for example, to recognize how the emotion of fear resticts cue utilizaton and focuses "attention on threats." By mobilizing responses that elicit heightened commitment to maintaining group boundaries, fear-driven forms of religious thought are well suited to bolstering a group's short-term fitness. The historical record indicates that most of those who embrace apocalyptic ideas do so out of love of family and cherished communal values. We might think, for example, of how such an apocalyptically charged anthem as Julia Ward Howe's *Battle Hymn of the Republic* generated an expansive sense of duty to a set of communal values (though leading to the tribalistic slaughter of thousands). Apocalypticism reinforces commitments necessary for the short-term viability of a community. Indeed, many who adhere to apocalyptic faith are motivated by a variety of other emotions besides simple fear. As for our relationship to God's will, it is important in this context that we make a distinction between end-times thought that has generally prophetic expectations (i.e., focusing on God's providential action to aid humans as they strenuously work to build a better future) rather than apocalyptic (i.e., focusing on destructive intervention by supernatural beings rather than constructive human action). We might further suppose that commitment to prophetic religious thought is motivated more by the arousal of such emotions as hope, compassion, or care than either fear or anger.

Yet, from the colonial demonization of Native Americans to contemporary denunciation of Muslims, the historical record is sufficiently clear that unrealistic and unwarranted fear has rendered apocalyptic thought maladaptive. Exaggerated attention to threat has served decidedly tribalistic functions. The labeling of Catholics, Jews, Masons, Deists, modernists, socialists, feminists, and advocates of peace organization as Antichrists has never functioned to promote "more inclusive wholes." Instead, apocalyptic name-calling has consistently strengthened the separatism or tribalism that has been integral to apocalyptic communities since biblical times. Demonizing enemies is a vivid instance of tribalism at work. Although the separation of clan groups is elementary throughout nature, humans today can ill afford the barriers to communication and cooperation that tribalistic outlooks create. We might remind ourselves of Garrett Hardin's important observation that "the essential characteristic of a tribe is that it should follow a double standard of morality—one kind of behavior for in-group relations, another for out-group."[61]

Fear-driven religiosity has time and again promoted this kind of tribalistic boundary posturing. It has made it possible to love one's family and religious community while hating all who are known to be in league with the Antichrist. Belief that Jews, Catholics, socialists, humanists, or feminists are in league with Satan has allowed uncivil conduct to masquerade as piety and devotion. Vigilance against the Antichrist not only legitimates aggression toward those outside one's own tribe but also helps "wall off" one's own unacceptable thoughts and desires. This has been particularly true in the last few decades when the signs of Antichrist activity have been variously located in ecumenical religious thought, modern computer systems, supermarket bar codes, rock music, and world peace organizations. Threats loom everywhere. Apocalyptic thought is adept at projecting these anxieties onto a mythic villain. As psychologist Paul Pruyser observed, "The human mind becomes automatically mythopoetic when it has to contend with threatened or actual attack upon a person's organismic integrity."[62] This is also what literary critic W. Warren Wagar had in mind when he suggested that apocalyptic thinking stems from a primitive level of human emotion containing fears of separation, powerlessness, loneliness, and failing. The mythopoetic language of evil adversaries, reigns of lawlessness and terror, catastrophe, and final victory over one's enemies is ultimately rooted in one's own primal fears and hungers. As Wagar put it, "A sense of powerlessness can invoke all the devils of thanatos: uncontrollable rage, bitter hatred, insatiable gluttony and lust, the desire to destroy supposed enemies and oppressors, self-loathing, and cravings for humiliation and death."[63]

The point here is that a spirituality in the flesh moves us well beyond the kind of analyses possible in a wholly constructivist approach to a topic such as apocalypticism. Whereas constructivism must finally bog down in discussions of the relativity of truth, power, or legitimacy, a fully interdisciplinary investigation prompts us to get on with the task of identifying criteria that might be used to assess religion's functional value. In this case, it seems hard to avoid the conclusion that fear-driven religiosity disposes us to apocalyptic, as opposed to prophetic, modes of religious life. The history of apocalypticism in America reveals just how frail human existence can be. It appears that the sea of human insecurities is teeming with beasts that arise to threaten our social and psychological well-being. Fear and anxiety mobilize perceptual and cognitive tendencies that focus on these threats and keep us ever-vigilant for cues about their presence in our midst. By identifying these threats in the outer world, such religiosity pushes back the threat of chaos and shores up our sense of membership in a valued group. The historical record indicates, however, that such fear-driven religiosity has rarely functioned in ways that lead to a productive engagement with life. Seldom have carriers of the apocalyptic tradition acted in ways that demonstrably worked for a richer universe, for the good that seems most organizable, or most apt to be a member of a more inclusive whole. A spirituality in the flesh, then, must begin by acknowledging that religion is often fueled by discrete emotions that are unlikely to yield thought or behavior most of us will deem noble. Such acknowledgement signals the recognition of life's higher possibilities.

3

Wonder and the Moral Emotions

The Genesis of Aesthetic Spirituality

We can further our understanding of the biological sources of religion by examining a mode of religiosity that contrasts sharply with apocalypticism. An ideal candidate for such a parallel inquiry is the distinctive spiritual outlook that historian Catherine Albanese has termed "nature religion."[1] Albanese uses this term to tie together a variety of religious perspectives that share a tendency to view nature as infused with immanent spiritual powers and meanings.

Albanese's concept of nature religion is similar to what intellectual historian Perry Miller had in mind when he identified a strain of American religious life that contains "an indestructible element which was mystical, and a feeling for the universe which was almost pantheistic."[2] Historian William Clebsch, too, finds a form of nature mysticism at the core of the most creative episodes in American religious thought. Clebsch referred to this distinctive form of religion as "aesthetic spirituality." Aesthetic spirituality, according to Clebsch, contrasts sharply with the predominant religious outlook of America's churches; it involves neither doctrinal creeds nor moral codes. The aesthetic religious posture emphasizes, instead, the inner experience of beholding God as spiritually present within the natural universe. It equates spirituality with "consciousness of the beauty of living in harmony with divine things."[3]

It is immediately clear that nature religion or aesthetic spirituality embodies a very different perceptual and cognitive style than apocalypticism. Aesthetic spirituality doesn't emphasize either scripture or doctrines. It doesn't require piety or submission to group authority. The two contrasting styles of spirituality—though both prevalent in American culture—share almost nothing in common. This raises an important question: why do styles of personal religiosity vary so greatly from one another? A multidisciplinary spirituality in the flesh seeks to supplement cultural explanations of such diversity by suggesting that different forms of religious thought might at least in part be motivated by quite different bodily programs. The variety of religious experience is, in part, due to the variety of bodily excitations.

The Moral Emotions

Evolution constructed brains to solve many adaptive problems other than those ensuring short-term physical survival. Evolution also favored emotional programs designed to solve recurrent problems that are more clearly cultural than physical. This is why it important that we distinguish between the very different emotional systems that exert motivational influences on perception and cognition. Psychologist Jonathan Haidt proposes that evolution favored a distinct set of motivational programs that he calls the "moral emotions." Moral emotions differ from those emotional programs designed to solve problems related to immediate physical safety in that they are designed to serve the interests or welfare of the social group to which a person belongs.[4] He points out that emotions such as disgust, contempt, shame, embarrassment, and guilt promote the long-term interests of a social group by inducing both loyalty and conformity to group activities.

According to Haidt, both awe and wonder are among the moral emotions that contribute to the formation, maintenance, and occasional restructuring of social groups. Haidt proposes, for example, that awe consists of a biologically based emotional reaction whose principal function is to prompt subordination to a powerful leader. As Haidt and his colleague Dacher Keltner argue, "Much as humans are biologically prepared to respond to certain fear-inducing stimuli (e.g., fast approaching objects, darkness), . . . humans are prepared to respond to awe-inducing stimuli (e.g., large stature and displays of strength and confidence)."[5] It appears that awe is thus a biological response to stimuli that are sufficiently vast (i.e., physical size, fame, authority, prestige) that they diminish our sense of self and challenge our accustomed frame of reference. The cognitive and perceptual changes peculiar to awe remind us that one of the principal functions of emotions generally is that they frequently serve as "place markers" designating individuals' roles and positions within social hierarchies.[6] Awe, as a social emotion, has an important role in the formation and maintenance of social hierarchies. The experience of awe is comprised of biologically based action tendencies that prompt subordination to the dominant individual by displaying passivity, heightened attention toward what is perceived as powerful, and imitation. Although awe has evolutionary origins in procuring subordination to powerful social others, it can also be detected in experiences triggered by vast stimuli arising from nature, art, and certain epiphanic experiences. Haidt and Keltner surveyed examples of various revelatory or epiphanic experiences such as are attributed to Arjuna in the *Bhagavad Gita* or to Paul in the New Testament. Haidt and Keltner found evidence suggesting that "awe can transform people and reorient their lives, goals and values.... awe-inducing events may be one of the fastest and most powerful methods of personal change and growth."[7]

Wonder belongs to the same family of emotions as awe. Wonder, like awe, is elicited by novel or unexpected stimuli that defy assimilation to pre-existing conceptual categories. Yet wonder differs from awe in that it is wholly lacking in fear or submission. Indeed, wonder often begins as a response to something that strikes us as intensely powerful, real, or beautiful—yet motivates sustained contemplation and engagement rather than subordination. Haidt even suggests that fellow researchers have inexplicably neglected the study of wonder precisely because it motivates response patterns that don't quite fit standard accounts of emotional functions. Haidt points out that wonder mobilizes physiological, perceptual, and cognitive changes that "enlarge the field of peripheral vision" and open our attention to a wider field of stimuli than we would ordinarily attend to. And, too, wonder-driven responses to certain kinds of beauty and perfection seem to "open our hearts and minds" to other persons in our social group.[8]

The motivational functions unique to emotions such as wonder illustrate why some researchers find it useful to distinguish between "positive" and "negative" emotions. Negative emotions (e.g., fear or anger) are those emotional programs triggered when new experiences fall short of expectations, thereby frustrating or threatening the organism's overall well-being. In contrast, positive emotions (e.g., joy, interest, or wonder) are those emotional programs triggered when new experiences exceed expectations. Positive emotions are associated with experiences that broaden an individual's thought-action repertoire and elevate an individual's level of pleasure or enthusiasm. Positive emotions have received less experimental attention than the study of negative emotions. A principal reason for this is that negative emotions are easier than positive emotions to differentiate according to their facial, autonomic, and behavioral components. Barbara Fredrickson argues that although research of positive emotions has lagged behind that of negative emotions, empirical evidence supports what she terms a "broaden-and-build" model that explains how certain positive emotions broaden an individual's thought-action repertoire.[9] As Fredrickson shows, emotions such as wonder expand a person's scope of cognition, increase her or his intellectual repertoire, and build a more extensive network of social relationships.

The ability of wonder to "broaden-and-build" a person's thought-action repertoire is connected with distinct changes in our perceptual and cognitive activities. The highly regarded psychologist Carroll Izard suggests that wonder is closely associated with joy and interest—two emotions that, like wonder, motivate enhanced affiliation with the surrounding environment. Certain environmental stimuli elicit heightened interest which "motivates exploration and learning, and guarantees the person's engagement in the environment. Survival and adaptation require such engagement. Interest . . . is the only emotion that can sustain long-term constructive or creative endeavors."[10] Wonder, because it also seems to be accompanied by many of the same emotional functions of joy, makes long-term engagement with the surrounding world intrinsically rewarding. Wonder imbues the world with an alluring quality, fostering increased openness and receptivity rather than immediate utilitarian action.

Wonder has certain similarities with other emotions that originate in what might be termed a "startle response." That is, like other emotions such as surprise or curiosity, wonder is part of the brain's inherited tendencies for agency detection in the face of uncertainty. As evolutionary biologist Richard Dawkins explains, "It is as if the nervous system is turned at successive hierarchical levels to respond strongly to the unexpected, weakly or not at all to the expected."[11] Several of our emotions are critically involved in responding to anomalous events by mobilizing responses aimed at "agency detection." As Scott Atran explains, "Cognitive schema for recognizing and interpreting animate agents may be a crucial part of our evolutionary heritage, which primes us to anticipate intention in the unseen causes of uncertain situations that carry the risk of danger or the promise of opportunity, such as predators, protectors, and prey."[12] Wonder, then, often arises in the perception of something novel, unexpected, or inexplicable. This is particularly true when we perceive something that strikes us as so vital or alive, so beautiful, or so true that we can not assimilate this experience into customary concepts of causal agency. We might go further and suggest that wonder differs from the emotions most frequently studied by evolutionary theorists in at least three important ways.[13] First, wonder is an emotion linked with approach and affiliation rather than avoidance. Wonder motivates a quest for increased connection with the putative source of unexpected displays of life, beauty, or truth. Wonder is thus some-what rare among the emotions in its functional capacity to motivate persons to venture outward into increased rapport with the environment.

Second, wonder differs from many other emotions in that it awakens our mental capacity for abstract, higher-order thought. Whereas curiosity typically directs cognition to understand agency by progressively identifying ever-smaller parts of the larger whole, wonder directs cognition to understand agency by seeking to identify some larger whole that might be responsible for the observed anomaly. Unlike curiosity, wonder prompts us to contemplate what might be behind, above, or beyond observed phenomena. Wonder thus awakens our mental capacity for linking perception with abstract interpreta-tions. Although such higher-order connections rarely contribute to our im-mediate physical survival, they are indispensable to humanity's chances for obtaining other kinds of satisfaction and fulfillment.

Third, wonder temporarily suspends utilitarian striving. Wonder renders us relatively passive and receptive, frequently giving rise to the sensation that we participate in a more general order of life.[14] Psychologists Richard and Bernice Lazarus also note that wonder causes a sense of mystery and produces both trust and a sense of belonging. Wonder, they observe, is frequently stimulated by sights of natural beauty or by the sudden recognition that life is a "gift." The sensation of wonder is experienced as intrinsically enjoyable. For this reason they suggest that wonder "can be likened to religious experience." Conceding that wonder is different from most of the emotions typically de-scribed in scientific literature, they conclude that it is "an emotional reaction that remains at the frontier of our understanding of the mind."[15]

This last feature of wonder—its capacity to deactivate temporarily our utilitarian striving to simultaneously open up a sense of participating in a more general order of life—is crucial to our understanding of its central role as a "moral" emotion. Wonder fosters receptivity and openness. These are traits that lead to both interpersonal and moral sensitivity. Human capacities for utilitarian striving and active mastery of the environment are certainly critical to our species' adaptive strength. Yet, when unchecked, they lead us to con-struct worldviews that are impervious and blind to the realities of the larger environment in which we live. Theologian Don Browning argues that active, goal-oriented cognition is mightily important to human survival. Yet it is also true that active modes of cognition are unable to help us understand how we connect with wider orders of life. Human well-being also requires receptive modes of awareness that enable us to "break out of this constructed world to some kind of larger vision."[16] Wonder, due to its peculiar ability to elicit sus-tained attention and receptivity, serves the adaptive purposes that Browning describes as "the capacity to get us in touch with the unitary and relational aspects of reality. It gives us a vision of our relatedness to the world, to other human beings, and to God."[17]

Wonder and the Capacity for Metaphysical Thought

Wonder emerged as part of humanity's genetically encoded responses to unexpected features of the environment. Whereas other emotional responses to uncertainty prompt us to identify agency or intentionality within the immediate environment, wonder instead prompts us to consider how our experience discloses agency or intentionality at a more general level of existence. What is peculiar to the emotion of wonder is that rather than leading to immediate defensive action, it leads to contemplation of why things are as they are. As such, wonder is the ontogenetic basis for the development of thinking that goes beyond the constraints of the immediate physical environment. It stimulates our efforts to contemplate ever-more general orders of existence. The human capacity for such thought appears intimately linked with the co-evolution of humanity's larger cerebral cortex and our cultural mode of existence. As larger cerebral cortexes made it possible to free ourselves from immediate stimulus-response reactions, we required cognitive skills to construct ever-more general models of ourselves and the world we live in. The motivational functions performed by wonder, then, are closely linked with the development of some of humanity's highest cognitive and cultural achievements. Not the least of these achievements is the emergence of both moral and metaphysical metaphysical reflection.

Wonder's role in generating modes of cognitive activity responsible for both moral and metaphysical thought can first be detected in early childhood with the appearance of children's "why" questions. The work of Jean Piaget is therefore relevant to understanding the origin and function of wonder in individual human life. Piaget's goal was to elaborate a broadly biological explanation of knowledge. Because he viewed knowledge as a form of adaptation continuous with organic adaptation, he set about studying the cognitive development of children as they adapted to ever-expanding environmental perplexities.[18] He closely observed children, particularly his own children, as they learned to make sense of the world about them. Of particular interest to Piaget was the sequential process through which children come to understand such things as causality, the relationship between parts and wholes, and the relationship between change and constancy. He eventually identified three distinct phases in the normal course of cognitive development: the sensorimotor phase (roughly, ages 0–2), during which infants relate to the world largely through reflexes and acquired motor habits; the phase of "concrete operations" (roughly, ages 2–11), during which young children learn to organize experience into fairly static configurations; and the phase of "formal operations" (beginning after the age of 12), when teens gradually learn to construct hypothetical models of reality that allow them to consider and compare ideas and thereby achieve a measure of mental control or direction over their lives. Subsequent researchers have challenged Piaget's argument concerning the universality of these phases and his relative neglect of the role that environmental conditions have upon the way that children learn to construct their reality. These limitations noted, Piaget's essential paradigms have nonetheless generated a great deal of what we know today about cognitive development and thus provide a helpful context for understanding how the emotional experience of wonder contributes to acquisition of specific kinds of cognitive skills.[19]

Piaget studied the way that children tried to solve various problems that arose while interacting with their natural and social environments. Each new problem disrupted the equilibrium that had previously existed between children and their world, thereby motivating them to acquire new cognitive understandings that would once again allow them to interact successfully with their surroundings. Piaget was thus interpreting cognitive development as a form of biological adaptation. He found it useful to explain this ongoing process of adaptation by drawing attention to the two alternating ways that we relate to our world: assimilation and accommodation. Assimilation represents our efforts to incorporate new experiences into the existing stock of ideas with which we fashion our goal-seeking behavior. When new experience can't be assimilated into existing cognitive schema, accommodation occurs. Accommodation refers to changes the individual makes to adjust to the environment. Accommodation signifies the way we modify our previous cognitive structures to include those new features of the environment learned through new or unexpected perceptions.

New experience often disturbs the equilibrium that formerly existed between a child's cognitive structures and the surrounding world. Cognitive development occurs as persons struggle to resolve this disequilibrium through some combination of assimilation or accommodation. The emotions of surprise, curiosity, and wonder are therefore critical to the overall course of cognitive development. All three emotions originate as reactions to unexpected events, mobilizing efforts to change cognitive structures in ways that will ensure our overall well-being. Surprise is the most general of these "orienting responses" and may easily combine with curiosity or wonder. William Charlesworth points out that Piaget's entire model of cognitive development hinges around the central role played by the emotion of surprise. Charlesworth explains that the emotion of surprise is a complex orienting response that has an "instigatory effect on attentional and curiosity behaviors" needed if unexpected "stimuli are to become part of and help reshape existing cognitive schemata."[20]

Surprise reactions have a general arousal effect. Surprise mobilizes selective attention to the environment and thereby alters our manner of attending to, and processing, sensory information. The emotion of surprise thereby ensures that the organism behaves in such a way as to produce new knowledge about problematic properties of the environment. Among other things, surprise instigates the process whereby we grow beyond concrete thought and become capable of more abstract, fully operational thought: "Under normal environmental conditions surprise reaction and subsequent attentional and curiosity behaviors are very hard to suppress, and that for this reason they seem to be good candidates for the mechanisms that insure that most individuals make the progression from sensorimotor intelligence to formal thought."[21]

Piaget was also aware that curiosity, like surprise, motivates cognitive growth. He frequently observed how curiosity propels children to interact proactively with their environment. Piaget often used the metaphor of "little scientists" to capture the way that curiosity drives children to investigate and create in the context of their interactions with the world. His point was that curiosity is rewarding in its own right. Curiosity draws children into sustained rapport with their environment. Curiosity motivates children not just to register experience passively, but to organize and interpret such experience. Of special significance is the fact that curiosity motivates sustained investigation of the relationship between ideas and experience. Curiosity therefore helps individuals refine their conceptions of the world to correspond more closely with the actual facts of experience.

Piaget's research focused primarily on the developmental acquisition of domain-specific knowledge rather than the ability to think in ways that stretch beyond domains. Thus Piaget, and cognitive psychologists in general, extol the role of curiosity in fostering the assimilation of environmental patterns into our working stock of behavioral strategies, but inadvertently denigrate cognitive activities that seek to make connections between different kinds of things or to put things together in higher order ways.[22] And these, of course, are the cognitive activities most directly stimulated by wonder. Fortunately, the total context of Piaget's work provide conceptual tools for understanding the developmental link between the emotion of wonder and our capacity for metaphysical thought. In his *The Language and Thought of the Child*, Piaget noted that the emergence of "why" questions in early childhood is linked with a capacity to think about the existence of an imperceptible reality behind the apparent perceptible world.[23] This observation draws attention to the fact that children are naturally curious about the purposes, intentionality, or teleology of things. Children have a natural tendency to infer the existence of a reality that in some way lies beyond or behind observed reality—and it is this more general sense of reality that enables them to unite objects together or to interpret their purpose or meaning.

This is an important observation. Children are motivated not only to understand local causal mechanisms but also to understand them in terms of some broader or larger context of meaning. This begins fairly early in childhood when children ponder time before they were born, what life was like in the age of dinosaurs, or what life will be like when they grow up.[24] All such cognitive operations require the construction of larger contexts based upon nonactual, fictional, and metaphysical possibilities of the past, present, or future. This process extends much further in late childhood and early adolescence when we first observe the movement from what Piaget labeled "concrete operations" to "formal operational thought." Formal operations depend upon the adolescent's ability to entertain abstract, possible constructions of reality that then guide hypethetico-deductive reasoning whereby multiple strategies can be entertained and compared. Thus, as Piaget notes, the adolescent differs from the child by becoming "an individual who thinks beyond the present and forms theories about everything, delighting especially in considerations of that which is not."[25] The highest levels of reasoning require the construction of a hypothetical model of existence, a structured whole that can be used to assess the meaning or value of the observed particulars of existence. As Piaget notes, at this important stage "reality becomes secondary to possiblity."[26] The existence of higher-order conceptions of reality frees us from sheer necessity and brute survival to consider what our existential and ethical response to life might optimally be.

The point here is that just as curiosity propels children to sustain their inquiries into the workings of physical reality, wonder is a prime ingredient in the emergence of higher-order conceptions of existence. Wonder disrupts cognitive equilibrium and prompts us to accommodate to the most general order of thinking possible—an order from which we might contemplate the intrinsic cause or intentionality of things. At least potentially, neither children nor adults have any problem distinguishing between the actual and the possible. The difficulty lies instead in discerning the boundaries of the possible.[27] We lack means of empirically testing our conceptions of the possible. For this reason, we typically rely on our own sense of plausibility and, of course, upon the mythic and theological traditions of our community. Beginning with Piaget, developmental psychologists have implicitly denigrated such cognitive processes, owing to their frequent connection with theological and mythic thought that strike researchers as forms of prelogical thinking.[28] Developmental psychologists have thus implicitly favored cognitive processes associated with assimilation (which can be empirically tested in our experience) to those associated with accommodation (which are not always susceptible to such empirical testing).[29] This brief foray into studies of cognitive development illuminates the fact that cognitive growth is defined by much more than the acquisition of skills for manipulating our external environment. From childhood on, humans are also curious in their own right, eager to accommodate to features of the environment that arouse their interest and that disclose something that strikes them as intensely powerful, real, true, or beautiful.[30] That is, we often find ourselves moved by a state of wonder to approach and make contact with the surrounding world. Moreover, we find pleasure or intrinsic reward in finding relatedness not just to discrete objects but to something more, some greater whole that connects and imparts meaning to otherwise separate objects. Wonder elicits sustained accommodation to the widest possible range of human experience even as it triggers the construction of cognitive categories that make it possible to seek what Aristotle described as "final" rather than "efficient" or "material" causes that affect our well-being.

It is important, too, to note how an emotion such as wonder strengthens our capacity for moral conduct. First, it does so by making it possible to envision general orders of existence in reference to which we might make moral judgments. Second, wonder elicits our prolonged engagement with life. By imbuing life with an alluring luster, wonder sustains our desire to connect with the surrounding world. For this reason the experience of wonder often leads to forms of empathy and selfless concern quite different than would arise in a life shaped solely by the active will. Ethical theorist Martha Nussbaum argues that wonder is the emotion that most clearly enables humans to move beyond self-interest to recognize and respond to others in their own right. Wonder, she writes, is the emotion that responds

> to the pull of the object, and one might say that in it the subject is maximally aware of the value of the object, and only minimally aware, if at all, of its relationship to her own plans. That is why it is likely to issue in contemplation, rather than in any other sort of action toward the object.[31]

Insofar as persons remain bound by ego-centered perspectives of the world, their ethical orientation is largely eudaemonistic (i.e., geared toward personal well-being as regulated by rational calculations of self-interest). Yet, "wonder, as non-eudaemonisitc as an emotion can be, helps move distant objects within the circle of a person's scheme of ends . . . seeing others as part of one's own circle of concern."[32] Nussbaum thus contends that no emotion matches wonder in its capacity to evoke true empathy or compassion. The very existence of living beings who appear to us as an ultimate limit to our own egoism awakens wonder at the way in which others embody the ultimate source of all life and vitality. As Nussbaum observes, "Wonder at the complex living thing itself " is what mobilizes our compassion and empathy.[33] Wonder re-draws our world of concern, establishing true mutuality with a wider sphere of life.

Emotional Episodes and the Genesis of Aesthetic Spirituality

Just as fear can be implicated in the biological impulse to reconstruct the world in apocalyptic ways, so can wonder be linked with the genesis of various forms of nature religion or aesthetic spirituality. A prime example of this connection can be found in the life and thought of John Muir (1838–1914). Muir, who later served as the founding president of the Sierra Club and was the principal instigator of the National Park System, moved to the United States from his native Scotland when he was just eleven.[34] John grew up in rural Wisconsin where he was afforded few opportunities to socialize with other youth, but was constantly surrounded by wildlife. Years later he recounted how "this sudden plash into wilderness—baptism in Nature's warm heart—how utterly happy it made us! Nature streaming into us, wooingly teaching her wonderful glowing lessons."[35]

Immersion in nature directed John's attention to unexpected phenomena. He remembers, for example, how he used to "wonder how the woodpeckers could bore holes so perfectly round, true mathematical circles." The odd path blazed by forest fires would set him "wondering why all the trees and everybody and everything did not share the same fate." Or, while watching mosquitoes select their targets, he was prompted to "wonder more and more at the extent of their knowledge."[36] Thus, from an early age John was constitutionally sus-ceptible to the emotion of wonder. He responded to unexpected perceptions of beauty, order, or vitality by setting these phenomena in ever-larger contexts. This sense of "something more" that mysteriously manifested itself in Wis-consin's flora and fauna was for him nothing less than a continuing stream of divine epiphanies. He was "urged on and on through endless, inspiring, Godful beauty."[37]

As John reached the age of twenty, he decided it was time to break away from his father's stern authoritarianism. One manifestation of his rebelliousness was a newfound interest in reading Shakespeare, Milton, and virtually every book he could put his hands on—other than the Bible, which his father took literally. A second avenue for exerting his independence was his penchant for tinkering with mechanical devices. His father found both of these to be careless diversions. But John persevered. In time, he invented several new mechanical devices such as clocks, thermometers, and a contraption that could arouse someone from sleep in the morning by jolting them out of bed. Finally, at the age of twenty-two and despite his father's objections, John gathered up his inventions and traveled to Madison so that he could display them at a state exposition. His inventions caught the attention of many of those who attended the exposition. A few encouraged him to develop his inventive prowess further and succeeded in talking John into enrolling in the University of Wisconsin.

While studying at the University of Wisconsin, John was greatly influenced by two professors who introduced him to the writings of the American Transcendentalists such as Henry David Thoreau and Ralph Waldo Emerson (whom the wife of one of these professors knew personally). These writings helped John build a bridge away from his father's narrow biblical religion to a wider world of thought and feeling. After a few years of taking classes (selected somewhat randomly rather than adhering to a fixed curriculum) and a brief sojourn through Canada to avoid the draft during the Civil War, John at last realized it was time to leave the University of Wisconsin for what he called "the university of the wilderness." Despite his aptitude for mechanical work, he feared spending any more of his time among machines. In his opinion, the world of machines strives to reduce the living flow of nature to rule and order. He yearned, instead, for more sustained immersion in Godful beauty.

A brief sojourn through several southeastern states finally led to California's Sierra mountain range. For the next seven years, these mountains were John Muir's home, or more accurately, his temple. For it was in the mountains that he was fully baptized in the higher powers at work in the universe. And it was in the mountains that he was instructed in a moral vision that enables us to remain faithful to those higher powers.

Muir's time in the Sierras was a catechism conducted by the emotion of wonder. It started the moment he began letting go of his accustomed way of seeing things and allowed himself to be guided by the fresh perceptions available to him. His journals and letters are striking in this regard. They provide insight into the sequence of unexpected perspectives that jarred Muir out of older perceptual patterns and invited him to view life from new, higher-order conceptual frameworks. The grand vistas of mountain ranges and wide valleys provided perspectives that readily invited him to widen the scales he might use to measure and interpret the significance of an object or event.

Muir's growing knowledge of geological time also enabled him to see life from unexpected perspectives. He might, for example, focus his attention on a simple raindrop. But as he began to view this raindrop against the vast context of geological time, he unexpectedly found himself awestruck: "How interesting to trace the history of a single raindrop!... since the first raindrop fell on the newborn leafless Sierra.... [each drop is] God's messenger, angel of love sent on its way with majesty and pomp and display of power that make man's greatest shows ridiculous."[38]

Muir was aware that his experiences in the Sierras were significantly altering his perception and cognition. Against the vast vistas afforded by the mountains, he was no longer able to organize experience with accustomed notions of time, background/foreground, and causality. He once wrote his brother that "the forest trees seemed to be running round in a circle chase and all the streams by the roadside seemed to be running uphill."[39] One of Muir's biographers, Michael Cohen, has observed that Muir was leaving the world of machines and entering a mystical perspective.[40] To Muir, nature now flowed in patterns which transcended scientific laws. When viewing mountain peaks at dawn, for example, Muir saw that they were "pervaded with the soul of light... they are made one, unseparate, unclothed, open to the Divine Soul, dissolved in the mysterious incomparable Spirit of holy Light."[41] The real way to apprehend nature, according to Muir, was in a perceptual mode filled with "rejoicing and wondering." Michael Cohen has aptly noted that "if a reader learned anything from [Muir's] narration, it was not what to see but how to see it.... He tried to make his readers powerful and enthusiastic observers, like himself. They would believe in the divine beauty."[42]

Immersion in nature was, to Muir, a sacrament much like baptism. It made all things new. As Stephen Fox observes, Muir's spiritual way of beholding nature made it possible for him to see "that the reductive tendency of modern science in breaking knowledge into ever smaller pieces of specialization obscured the whole picture."[43] Muir saw unities, not fragments. His wonder-driven sensibility took him beyond an anthropomorphic vision of nature. Having shifted to a perceptual frame of reference that wasn't circumscribed by the human ego, Muir acquired a truly biocentric vision of nature. He could see that humans were but one small part of a vaster whole. As he put it, the "freshness of perception" which the wilderness inspires in us helps us to "lose consciousness of our separate existence; you blend with the landscape and become part and parcel of Nature."[44] The wonder-driven changes in Muir's perceptual and cognitive orientation to the world drew him beyond an egocentric or even anthropocentric perspective of the world. He became, in other words, maximally aware of the intrinsic value of all forms of life and minimally aware of their relationship to human desires or aspirations. Wonder led him to see the value of nature wholly independent of human need or desire. He came to see that rattlesnakes, tarantulas, floods, and earthquakes deserve to be viewed as central to God's creative intentions as humans.

Muir's wilderness experiences sensitized him to natural forces that are different from those recognized by science or by our churches. His peculiar way of apprehending nature through "rejoicing and wondering" made it possible to identify patterns or harmonies not otherwise discernible. Thus, even though Muir embraced Darwin and was a thoroughgoing evolutionist, he was yet unwilling to reduce nature to purely mechanical forces. Where Darwin saw a world controlled purely by the interplay of chance and struggle, Muir perceived only the wholeness of nature and the "mystery of harmony." Muir's distinctive perceptual and cognitive orientation to experience looked past material and efficient causes of events and instead focused on the causal presence of a "higher" harmony: "Evolution!—a wonderful, mouth-filling word, isn't it! . . . Somewhere, before evolution was, was an Intelligence that laid out the plan, and evolution is the process, not the origin, of the harmony."[45]

Life in the wilderness taught Muir that nature functions as a unified organism. This vision carried with it a pantheistic sense of the sacredness of all being—putting Muir at the forefront of nineteenth- and early-twentieth-century thought about the environment. This spiritual sensibility carried over into his efforts to establish the National Parks movement and with his founding of the Sierra Club, one of the most important conservationist societies in history. As the entry on Muir in *The Encyclopedia of Nature and Religion* concludes, "Even when losing important battles, Muir's passionate writing contributed to shifts in public perceptions that help account for the continuing strength of preservationist sentiment in the United States. His thought has become nearly canonical within the contemporary environmental movement—and deep ecologists have posthumously adopted Muir as a central intellectual and spiritual elder—precisely for his 'resacralization' of nature—a perceptive task they view as a prerequisite to the re-establishment of proper human behavior toward the natural world."[46] It seems, then, that Muir's lasting contribution to the world was not just what to see in nature but how to see it. Muir taught us that learning to behold nature in a manner permeated by "rejoicing and wondering" is the important first step toward becoming a citizen of an ecologically healthy universe.

A more recent progenitor of nature religion was Rachel Carson (1907–1964).[47] Shy and soft-spoken, Carson became the leading voice of the environmental movement that gained momentum in the 1960s. She grew up in a small town outside Pittsburgh, Pennsylvania. She later recalled that she was "rather a solitary child and spent a great deal of time in woods and beside streams, learning the birds and the insects and flowers."[48] Upon graduation from high school, Carson entered Pennsylvania College for Women (now Chatham College) to major in English and become a writer. Midway through her junior year, however, she changed her major to zoology. At the time, it appeared that Rachel was abandoning her literary aspirations. She graduated from college with high honors and decided to pursue a master's degree in marine zoology at Johns Hopkins. There were few careers open to women in the 1930s—even to those with graduate degrees. Carson was fortunate to land a civil service position as a writer and editor with the Fish and Wildlife Services. One of the first two women ever to be hired by this governmental agency, Carson slowly worked her way up the bureaucratic ladder. She was initially hired as assistant aquatic biologist before being promoted to the positions of associate aquatic biologist, aquatic biologist, information specialist, and biologist and chief editor.

One of Carson's projects on marine life led to an article that was eventually published in the *Atlantic Monthly* in 1937. Simon and Schuster approached her after the article appeared and signed her to a contract for her first book, *Under the Sea-Wind*. In 1951, Rachel published a second book, *The Sea Around Us*. The book was a huge commercial success, staying near the top of the best-seller list for eighty-six weeks. The royalties from this book allowed her to resign from her governmental position and devote herself full-time to a life of writing about her abiding reverence for life.

Carson was a careful, deliberate writer. Her goal was not just to convey information. She strove to introduce her readers to a new way of seeing the world. She wrote, for example, "Whenever I go down into this magical zone of the low water of the spring tides, I look for the most delicately beautiful of all the shore's inhabitants . . . In that fairy cave I was not disappointed. . . . Here were creatures so exquisitely fashioned that they seemed unreal, their beauty too fragile to exist in a world of crushing force."[49] Her intention was to describe the unexpected beauties found in nature in such a way that she might prompt wonder in her readers. She sensed the tragedy in the fact that "most of us walk unseeing through the world, unaware alike of its beauties, its wonders, and the strange and sometimes terrible intensity of the lives that are being lived about us."[50]

Carson's writing evoked emotions that would elicit an abiding reverence for life. It was not just the sea that she wrote about. It was a way of seeing the sea—a way that disrupted our short-sighted utilitarian frameworks and allows us, instead, to see how our entire existence connects with the cosmic flow of life. To see the recurring patterns through which the sea has spawned life for thousands of years "is to have knowledge of things that are as nearly eternal as any earthly life can be. These things were before ever humans stood on the shore of the ocean and looked out upon it with wonder; they continue year in, year out, through the centuries and the ages, while humanity's kingdoms rise and fall."[51] Viewing the world "in the long vistas of geologic time" altered Carson's vision in such a way as grant the natural universe a value independent of human use. When seen against the cosmic background, "this same earth and sea have no need of us." Such vision reverses figure and ground, making human problems and motivations less relevant to the flow of life: "Perhaps if we reversed the telescope and looked at humans down these long vistas, we should find less time and inclination to plan for our own destruction."[52]

Experiences of wonder led Carson to what might be called an ethics of appreciation rather than an ethics of obedience to moral authority. Carson believed that moral conduct flows naturally from emotions producing empathy and identification. She observed that "in the artificial world of our cities and towns, we often forget the true nature of our planet and the long vistas of its history."[53] The unexpected beauty of nature, however, jars us out of everyday utilitarian rationality and elicits emotions that set us in search of meanings that somehow lie just beyond sensory appearances:

> Underlying the beauty of the spectacle there is meaning and signif-
> icance. It is the elusiveness of that meaning that haunts us, that
> sends us again and again into the natural world where the key to the
> riddle is hidden. It sends us back to the edge of the sea, where
> the . . . forces of evolution are at work today, as they have been
> since the appearance of what we know as life; and where the spec-
> tacle of living creatures faced by the cosmic realities of their world is
> crystal clear.[54]

Carson's lifelong mission was to teach her readers how to feel about nature. As her biographer, Linda Lear, explains, "Wonder and awe were, for her, the highest emotions."[55] While outlining one of her major articles, Carson jotted down the basic creed that guided her personal and professional life: "Once you are *aware* of the wonder and beauty of earth, you will want to learn about it." The article went on to elaborate how the emotion of wonder produces a proper reverence for life: "Once the emotions have been aroused—a sense of the beautiful, the excitement of the new and the unknown, a feeling of sympathy, pity, admiration or love—then we wish for knowledge about the object of our emotional response. Once found, it has lasting meaning."[56] Carson placed her final hope for the survival of life on the empathy, compassion, and care aroused by the emotion of wonder. "I believe," she wrote, "that the more clearly we can focus our attention of the wonders and realities of the universe about us, the less taste we shall have for destruction."[57]

What Rachel Carson teaches us is that wonder is a profoundly functional emotion. This is in sharp contrast to the position taken by many contemporary scientists such as Richard Dawkins, Scott Atran, and Steven Pinker. In their view, the highest and best mental faculties produced by evolution have to do with utilitarian rationality, not the kind of mental processes mobilized by wonder. Dawkins, for example, acknowledges humanity's "appetite for wonder," but insists that this appetite is something that only "real science ought to be feeding" or it will lead only to delusion.[58] Atran and Pinker similarly believe that wonder is an example of the application of mental tools to problems other than those the mind was designed by natural selection to solve.[59] Carson saw the matter quite differently. She acknowledged that humanity's technological rationality is sufficiently developed that we are now capable of taking over many of the functions of God. Yet, she cautioned, "As humans approach the 'new heaven and the new earth'—or the space-age universe . . . they must do so with humility rather than arrogance." To this she added, "And along with humility I think there is still a place for wonder."[60]

Carson placed humility and wonder at the core of her spiritual orientation to life. She told a group of journalists that the emotions aroused by natural beauty have "a necessary place in the spiritual development of any individual or any society." She continued, "I believe that whenever we substitute something human-made and artificial for a natural feature of the earth, we have retarded some part of humanity's spiritual growth."[61] Carson was a deeply spiritual person. Yet she believed that genuine spirituality emerged from wonder at the facts of nature, not from submitting our minds to ancient scriptures. Thus humility, wonder, and a reverence for life—not adherence to institutional religion—were for her the spiritual virtues suited to the ongoing flow of life.[62]

Carson found herself in midlife suddenly faced with responsibility of caring for the future. When her niece passed away, Carson assumed the task of raising her grandnephew, Roger. It was while reflecting on how best to raise Roger that she penned an article for *Woman's Home Companion* titled "Help Your Child to Wonder." This article, later published with photographic illustrations as *A Sense of Wonder*, captured Carson's maturing vision of how we might help a new generation develop a reverence for life. She began this discourse by noting: "A child's world is fresh and new and beautiful, full of wonder and excitement. It is our misfortune that for most of us that clear-eyed vision, that true instinct for what is beautiful and awe-inspiring, is dimmed and even lost before we reach adulthood." She then ventured:

> If I had influence with the good fairy who is supposed to pre-
> side over the christening of all children I should ask that her gift to
> each child in the world be a sense of wonder so indestructible that
> it would last throughout life, as an unfailing antidote against the
> boredom and disenchantments of later years, the sterile preoccupa-
> tion with things that are artificial, the alienation from the sources of
> our strength.[63]

Carson understood well the kinds of skepticism that staunch rationalists such as Dawkins, Atran, or Pinker might have about the importance of the emotion of wonder. Wonder is surely not linked with early humanity's hunt-ing and gathering survival tasks. She was quite aware that wonder sets us in search of meanings and truths that lay just beyond the boundaries of human existence. Yet this is precisely why she believed wonder to be a virtue necessary for the long-term survival of our species.

> What is the value of preserving and strengthening this sense of
> awe and wonder, this recognition of something beyond the bound-
> aries of human existence? Is the exploration of the natural world just
> a pleasant way to pass the golden hours of childhood or is there
> something deeper?
>   I am sure there is something much deeper, something lasting
> and significant. Those who dwell, as scientists or laymen, among the
> beauties and mysteries of the earth are never alone or weary of
> life. . . . their thoughts can find paths that lead to inner contentment
> and to renewed excitement in living. Those who contemplate the
> beauty of the earth find reserves of strength that will endure as long
> as life lasts.[64]

Carson did not expect wonder to lead to the same types of truth that we expect from science or logical analysis. As she wrote elsewhere, wonder instead awakens a passion for "some universal truth that lies just beyond our grasp. . . . The meaning haunts and ever eludes us, and in its very pursuit we approach the ultimate mystery of Life itself."[65] The truth to which wonder points us is noetic and transient. Yet it is precisely this kind of universal truth renews excitement in living and unlocks reserves of strength with which we might care for life around us. The ongoing pursuit of a truth "just be-yond our grasp" engages us in life; it draws us out into sustained activity on behalf of the larger world. Carson believed that the sense of wonder was uniquely designed to arouse and sustain a reverence for life. Her cautionary message was that a life without wonder puts humanity's long-term future in jeopardy.

Assessing Wonder-Driven Religiosity

In the previous chapter we noted that there is no such thing as emotion-free cognition—religious or otherwise. It is not a question of *whether* emotions influence our religious thinking, but instead a matter of *which* emotions most strongly mobilize the subprograms that influence our perception and cognition in specific ways. Wonder, as an emotional response to unexpected phenomena, gives rise to certain kinds of religious sensibilities. If there are indeed prototypical characteristics of a religious outlook shaped by wonder, then it is fitting that we try to assess the relative value of wonder-driven religiosity for humanity's overall well-being.

William James sketched out how we might go about assessing religion in his *The Varieties of Religious Experience*. James suggested that we might gauge religion according to three separate criteria. Assessments of religion must be based "on our own immediate feeling primarily; and secondarily on what we can ascertain of their experiential relations to our moral needs and to the rest of what we hold as true. *Immediate luminousness*, in short, *philosophical reasonableness*, and *moral helpfulness* are the only available criteria."[66] Taken together, these pragmatic criteria permit us to gauge the extent to which the sensibilities elicited by wonder enhance—or constrain—humanity's pursuit of the widest possible range of objective and subjective satisfactions.

That wonder, if even for the briefest duration of time, ushers in "immediate luminousness" is warrant for considering it among humanity's most sublime emotions. Its value to human life can be justified on this criterion alone. Experiences of wonder arrest our active will. They make possible the quiet contemplation of a grander scheme of life that strikes us as responsible for life's beauty, order, and vitality. Wonder thereby evokes the subjective sense that we have established harmonious relationship with the widest possible range of human experience. Wonder is thus accompanied by joy and by feelings of expansiveness. Our lives seem to open up to new possibilities. Experiences of wonder prompt sensations of intimate continuity with sources of beauty, order, and vitality unexpected in a purely rational approach to life. All of this makes for experiences of "immediate luminousness." There can be no question but that they have an immediate subjective feel that strikes us as rewarding in their own right without further need for outside validation.

What further justifies the "immediate luminousness" of experiences of wonder is their ability to make possible certain existential orientations to life that we would otherwise go without. In *Experience and God*, theologian John E. Smith argues that distinctively religious orientations to life arise in those rare moments that "occasion wonder." Smith observes that most of our life is profane. By profane, Smith means the taken-for-granted aspects of everyday life. Profane existence is ordinary. Because it is ordinary, it fails to evoke consideration of the more-than-ordinary horizons of life that might reveal to us the meaning or purpose of existence. Smith contends that we have an enduring desire to experience, even if only momentarily, an utterly different order of existence that somehow stands beyond the profane, an order of existence that is best termed the "sacred" or the "holy." Smith explains that "the daily round of events is ordinary enough and gives no occasion for wonder or special concern. In the ordinary events there is no question of judgment on life as a whole. . . . [they] harbor no mystery, nor call forth the sense that beyond and beneath our life is a holy ground."[67]

Smith's point is that experiences that "give occasion for wonder" provide glimpses of the sacred not available to those less influenced by this emotional response. Wonder-filled experiences take us beyond ordinary events to consider judgments on life as a whole. They harbor mystery, calling forth a sense of what is beyond or beneath ordinary experience. Erich Fromm made a very similar point when he observed:

> One aspect of religious experience is the *wondering*, the marveling, the becoming aware of life and of one's own existence, and of the puzzling problem of one's relatedness to the world. . . . Socrates' statement that *wonder is the beginning of* all wisdom is true not only for wisdom but for the *religious experience*. One who has never been bewildered, who has never looked upon life and his own existence as phenomena which require answers and yet, paradoxically, for which the only answers are new questions, can hardly understand what religious experience is.[68]

The second pragmatic criterion, philosophical reasonableness, provides a more complex perspective on wonder-driven orientations to life. Most biological and psychological researchers equate wonder-driven cognition with mistaken notions about cause and effect. Richard Dawkins speaks for many scientifically minded persons when he argues that "real science" ought to be feeding our appetite for wonder, not religion. Dawkins and other champions of the scientific method typically characterize wonder-driven thought as a fanciful diversion from the real facts about existence. This is why many developmental psychologists assume that wonder-driven types of cognition will (and should) gradually be discarded as we make the psychological transition from childish thinking into adult rationality. Yet, viewed from another perspective, wonder can be seen as one of the emotional sources of humanity's highest cognitive achievements. Cognitive development requires the construction of realms of possibility. Much of adult life requires our ability to formulate conceptions of more general orders of life in terms of which specific events or behaviors can be assigned meaning and value. Indeed, the highest conceptions of justice, dignity, and worth all require highly developed notions of a general order of existence that in some fundamental way lies "beyond" the observed parts of life. The important point here is that philosophical claims accompanying wonder must be assessed according to standards derived from enhanced accommodation to—not assimilation of—the wider environments we inhabit.

We must acknowledge, however, that wonder-driven cognition is rife with magical qualities. From most philosophical perspectives, magical thinking is an immature and irrational cognitive orientation to the world. Magical thinking encourages an utterly egocentric view of the world that can border on pathology. Moreover, magical thinking thwarts the assimilation of experience into a developing repertoire of reality-based conceptions of how the world operates. Yet, cognitive psychologists have also recognized that magical thinking is potentially valuable when considered from the standpoint of enhanced accommodation to experience.[69] Magical thinking involves a blurring of the usual boundary between the "inner self" and the "external world." This allows persons to feel a basic symmetry between their inner life (i.e., thoughts and desires) and the surrounding world. Wonder, and the magical blurring of distinct boundaries it sometimes occasions, thus promotes certain mental dispositions conducive to psychological well-being: a sense of seamless continuity with the world, felt-participation in a larger whole, relatedness to things of meaning, having a sense of control over life, and basic trust that the universe is responsive to our needs and desires. Magical thinking therefore has some adaptive qualities. While it is not philosophically reasonable to live permanently in a world with such blurred boundaries, it is nonetheless quite reasonable to strive for a life that periodically benefits from the affiliative nature of wondrous experience.

It appears, then, that even the elements of fantasy and illusion to which wonder often leads have some element of philosophical reasonableness. But this is not to say that abiding in wonder alone is an appropriate existential response to the ultimate context of experience. Wonder, without the balancing emotion of curiosity, will eventually lead to unproductive relationships with the world. As Piaget discovered, curiosity, too, arises amidst unexpected perceptions. Curiosity, however, turns our perception and cognition toward the ever-smaller parts that make up the totality of experience. Curiosity leads to the fine-tuning and adjustment of ideas so that they better correspond with things as they are independent of our desires and wishes. It is the emotion of curiosity, not wonder, that puts us into working touch with reality and ensures the development of productive relationships with the world over the long run. Abiding in wonder alone, therefore, is never an appropriate philosophical response to life. Without being balanced by curiosity, wonder runs the risk of leading us only to fantasy and illusion. This, of course, is so often the case with religion. When religion eschews intellectual curiosity, it loses its connection with empirical data and lived human experience. Adaptive strategies based on wonder alone are at considerable risk of steering humans away from the broadest range of experience. The basic danger of religion is that it reifies what "possibly exists." Severed from curiosity, wonder-driven religiosity runs the risk of tunnel vision. Unbalanced by curiosity, wonder all too often severs us from productive relations with the surrounding world even as it seeks to accommodate us to a nonexistent illusion.

This leads us to one last issue concerning the "philosophical reasonableness" of wonder-driven cognition. While it is true that wonder-driven thought carries considerable philosophical risk, so, too, does thought that is wholly devoid of wonder. This is particularly true of systems of thought that are overtly religious or theological in nature—yet lack any element of wonder. Wonder imparts a noetic quality to cognition. It also invests the "object of consciousness" with intrinsic value, leading us to seek closer, more harmonious relationship to this object of consciousness. For these reasons, wonder gives religious thought a leading or heuristic quality—a quality that can arguably separates mature from immature forms of religious thinking.[70] Wonder instills fascination with its object, yet recognizes that this object in some fundamental way eludes literal designation. Wonder has a tendency to ward off literalism in religious thought (as well as the authoritarianism that so often accompanies literalism). This is a particularly important point because, as Marjorie Taylor and Stephanie Carlson have found, some religious groups actively suppress the kind of cognitive openness generated by wonder.[71] Many conservative religious communities suppress nonlinear thought because it violates their clear bifurcation of the secular and sacred. This gap separating us from the sacred, they maintain, can not be bridged from the human side— leaving us dependent upon the mediating functions performed for us through scriptural or ecclesiastical authority. Assuming that mature spirituality ought to enliven rather than deaden the human intellect, some degree of wonder is indispensable to philosophically reasonable religious thought.

We might now turn to the connection between experiences of wonder and our third pragmatic criterion, their relationship to our moral needs. Wonder, like joy and interest, is characterized by its rare ability to elicit prolonged engagement with life. Experiences of wonder succeed in motivating creative and constructive approaches to life by imbuing the surrounding world with an alluring luster. Experiences of wonder enable us to view the world as it exists independent of our own immediate needs. They thereby foster empathy and compassion. It is true that wonder, per se, is likely to issue in contemplation rather than immediate action. Yet, as we saw in the lives of Muir and Carson, this is not to suggest that wonder leads to passivity or an evasion of moral responsibility. Their lives provide ample evidence that wonder pulls objects that would otherwise be of remote interest into our own circle of concerns.

As Martha Nussbaum alerted us, wonder responds to the pull of the surrounding world. It induces modes of cognition in which "the subject is maximally aware of the object, and only minimally aware, if at all, of its relationship to her own plans."[72] We saw this repeatedly in the lives of Muir and Carson. Their lives illustrated a way of seeing the world around us. Compassion and empathy predominated over utilitarian self-interest. And both came to ascribe sacredness to nature itself, making religiosity neither more nor less than an ever- fresh sensibility for what Carson termed "the ultimate mystery of Life itself."[73]

Experiences of wonder are principal sources of what historians variously call nature religion or aesthetic spirituality. They repeatedly give rise to an enduring sensibility for the sacredness of nature—a sensibility that is mystical, and inculcates a feeling for the universe which is almost pantheistic. What is more, when assessed for its overall functional value in human existence, this wonder-driven sensibility seems to comport well with pragmatic criteria for healthy and responsible living. Insofar as all religious thinking is guided by one or another emotional response toward life, it would seem that wonder would be among the principal elements of any normatively conceived spirituality in the flesh.

4

The Chemistry of Consciousness

Neuroscience and Metaphysical Illumination

Biologically based explanations of religion assume that our brains are implicated in the construction of spiritual thought and feeling. We have already examined how our emotional programs influence the way we think or feel about ourselves and our place in the wider universe. A comprehensive spirituality in the flesh must examine the many other ways that our neurochemistry makes it possible for us to construct specifically religious images of the world.

The Biology of Belief

One of the world's leading geneticists, Dean Hamer, recently added a new dimension to a biological understanding of religion. Hamer has pinpointed a specific gene that he claims triggers spiritual experience and belief. It is important to note that Hamer doesn't claim that he can explain all of religion. He limits himself to explaining a single measure of spirituality: a sense of self-transcendence. Hamer believes that one of the most crucial variables affecting the degree to which a person embraces religion is the capacity for self-transcendence, which he defines as the capacity to feel connected with something outside ourselves, such as wider causes or the universe itself. Using this measure of spirituality, Hamer has marshaled fascinating evidence in support of his claim that the capacity for faith is hardwired into our genes.

The premise of Hamer's argument is that spirituality is associated with specific kinds of changes in our sense of self. For Hamer, humans are spiritual to the extent that they feel connected with the whole of creation rather than having a sense of being a distinct or separate self. Hamer then turned to neuroscience to identify the distinct brain processes that regulate our consciousness in general, and specifically our sense of self. He discovered that a very particular gene labeled VMAT2 influences the ebb and flow of the monoamines that regulate these brain processes. In some individuals, VMAT2 makes only modest alterations in monoamine signals and therefore persons construct a sense of self that has sharp, distinct boundaries separating the self from the surrounding world. Such a person would not be inclined to spirituality since he or she does not easily feel connected to, or "at one" with, the wider universe. Yet, in other individuals, the VMAT2 gene enables monoamine signals to be more dramatic, causing dopamine, serotonin, and noradrenaline to have stronger affects on consciousness. Hamer notes, "The result is a radical shift in the communication between the front and the back of the brain—a shift that, in this individual, brings a profound sense of joy, fulfillment, and peace."[1] In this limited sense, then, VMAT2 might be called "the god gene." Differences in the VMAT2 gene are predictors of the degree to which a person is likely to have experiences of "self-transcendence" and to this extent would consider herself religious.

Hamer conducted a series of research studies by measuring persons according to a scale of self-transcendence developed by psychiatrist Robert Cloninger. Hamer detected a clear association between the VMAT2 gene and the brain processes that may alter our sense of self in ways that foster spiritual thoughts and behaviors. His findings support the view that spirituality—at least in part—is hardwired in our genes. Some of us are biologically more inclined to spirituality than others. Hamer wishes to be clear that he is not offering a narrow, monocausal view of something as complex as religion. He freely admits that genes explain only half the variation found among subjects measured according to the self-transcendence scale. Genes and the environment combine to influence all complex behaviors in humans. He is thus making a more limited claim for genetics, contending that we have "a genetic predisposition for spiritual belief that is expressed in response to, and shaped by, personal experience and the cultural environment."[2] Or, put a bit differently, he is advancing the view that spirituality is "a complex amalgamation in which certain genetically hardwired, biological patterns of response and states of consciousness are interwoven with social, cultural, and historical threads."[3]

Hamer believes humans inherit this gene because it conferred selective advantage upon our ancestors. He suggests that spiritual states of consciousness provide humans with an innate sense of optimism, making us willing to persevere even through difficult experiences. He further speculates that spirituality of this kind promotes health and accelerates recovery from disease. The long course of natural selection thus hardwired humans for religious faith because such faith enhances our individual and collective chances of survival.

Historians and philosophers of religion need to pay attention to research such as Hamer's. Hamer readily admits that genetics alone do not explain religious behavior. As he puts it, "Our genes can predispose us to believe. But they don't tell us what to believe in."[4] Even if Hamer's research eventually earns widespread acceptance, it will need to be supplemented by historical and cultural studies that further illuminate the conditions that encourage, suppress, or redirect the expression of these dispositions toward religiosity. Yet, we would be wise not to ignore the fascinating data that both Hamer's work and the well-known University of Minnesota study of identical twins have amassed to support the contention that a great deal of human religiousness is hardwired in our DNA.[5] Scholars of religion who ignore such research will appear increasingly out of date.

Just three years before Hamer published his *The God Gene*, two researchers at the University of Pennsylvania concluded a similar study titled *Why God Won't Go Away: Brain Science and the Biology of Belief*. Andrew Newberg, director of nuclear medicine at the university's hospital, and psychiatrist Eugene d'Aquili designed an unusual experiment to study what happens in the brains of persons undergoing a spiritual experience. They enlisted the service of eight Tibetan Buddhist meditators who served as laboratory subjects. The meditators were left alone in a room with burning incense and candles. They were instructed to pull on a string when they believed they had reached the peak of their spiritual experience. At the moment they signaled to indicate they had entered into a mystical state, Newberg injected them with a radioactive tracer through a long intravenous line. This tracer, with the assistance of a sophisticated brain imaging device known as a SPECT (single photon emission computed tomography) camera, allowed Newberg and d'Aquili to observe precisely what was happening to the brain during meditation.

Newberg and d'Aquili discovered that meditation increased the flow of blood to what they call "the attention association area" of the brain located in the frontal cortex. This finding was consistent with their expectations, since this area of the brain is associated with focusing and concentration, which is exactly what the meditators were trying to do. What Newberg and d'Aquili didn't expect, however, was that at the same time there was a decreased amount of brain activity in the "orientation association area" located in the posterior superior parietal lobe. This area of the brain is implicated in our ability to locate ourselves in physical space by sensing the physical boundaries of the self. They realized that these two changes would collectively have a profound effect on a person's consciousness. If a person's attention association processes are aroused while he or she is simultaneously being deprived of information normally used to define the boundaries of the self, the brain would construct quite novel images of the self's relationship to the surrounding world. In such situations,

> The brain would have no choice but to perceive that the self is end-less and intimately interwoven with everyone and everything the mind senses. And this perception would feel utterly and unques-tionably real. This is exactly how [our experimental subject] and generations of Eastern mystics before him have described their peak meditative, spiritual, and mystical moments.[6]

Newberg and d'Aquili showed that the redirection of a tiny amount of electrochemical activity in the brain can produce vivid sensations of becoming one with the universe. They postulated that there is something like a contin-uum of mystical experiences, each representing progressively greater degrees of deactivating the orientation association area. A relatively small redirection of electrochemical activity from the orientation association area might result in simple aesthetic experiences. Yet, if the orientation association area is almost completely shut down, persons might have an experience that mystics vari-ously describe as "cosmic consciousness" or "absolute unitary being." Newberg and d'Aquili further conjectured that religious myths and rituals have been passed down over the centuries because they are particularly adept at triggering these fundamental neurological processes. They explain that when religious ritual is effective, "it inclines the brain to adjust its cognitive and emotional perceptions of the self in a way that religiously minded persons interpret as a closing of the distance between the self and God."[7]

Newberg's and d'Aquili's research supports a fairly strong biological in-terpretation of the nature and function of religion. They argue that religious behavior promotes individual nad group health and for this reason it is es-sentially adaptive. In their view, "natural selection would favor a brain equip-ped with the neurological machinery that makes religious behavior more likely."[8] Newberg and d'Aquili make the bolder claim that religion is struc-tured by a few biological universals. They believe that a neuropsychological approach to religion makes it possible to identify certain core elements uni-versally present in all religions. In their view, all myths, all rituals, and all mystical experiences—though expressed in culturally unique ways—are an-chored in neuropsychological states that are materially the same.

Neurobiologically and philosophically, there cannot be two versions of this absolute unitary state. It may look different, in retrospect, according to cultural beliefs and personal interpretations—a Catholic nun, for whom God is the ultimate reality, might interpret any mystical experience as a melting into Christ, while a Buddhist, who does not believe in a personalized God, might interpret mystical union as a melting into nothingness. What's important to understand, is that these differing interpretations are unavoidably distorted by after-the-fact subjectivity. . . . there is only absolute unity, and there cannot be two versions of any unity that is absolute.[9]

It seems a bit premature to jump to such strongly biological versions of the origins of religious belief and experience. A comprehensive spirituality in the flesh can't ignore the variability of human experience and must keep in closer connection with the cultural and historical contexts into which all experience is embodied. The fact that certain neurological machinery makes religion possible or more likely doesn't make religion inevitable. Yet Newberg and d'Aquili have done us a great service by alerting us to the important fact that there is a neurobiological dimension to all human experience—including spiritual experience. This, of course, is undoubtedly true and must guide any approach to the embodied nature of religious experience.

Several innovative studies of religion have appeared in recent years based on research findings in evolutionary psychology, cognitive psychology, and neurophysiology. Among them are Scott Atran's *In God We Trust*,[10] Pascal Boyer's *Religion Explained*,[11] Steven Pinker's *How the Mind Works*,[12] Jensine Adresen's *Religion in Mind*,[13] and David Sloan Wilson's *Darwin's Cathedral*.[14] All of these offer fairly strong versions of the biological interpretation of religion. As a consequence, they have generated provocative hypotheses concerning religion in general, but they are far less helpful when it comes to understanding or evaluating particular episodes of religion. To understand more fully the biology of belief, we need to explore more rigorously the fully embodied context of spiritual states of consciousness.

Native Americans' Narcotic Complex

Dean Hamer notes that several psychoactive drugs mimic the monoamine serotonin. The effects that these drugs have on the nervous system therefore give us some empirical evidence about how altered monoamine signaling transforms consciousness. He recounts, for example, a famous experiment conducted in a chapel at Boston University that demonstrated how a small capsule of psilocybin triggered vivid spiritual experiences in those who in-gested them.[15] Hamer further notes that these altered states of consciousness did more than momentarily affect subjects' moods and attitudes. These chemically altered states were able to produce long-term effects on the ex-perimental subjects' spiritual beliefs and attitudes. Hamer concludes that if we want to delve further into the biology of spirituality, we need to understand more about how changes in brain chemistry alter consciousness in ways that are identifiably—and predictably—spiritual.

A test case for exploring how chemical changes in the brain give rise to distinct modes of spirituality can be found in Native American religious history. We should be careful from the outset that it is difficult to make generalizations about Native American religion. There were thousands of separate ethnic groups that inhabited North America prior to European settlement. They were geo-graphically separated and used hundreds of different languages. Some were hunting and gathering societies, whereas others developed fairly advanced ag-ricultural economies. We are also dealing with traditions that continuously de-veloped over the 15,000 to 20,000 years since these various peoples first arrived on the North American continent. Few statements apply to all of these cultures. There is, therefore, no such thing as *the* Native American religious tradition. We must be content with summaries and generalizations that fit some, but never all, of the many Native American societies that have existed over time.

Harvard botanist Richard Schultes points out that whereas Europe had known of only a half dozen mind-altering drugs prior to the seventeenth century, the native peoples of North America had used somewhere between eighty to a hundred such substances.[16] Accounting for this statistical anomaly is difficult, since European cultures were directly contiguous with a greater landmass and an even wider variety of climates. Anthropologist Weston La Barre has made a compelling argument that historical and cultural factors (rather than geographical or agricultural) explain why North Americans were more interested in identifying intoxicating plants.[17] He suggests that there was a "narcotic complex" underlying many Native American cultural systems:

> The striking discrepancy between the Old and New Worlds in the numbers of known psychotropic plants must rest on ethnographic rather than botanical grounds. It is, in fact, the ubiquitous persistence of shamanism in aboriginal hunting peoples of the New World that provides the solution. . . . It should be noted that ecstatic-visionary shamanism is, so to speak, culturally programmed for an interest in hallucinogens and other psychotropic drugs.[18]

La Barre is almost certainly correct that cultural forces favored the continuing existence of a "narcotic complex" in the New World. Indeed, the religious elements of Native American culture bestowed normative status upon certain extraordinary states of mind. As La Barre explains, Native Americans preserved the shamanic ideology of ancient hunting peoples, whose "epistemological touchstone for reality was direct psychic experience of the forces of nature."[19] And, in turn, this "epistemological" orientation prompted Native Americans to seek out these extraordinary states of mind through the use of psychoactive (what La Barre termed psychotropic) drugs such as beer, mushrooms, datura, mescal beans, tobacco, and peyote.

The last of these two botanical substances—tobacco and peyote—serve as particularly helpful examples of how a spirituality in the flesh helps us explain and assess some of the concrete instances in which chemical alterations of consciousness give rise to distinct forms of religiosity.

There is abundant evidence to indicate that "tobacco is the supernatural plant par excellence of the American Indian, for tobacco was used aboriginally everywhere it would grow in the New World—that is, from middle Canada southward to Patagonia."[20] The tobacco used by Native Americans varied from region to region, as there were at least nine species of *Nicotiana* indigenous to North America alone (although *Nicotiana rustica*—a species much stronger than the *Nicotiana attenuata* used commercially today—was the most widely used).[21] What further complicates matters is the fact that tobacco was frequently used in mixtures with other ingredients such as the kinnikinnick used by the Oglala Sioux. In some instances, datura and other powerful substances might be added to tobacco to prepare a particularly potent smoke.

It is, therefore, difficult to be absolutely certain about the botanical and pharmacological properties of Indian tobacco mixtures. We are reasonably certain, however, that the tobacco species employed by Native Americans produced strongly intoxicating effects. In all likelihood they contained large amounts of the harmala alkaloids, which can severely alter neural transmission in the visual system and have pronounced hallucinogenic effects. The nicotine in native tobaccos was also a powerful stimulant. It acts through specialized cell formations in the brain and muscle tissues to produce changes in heart rate, alter brain wave patterns, elevate blood pressure, and release hormones affecting the central nervous system.[22] It is thus not surprising that the exhilaration and euphoria caused by native tobacco prompted Native Americans to associate it with states of consciousness that connect us with supernatural power. As Weston La Barre observes, "That tobacco alters the psychic state, however feebly, was enough for the American Indian to believe it had supernatural power and to use it in sacred contexts."[23]

Prior to modern times, Native Americans used tobacco only in sacred, never secular, contexts. Tobacco was thought to be a gift from the gods and as pleasing to them as it was to humans. For this reason tobacco was present in almost every ceremony designed to communicate with the supernatural realm. Florida Indians used tobacco in shamanistic divination, while the Seminoles and Iroquois presented tobacco as an offering to the gods.[24] Paul Radin has shown that Winnebago warriors used tobacco when addressing the spirits of those whom they had conquered in battle.[25] And, too, sacred smoking almost always attended quests for a vision of a guardian spirit. Accompanied by purifying baths, solitude and nightly vigil, tobacco smoking assisted the supplicant in transporting himself beyond the familiar world.

Tobacco smoking was a nearly universal feature of North American shamanism. This was true not only for attaining ecstatic states of awareness but also for performing sacred curing rituals. Willard Park has described how Paviotso shamans stored tobacco mixtures in a kit that included their pipes, rattles, and other healing paraphernalia.[26] In the curing rite, the shaman sat beside the patient and lit his pipe. After a few moments, he began to sing, and at the beginning of the sixth song, he picked up his rattle and shook it in rhythm with the song. A bit later, the shaman took several more puffs from his pipe and then passed it counterclockwise among those gathered for the curing rite. If anyone refused to smoke, the shaman stopped the performance until that person was coerced into compliance. The pipe was repeatedly circulated in this way about every half hour as long as the curing rite continued, which was often until the next morning. It was the shaman's job to enter into trance to diagnose the cause of the illness (e.g., soul loss, object intrusion, sorcery, etc) and then to discern the action necessary to restore proper connection with the spirit world. For this, he had to sustain his personal power, a task requiring continued use of his special tobacco mixtures.

Tobacco was also utilized in rituals for solemnizing oaths. Tobacco was thought to summon potent spiritual power that could then be infused into the bonds established by the oath. Breaking the oath would consequently unleash disastrous consequences upon the guilty party. Among the Woodlands and Plains Indians, chiefs met to smoke the sacred calumet, or peace pipe, in order to invoke supernatural sanctions for the oaths being taken. The calumet was an elaborately decorated shaft, sometimes as long as four feet. Custom dictated that if the calumet was offered and accepted, the act of smoking would make any engagements sacred and inviolable. It was thought that anyone who violated this agreement could never escape supernatural punishment. Citing eighteenth-century sources, Ralph Linton describes that "by smoking together in the calumet the contracting parties intend to invoke the sun and the other gods as witnesses of the mutual obligations assumed by the parties, and as a guaranty the one to the other that they shall be fulfilled."[27] In this way tobacco rituals forged long-lasting social relationships.

The pipe, no less than the tobacco itself, came to be viewed as an instrument of sacred power. The pipe was a symbol of the universe and more specifically humanity's place in the universe. Its use connected humans with the spirits and with one another. Joseph Epes Brown observes:

> In filling a pipe, all space (represented by the offerings to the powers of the six directions) and all things (represented by the grains of the tobacco) are contracted within a single point (the bowl or heart of the pipe), so that the pipe contains, or really *is* the universe. But since the pipe is the universe, it is also man, and the one who fills the pipe should identify himself with it, thus not only establishing the center of the universe, but also his own center; he so "expands" that the six directions of space are actually brought within himself. It is by this "expansion" that a man ceases to be a part, a fragment, and become whole or holy; he shatters the illusion of separateness.[28]

It is impossible in such rituals to distinguish clearly where the pharamacological properties of tobacco end and cultural shaping of experience begins. Both the chemistry of tobacco-altered consciousness and cultural symbolism contribute to the "expansion" by which ritual participants become whole or holy.

This same interconnection of chemistry and culture contributes to the ecstatic states found in peyotism. The religious use of peyote has been common in Mexico for centuries. Yet, prior to the 1890s, only five or six tribes inhabiting lands that are now within the borders of the United States were known to ingest this carrot-looking desert cactus. In just the next thirty years, however, peyote rituals became a prominent religious activity in an additional thirty tribes, concentrated in the Plains but stretching from the Southwest to Wisconsin. The story of the emergence and rapid spread of peyotism among these tribes constitutes a fascinating chapter in the history of American religion—a story best understood with sensitivity to the embodied nature of human consciousness.

The small "buttons" that grow on the peyote cactus contain at least nine psychoactive alkaloids, some of them strychnine-like in physiological action, the rest morphine-like.[29] The most important of these alkaloids from the standpoint of human neurophysiology is mescaline. Mescaline slows the pulse, gives the sensation of immobility, and produces a variety of visual effects, including visions of geometrical patterns and bright colors. Peyotline and anhaline are two of the other alkaloids, both of which have sedative, paralyzing effects that often induce hypnotic susceptibility. Four other alkaloids—anhalonidine, anhalonine, lophophorine, and anhalamine—produce a dull pain in the head, nausea, and generally disrupting influence upon the central nervous system.

Ingesting peyote buttons understandably induces initial nausea, often accompanied by vomiting. Peyote ingestion also causes general stimulation, with the face becoming flushed, the pupils dilated, and an overall sense of being "light-headed." As the intoxication increases, there is a tendency to overestimate time, possibly caused by the rapid flow of ideas and the inability to fix attention. Perhaps the most distinctive feature of peyote intoxication is visual hallucination, principally of a kaleidoscopic display of color. These colors are constantly in motion, assuming a variety of geometric shapes. Yet another effect of peyote is synesthesia, or the translation of one kind of sensory experience into another kind. For example, sounds may be perceived in terms of colors, or an individual might either "taste" or "touch" something they are seeing. An individual's overall psychic state may range from hilarity to confusion. Many individuals hallucinate animals that may appear so monstrous as to be frightening or so ridiculous as to be hilarious. For the most part, however, emotions and the overall experience of well-being is controlled not by sheer physiological changes but rather by the cultural setting in which the intoxication takes place.

Between 1890 and 1920, the ritual use of peyote spread from Mexico into the United States for a variety of religious, social, and psychological reasons. The most important factor in this northward migration of peyote rites was the systematic segregation of Indians onto government reservations. By 1890, traditional tribal cultures had come under tremendous strain. Native American tribes had formerly been distinct and even competitive. When merged together onto reservations, these tribal cultures found themselves stripped of their former identities. There was a widespread need for rituals that were essentially Indian in origin and fitted to the Indian mode of thought, while still sufficiently amenable to a new cultural state of life. Set against this historical context, it is not surprising that peyotism had its fastest diffusion among the Plains Indians of Oklahoma, Kansas, Nebraska, South Dakota, and Wisconsin. Nearly all North American Indians made use of visions. Visions, usually induced by fasting and other ascetic ordeals, were part of puberty rites in which young men gained their guardian spirits. Visions were also central to many curing rituals during which shamans availed themselves of supernatural power. On the Plains, however, visions were not confined to puberty rites. Nor were visions the exclusive property of shamans as in some regions of the United States. Instead, visions were thought to be part of an adult male's

ongoing connection with the spirit world and were sought for hunting purposes, before battle, at times of mourning, and for divination purposes. As
Ruth Shonle observes,

> The underlying belief in the supernatural origin of visions is im-
> portant among the factors contributing to the diffusion of peyote.…
> Peyote did not have to win its way into a system of religion which
> was without visions. Rather it facilitated obtaining visions already
> sought. It was holy medicine given to the Indian that he might get
> into immediate touch with the supernatural without the long period
> of fasting.[30]

Peyotism manifested itself differently depending on the tribal context.
What is often called "the Americanized" form of peyotism developed first
among the Kiowa and Comanche in Oklahoma. This version of peyotism
shifted the emphasis away from the shaman to every participant's quest for
visionary power. Doctoring was still an important feature of the ritual, but
healing was subordinated to the more general goal of establishing harmony
with supernatural power. This Americanized form of the peyote ceremony is
held in a traditional tipi, with the door facing east.[31] The peyote buttons are
blessed through prayer and consecrated for use in bringing health to all who
will ingest them. Participants ordinarily prepare for the ceremony with ob-
servances intended to purify themselves, such as special diets or sweat baths.
Any member of the peyote cult may rise to the position of ritual leader, known
as the "roadman." The roadman is assisted by a drummer, a fireman, and a
cedar man. Women assist in erecting the tipi, preparing food, and are sometimes permitted to attend the meeting and eat peyote and pray.

The precise order and content of the ceremony varies by tribe and the
idiosyncratic preferences of the roadman. Ceremonies begin in earnest when the
roadman makes a tobacco cigarette and passes it clockwise around the tipi while
offering a prayer to the power of the peyote. The other participants then begin to
pray silently to the "earth-creator" or "earth-lord." Following these initial prayers,
participants begin to eat the dried buttons of the peyote plant, followed by
drumming and singing. The roadman's initial song, chanted in a high nasal
tone, implores, "May the gods bless me, help me, and give me power and
understanding."[32] Throughout the night more peyote buttons are eaten (while
most participants eat about twelve buttons throughout the night, others may
consume as many as thirty) and prayer intensifies. Weston La Barre recounts:

> At intervals older men pray aloud, with affecting sincerity, often with
> tears running down their cheeks, their voices choked with emotion,

and their bodies swaying with earnestness as they gesture and stretch
out their arms to invoke the aid of Peyote. The tone is of a poor and
pitiful person humbly asking the aid and pity of a great power,
and absolutely no shame whatever is felt by anyone when a grown
man breaks down into loud sobbing during his prayer.[33]

Depending on regional traditions and the roadman's proclivities, the
peyote ritual may also include ceremonial dancing, divination, or quiet meditation. There is almost always some concern to use the peyote ceremony for the
purpose of healing. Ingesting peyote is thought to help persons make contact
with healing power. Cures of almost every kind have been attributed to the
power generated in peyote ceremonies. Yet the most intriguing feature of
American peyotism is its overt emphasis upon preaching and moral instruc-
tion. Participants admonish one another to forego vices, particularly in regard
to abstaining from alcoholic beverages. This preaching element of the peyote
ritual escalated with the introduction of Christian elements into the ceremony.
As early as the 1890s, the Bible was being introduced into the liturgical format
of the peyote "singing." Prayers once made to Indian spirits were increasingly
redirected to the Christian god. Traditional elements continued, but their symbolism changed dramatically. The fire in the tipi became associated with the
Light of Christ; the water drunk at midnight became associated with Christ's
alleged midnight birth; the roadman's gestures to the four directions became a
way of announcing the birth of Christ to all the world; and the meal eaten in the
early morning became a sacrament for all those who are saved in Christ.

The incorporation of Christian elements continued throughout the twentieth century. True, some peyotists retained the traditional rituals and even
denounced efforts to adapt the ceremony to the culture of Euro-Americans. Yet,
on the whole, the gradual "Christianization" of peyotism is a portal through
which we can view the continued pressures placed upon Native Americans to
assimilate into white, Christian America. The special value of the peyote ritual
was that it ostensibly represented Native Americans' distinctive spiritual heritage. Indeed, Weston La Barre argues that "despite the apparent and superficial
syncretism with Christianity, peyotism is an essentially aboriginal American
religion, operating in terms of fundamental Indian concepts about powers,
vision and native modes of doctoring."[34] Furthermore, these concepts of
powers, vision, and doctoring are all intimately associated with the "narcotic
complex" that has endured in Native American culture for centuries.

In sum, we can not lose sight of the fact that the chemistry of ecstatic states
of consciousness has always achieved its effects in tightly structured ritual
contexts. The very emergence of peyotism among tribes north of the Rio

Grande appeared part and parcel with the need to make sense of the cultural crisis born of forced capitulation to Euro-American culture. Peyote rites are a response to this crisis and have provided a vehicle for both religious and cultural renewal during a bleak period in Native American history. The rites enable individuals to reorganize their lives in ways that are both individually and communally healthy. Peyotism validates Indian tradition by fostering individual religious experiences that are directly linked with inherited religious patterns. It does so, furthermore, by heightening the sense of social solidarity among participants. Peyotism thus functions among American Indians north of the Rio Grande in ways that are very similar to what Barbara Myerhoff found among the Huichol in Mexico: that the ritual ingestion of peyote "evokes the timeless, private, purposeless, aesthetic dimension of the spiritual life, mediating between former and present realities and providing a sense of being one people, despite dramatic changes in their recent history."[35]

Marijuana and the Religious Counterculture

The largest group of religious Americans today—and throughout the nation's history—is the unchurched.[36] Over thirty percent of all Americans have no formal religious affiliation, yet are nonetheless deeply interested in spiritual matters. Some of these persons are still drawn to Christianity or Judaism. Yet most of them, a full 20 percent of the total population, can be considered spiritual seekers. They don't believe that any organized religion has a monopoly on truth. For this reason, they remain open to new spiritual teachings. They are, for example, apt to find merit in the spiritual ideas associated with Eastern religions, alternative healing philosophies, self-help psychologies, books on the occult or supernatural, pagan religions, deep ecology, or radical feminism. Rather than emphasizing loyalty to inherited tradition, seekers celebrate both pluralism and eclecticism as hallmarks of a vital spirituality.

Today's spiritual seekers have had their counterparts in other periods of American history. For example, Transcendentalism, mesmerism, spiritualism, and Theosophy were all metaphysical movements that provided a vocabulary for seekers throughout the nineteenth and early twentieth centuries. And, during the 1950s, members of the Beat movement frequently connected these metaphysical interests with other countervailing viewpoints such as European existentialism and Zen Buddhism.[37] What is not so clear about America's enduring religious counterculture is precisely how people come to be inducted into these alternative belief systems. Organized religion typically makes use of a gradual process of indoctrination that begins shortly after birth. Sunday school classes, weekly attendance at worship services, confirmation programs, sermons, and church publications are among the many ways that our nation's formal religious institutions induct each new generation into its belief system. Unchurched spirituality has evolved a number of mechanisms for transmitting its distinctive teachings: weekend seminars, evening lectures offered at rented facilities or liberal churches, retreat centers, and publications found in the metaphysical or "New Age" section of bookstores. Yet, to these methods of inducting new "recruits" into the religious counterculture, we might add the altered states of consciousness induced by psychedelic substances—both major and minor.

The historical connection between mind-altering drugs and "seeker spirituality" goes back at least as far as the career of the psychologist and philosopher William James. In 1882, James recounted his personal experience with nitrous oxide gas. He had become interested in the use of nitrous oxide while reviewing a book entitled *The Anaesthetic Revelation and the Gist of Philosophy* written by the amateur philosopher Paul Blood. The book advanced Blood's claim that after breathing nitrous oxide he had a direct "insight of immemorial Mystery." Blood was convinced that he had stumbled upon a pharmaceutical pathway to experiences "in which the genius of being is revealed." The epiphany to which he had been treated disclosed how all is in God and God is in all. The gist of his anaesthetic philosophy was thus quite simple: "The kingdom of God is . . . within you; it is the Soul."[38]

William James was above all an empiricist. Among other things, this meant that all ideas must be tested by experience. So, with respect to Blood's claims, he decided to experiment for himself. The results were impressive. He claimed that although the effects will vary from person to person, there is nonetheless a general pattern to the subjective experience induced by nitrous oxide: "With me, as with every other person of whom I have heard, the keynote of the experience is the tremendously exciting sense of an intense metaphysical illumination."[39]

This metaphysical illumination eventually led James to the principal conclusion of his famous *The Varieties of Religious Experience*. First published in 1902, *The Varieties* argues that personal, mystical experience is the core of authentic religion. All the various creeds and rituals associated with the world's organized religions are, according to James, but secondhand translations of the mystical experiences from which they first arose. Mystical experiences disclose the defining attributes of religion, James argued, because in contrast to non-religious constructions of experience they evoke belief (1) that the visible world is part of a more spiritual universe from which it draws its chief significance and (2) that union or harmonious relation with that higher universe is our true end. And, importantly, James confessed that such distinctively religious convictions first came to him in his own earlier experiment with nitrous oxide:

> Some years ago I myself made some observations on this aspect of nitrous oxide intoxication, and reported them in print. One conclusion was forced upon my mind at that time, and my impression of its truth has ever since remained unshaken. It is that our normal waking consciousness, rational consciousness as we call it, is but one special type of consciousness, whilst all about it, parted from it by the filmiest of screens, there lie potential forms of consciousness entirely different.[40]

The alternative spiritual traditions in America have, following James's lead, tended to equate spirituality with the quest for mystical forms of consciousness. The use of psychedelic drugs, such as mescaline and LSD, has played a major role in such mystical quests. Aldous Huxley, Timothy Leary, Alan Watts, Allen Ginsberg, and Stanislav Grof are but a few of the many "high priests" who have advocated psychedelics as a direct route to metaphysical illumination.[41] Members of the Baby Boom generation heard these testimonials and understood that they were integral to the counterculture that gained momentum in the 1960s and 1970s. What we now label "seeker spirituality" has important roots in this era's religious experimentalism that fostered (1) a shift from mainline to nonconformist religion, (2) a rediscovery of natural rather than revealed religion, (3) a new appreciation for Eastern religious thought, and (4) a tendency to attribute spiritual importance to nonrational modes of thought and perception.[42]

For those who used them, psychedelics provided an experience-based rite of passage to the religious counterculture. They dissolved normal waking states of consciousness, transporting the initiate into an entirely new mode of thinking and feeling. This new way of perceiving reality was charged with excitement, mystery, and intrigue. Many believed that they had left behind the superficial world of "orthodox" science and religion and had, instead, for the first time encountered reality in a genuine, authentic way. Direct experience of the "true" shape of reality legitimated the transition from consensus to alternative religion. Cultural anthropologist Marlene Dobkin de Rios points out that drugs will be considered with awe and respect in any society that values firsthand experience as the true way to knowledge: "In those societies where plant hallucinogens play a central role, one learns that the drug user believes that he or she can see, feel, touch, and experience, the unknown."[43]

The fascination with extraordinary states of consciousness led to interest in Eastern religions, whose meditation practices struck Americans as another path to cleansing the doors of perception. A recent survey of over thirteen hundred Americans engaged in Buddhist practice showed that 83 percent had taken psychedelics.[44] The vast majority of these Buddhist practitioners believe that psychedelics provide a glimpse to the very same reality opened up by disciplined meditation. Ram Dass (a.k.a. Richard Alpert, who was Timothy Leary's early psychedelic research partner) explains, "From my point of view, Buddhism is the closest to the psychedelic experience, at least in terms of LSD. LSD catapults you beyond conceptual structures. It extricates you. It overrides your habit of identifying with thought and puts you in a nonconceptual mode very fast."[45]

Even those who never used major psychedelics were influenced by the psychedelic movement. Psychedelics were a cultural icon. The multisensory nature of the era's art, films, and music affected even those who never saw a mushroom or tab of LSD. No one was surprised to learn that Paul McCartney, John Lennon, and George Harrison of the Beatles had all tried LSD. Their albums, particularly "Sgt. Pepper's Lonely Hearts Club Band," made altered states of mind exotic and alluring to an entire generation. Subjectivity and experimentalism were fast becoming hallmarks of the pursuit of spiritual authenticity.

Many in this era sensed that mainstream religion lacked a mystical dimension and had, consequently, lost its connection with authentic truth. Youthful seekers yearned to break out on their own quests for a firsthand experience of a higher reality. They yearned to open up inwardly in search of the hidden reaches of the universe. First, however, they had to learn to expand personal consciousness. It is for this reason that marijuana became the counterculture's drug of choice. True, marijuana lacked the hallucinatory or vision-giving powers of the major hallucinogens such as LSD or psilocybn. It could, however, be used more casually and more frequently. It was also a great deal safer. Smoking marijuana was, furthermore, a more communal experience than ingesting potent drugs that fostered personal withdrawl. Passing a joint created unique social settings that allowed young cultural rebels to bond with a countercultural community explicitly formed to experiment with altered states of consciousness.

The popularity of marijuana as a "minor" psychedelic is not difficult to understand. The plant, known scientifically as *cannabis sativa*, produces an isomer known as 1-delta-9-tetrahudrocannabinol (commonly known as THC), which is thought to be the principal agent responsible for the physiological and psychological effects of marijuana use. The THC content of marijuana plants varies considerably, from 0.5 percent to over 6 percent; the THC content of hashish oil (made from the resin of the plant's flower tops) is often as high as

50 percent. The actual physiological effects of smoking marijuana are poorly understood. In fact, the only two established findings concerning marijuana smoking are that it causes a mild reddening of the eyes and a temporary increase in heartbeat. The psychological effects vary according to both the set (the subject's overall personality, beliefs, past experiences) and setting (the immediate environmental context). Nonetheless, a commission appointed by the Canadian government to study marijuana use found that there are near-universal reactions to THC intoxication:

> [H]appiness, increased conviviality, a feeling of enhanced interper-sonal rapport and communication, heightened sensitivity to humour, free play of the imagination, unusual cognitive and ideational asso-ciations, a sense of extraordinary reality, a tendency to notice aspects of the environment of which one is normally unaware, enhanced visual imagery, an altered sense of time in which minutes may seem like hours, enrichment of sensory experiences, increased personal understanding and religious insight, mild excitement and energy.[46]

Almost every one of these symptoms is capable of bestowing the impres-sion of having stepped beyond one's ordinary limits. Marijuana, by unleashing "unusual cognitive and ideational associations," imparts the subjective feel of creativity and aesthetic insight. Subjects have "a sense of extraordinary reality" as though becoming aware of aspects of the universe normally screened from consciousness. They suddenly recognize the existence of a "more" to every-day experience—a "more" that will quite possibly be interpreted as revealing more-than-worldly realities from which our everyday lives draw their chief significance.

All of these effects help explain why marijuana use helps bond individuals to alternative religious beliefs and to small groups of fellow seekers. Psychol-ogist Charles Tart studied the experience of "being stoned" and found that subjects report an enhanced sense of tactual sensations. These subjects also reported that their senses of taste and smell were more intense. And, more important, Tart found that marijuana intoxication caused persons to become more intensely aware of their thought process. Being stoned gives persons the sense that their thoughts are more original, intuitive, and profound (even though many researchers note that these same individuals often later confess that marijuana only gave them the *feeling* of being more original). Tart con-cluded that, on the whole, "marijuana intoxication characteristically produces a childlike openness to experience and a sense of wonder and awe, in contrast to the usual businesslike manner in which we classify events and people strictly in terms of their importance to us."[47] This childlike wonder at the universe gives marijuana users the sensation of having a firsthand encounter with life's deeper meanings and beauty. It expands their sense of interiority, helping them to feel that they have momentarily established a more authentic relationship to the universe.

William Novak also studied marijuana use and came to some interesting conclusions about the connection between drugs and alternative spirituality. Novak wrote that "for some, marijuana has served as a teacher whose principal lesson has been that life holds multiple forms of reality."[48] Marijuana, it seems, was instrumental in affording religious seekers a "pluralism of perspectives." In our normal waking state, we connect incoming sensory data with previously acquired ideas and concepts. Marijuana users, however, report that they find it difficult to fix their attention. As a consequence, they find themselves connecting the same sensory data to two or more different sets of concepts. This gives them the sensation that there is not just one reality but several realities, depending upon their current frame of mind. One subject reported to Novak, "When I'm very stoned, I find myself switching constantly between two or more frames of mind."[49] Another subject commented, "When I'm high, the ideas keep coming. Some times I wonder whether marijuana actually creates these ideas—or whether, perhaps, it functions more like a magnet, drawing together the various iron filings of thought from different parts of my mind and bringing them together."[50] These multiple associations give experience a highly symbolic character. Marijuana users frequently conclude that life is multivalent or multidimensional. They typically believe that even though the normal waking state of consciousness attends to the "material" meaning of experience, there are nonetheless other forms of experience better suited to discovering insights about life's intrinsic beauty and spiritual purpose.

The "multiple perspectives" that emerge when smoking marijuana helped many Baby Boomers appreciate alternative myths and worldviews. The pluralistic way of viewing experience they learned from using marijuana turned many away from religious belief systems that proclaim one, absolute truth. Instead, many marijuana users tended to see beliefs as symbolic, rather than literal. Smoking marijuana was therefore a ritual activity that helped connect young seekers to the mystical philosophies of Alan Watts, Aldous Huxley, Carl Jung, Carlos Castenada, Zen Buddhism, and Vedanta Hinduism. These exotic forms of spirituality all suggested that authentic spirituality stems from inner, personal experience. They also implied that the mainline churches had somehow lost touch with the experiential basis of religion. Learning to get high was thus simultaneously learning to piece beneath social institutions to discover a deeper fount of spiritual and moral truth. As one user put it:

It's difficult to talk about marijuana and religion because I have a hard time separating them out. Authentic religion, when you sweep away all the extraneous stuff of politics and institutions, is about transcendence, heightened awareness, ecstasy, and goodness. Religion and marijuana both involve going beyond the rational, material, and normative concerns of existence. Religion is the original altered state of consciousness.[51]

Most marijuana users during the 1960s and 1970s knew they formed a distinct American subculture. They were more likely to be liberal in politics and less likely than other Americans to be affiliated with a religious organization.[52] The longer and more often people smoked marijuana, the more likely they were to bond or connect with the eclectic cluster of metaphysical ideas underlying the era's "alternative spirituality" movement.[53] In the 1960s and 1970s, the actual act of smoking marijuana was frequently a rite of passage into the religious underground. Persons who took their first "joint" were aware that they were thereby signifying their desire to join an elitist, clandestine, and self-consciously countercultural segment of American society. They knew that they were joining a community that valued nonconformity, peacefulness, and quiet introspection. They were in some fundamental way bonded to others who shared their belief that altered states of consciousness lead to metaphysical illumination.

Many of these connections between drug-induced intoxication and seeker spirituality still hold. But it is hard to avoid the impression that at some point during the late 1970s or early 1980s, the zeitgeist changed. The physical effects of psychedelics (major or minor) remained constant, but the cultural setting changed. And with this change came noticeable changes in the subjective experience. As marijuana became more pervasive across all groups of Americans, its physiological effects lost their connection with specific ranges of religious and philosophical ideas. Marijuana and other mind-altering substances became just a more potent version of the intoxication associated with alcohol. Rowdiness, not quiet introspection, became an increasingly common manifestation of altering consciousness.

An important lesson of this historical trend away from the 1960s' counterculture is that neither constructivist nor biologically oriented interpretations of religion are alone sufficient. The "chemistry of consciousness" can tell us much about whether persons are inclined to think in ways we commonly define as spiritual. But it can not alone tell us whether persons will indeed come to think that way. Nor can it tell us how long such spiritual sensibilities (if aroused) will last, how intense they will be, or to which specific ideas they will lead. A spirituality in the flesh must take account of the many ways our thought and behavior are embedded, and avail itself of biological, psychological, cultural, and historical modes of interpretation.

The Chemistry and the Politics of Consciousness

Attention to the neurochemistry of consciousness deepens our theoretical understanding of religion. Theories of religion must first and foremost perform a descriptive function, highlighting elements of religious thought and behavior that may not be obvious to the casual observer. Broadly biological explanations of religion are especially helpful in this regard. They alert us to the cunning ways that evolution selected for various kinds of genetic codes that guide us to adaptive behavior. Our brains are hardwired to ensure that our evolutionarily recurrent needs are met. We need, for example, to be induced to subordinate our immediate personal interests to the long-term interests of the group. And, once natural selection gave rise to organisms with complex brains, a wide new range of needs emerged. Many of these needs (variety, aesthetic delight, philosophical contemplation, etc.) are not themselves directly related to biological fitness, but they are born of the biological capacities that biological evolution did bestow upon us. It is true, of course, that we can meet most of these needs without the induction of specifically religious states of consciousness. But religion has proven to be especially capable of co-opting our biological capacities and using them in ways that meet a rich and varied set of needs born of the (evolutionarily designed) human condition.

Dean Hamer, Andrew Newberg, and Eugene d'Aquili are but a few of the researchers who have proposed specific theories about how our neural chemistry helps the brain achieve important biological goals. Their work, in conjunction with the vast scientific literature analyzing altered states of consciousness, goes a long way toward demonstrating how the chemistry of consciousness makes religiosity a nearly universal human trait. Such studies have generated a great deal of information explaining how certain kinds of altered neural functioning dispose humans to think and feel in religious ways. They show, for example, that one of the principal ways that states of consciousness differ from each other is the ratio between the brain's "sensory intake" mechanisms and its "sensory processing" mechanisms. Every pharmaceutical agent and every ritual activity (e.g., drumming, chanting, dancing) exerts specific effects upon either the brain's intake or its processing mechanisms. Some result in hyperarousal. Others lead to hypoarousal. Attention to this "cartography of consciousness" can illuminate many of the subtle features that distinguish specific kinds of religious awareness.[54] A great deal about the experiential contours of Zen *satori*, Yoga's *samadhi*, or the ecstasy of peyotism can be learned from the neurochemistry of distinct states of consciousness.

Many scientifically inclined scholars have employed these kinds of explanatory models without sufficient attention to the equally important factors of set and setting. The results of such inquiry have been disappointing, wholly ignoring the role of acquired cognitive sets in interpreting human experience. Scholars in the humanities would seem well poised to remedy such excessive reductionism by incorporating historical, philosophical, and cultural perspectives. It is also important to note that descriptive accounts of religion that ignore the chemistry of consciousness will appear increasingly anemic.

Theories of religion should be more than descriptive. They should also be able to help us assess the value of religious thought and behavior. The most important benefit of a comprehensive spirituality in the flesh is that it moves beyond description and sets a context within which we might venture toward analysis or assessment. The context is strictly functional. It assesses religion not according to the "truth" of its beliefs but in terms of how it promotes life over time and through larger cultural or ecological communities. This hardly means that we now have access to firm or unchanging factual information that can be brought to bear upon religion. Wide differences of opinion will always exist about what "promoting life" actually means (e.g., The life of which organisms? What behaviors best signify that life has indeed been promoted?). The natural and social sciences can, however, keep us focused on a common agenda: trying to understand whether or to what degree religion promotes life, more life, a richer and more satisfying life. They do this, moreover, by establishing empirical measures of selected variables that demonstrably affect either personal or communal development. Philosophical and cultural considerations—far from being excluded in such a broadly biological agenda—become central to the interpretive task. We saw this already in our previous attempts to evaluate the significance of specific emotions such as fear or wonder in generating religious orientations to life. We can utilize a similar perspective for assessing the connection between the chemistry of consciousness and metaphysical illumination.

Our normal waking state of consciousness has been shaped by natural selection to achieve the basic goals of biological survival. Our sensory organs selectively ignore all aspects of the environment that are not relevant to those tasks. Altered states of consciousness temporarily deautomatize our accustomed modes of registering sensory data. Thus, as psychiatrist Arthur Deikman has noted, even the most subtle changes in our neurochemistry cause us to enter "altered modes of consciousness whose stimulus processing may be less efficient from a biological point of view but whose very inefficiency may permit the experience of aspects of the real world formerly excluded or ignored."[55] A spirituality in the flesh may never know what the "real world" is and, therefore, whether any particular mode of consciousness truly corresponds to some objectively existing ontological reality. But it can ask whether configurations of the world that were formerly excluded from awareness can reliably contribute to the overall promotion of life. Thus, for example, Hamer, Newberg, and d'Aquili have all argued that humans inherit genetic tendencies toward religious states of consciousness because these religious states serve important biological functions. The question of the theological truth of these states of consciousness is thus subordinated to considerations of their functional value. The same type of analysis can be extended to other religious states of consciousness, including those induced by psychedelic substances.

Altering the normal ratio of sensory intake to sensory processing radically alters cognition. There is less stability in the way we configure our thoughts and feelings. Confusion often reigns. Yet for some persons, and especially for those who are in a cultural setting that is supportive of these changes, the alterations are accompanied by a heightened sense of the vitality or freshness of experience. Experience may take on new, special meanings. Ronald Shor explains that in altered states of consciousness "(a) experiences cannot have their usual meanings; (b) experiences may have special meanings which result from their isolation from the totality of general experiences; and (c) special orientations or special tasks can function temporarily as the only possible reality for the subject in his phenomenal awareness as a result of their isolation from the totality of general experience."[56]

Knowledge about the chemistry of consciousness can inform our evaluation of drug-induced ecstasy. As the normal waking state changes, experience cannot have its usual meaning. Neurochemical and cultural factors interact to imbue altered states with new meanings. We know, for example, that religious communities provide ritual structures that transform sheer intoxication into spiritual renewal. According to anthropologist Felicitas Goodman, "Religious communities that use drugs [to induce ecstasy] teach their members how to switch from intoxication to religious trance."[57] Ritual leaders such as the roadman in peyote ceremonies or "high priests" such as Leary or Watts help newcomers interpret novel sensations in the ready-made categories of a specific religious worldview.

The meaning of altered states of consciousness is not solely derived from the cultural context. Neurochemistry exerts considerable leverage on how we think. The meaning we attribute to experience is at least partially determined by our neurophysiology. For example, most altered states are accompanied by an intensification of smell, sound, color, and tactile sensations. This alone predisposes persons to believe they have transcended the superficial world of socially defined reality and thereby a more authentic grasp of reality. And although alcohol, tobacco, marijuana, and cocaine have very different chemical effects on the nervous system, evidence suggests that all trigger a sharp increase in the brain's levels of dopamine. Dopamine is the agent most responsible for the exhilarating rush, pleasure, and elation that overtakes the nervous system after ingesting these drugs. Some of us might interpret the effects of dopamine to be evidence that a person has confused chemically induced euphoria with spiritual insight.[58] Alternatively, others might argue that abnormal states of mind lead to unreliable perceptions that have little chance of corresponding with objective reality.[59] It is legitimate to ask whether the kinds of self-transcendence that Hamer believes are triggered by the action of monomines produces metaphysical illumination or simply self-deception.

Adjudicating between rival "truth claims" requires careful philosophical reflection. It is one thing to note the connection between the chemistry of consciousness and particular kinds of religious beliefs. It is quite another thing to make judgments about these beliefs on the basis that they originated in altered neurochemical activity. William James displayed unusual perspicacity as both a psychologist and a philosopher when he cautioned that we cannot dismiss an insight as invalid solely on the basis of the neurological conditions under which it originated.

> Let us play fair in this whole matter, and be quite candid with ourselves and with the facts. When we think certain states of mind superior to others, is it ever because of what we know concerning their organic antecedents? No! It is always for two entirely different reasons. It is either because we take an immediate delight in them; or else it is because we believe them to bring us good consequential fruits for life. When we speak disparagingly of "feverish fancies," surely the fever-process as such is not the ground of our disesteem—for aught we know to the contrary, 103 degrees or 104 degrees Fahrenheit might be a much more favorable temperature for truths to germinate and sprout in, than the more ordinary blood-heat of 97 or 98 degrees.[60]

James is surely right. For aught we know, the states of consciousness triggered by VMAT2 or by decreased activity in the orientation association area are more favorable for metaphysical truths to germinate than the normal waking state. The real issue is not the chemistry of consciousness but the politics of consciousness; that is, the battle over who gets to determine what kinds of subjective delight are to be most valued or which fruits for life are most consequential. No a priori bias toward the normal waking state can fairly consider these points. As Ronald Shor explained, in altered states of consciousness (1) experiences cannot have their usual meanings and (2) experiences may have special meanings which result from their isolation from the totality of general experiences. Mystics and nonmystics alike have the right to stipulate specific measures of delight, meaning, or consequential fruits for the purpose of making comparative assessments. All such stipulated measures deserve their day in court. The special meanings arising from religious states should be considered hypotheses as worthy of consideration as any others. If we choose to ignore these hypotheses because of our commitment to prefixed notions of rationality, we do so at our own philosophical risk. It is at least possible, after all, that these special meanings embody metaphysical illumination available in no other way.

5

Sexuality and Religious Passion

The Somatics of Spiritual Transformation

The drive to continue life is encoded in our DNA. Sexuality represents a powerful life force within us, constituting our body's grand biological imperative. Our biological desires connect us with the grand drama of cosmic creation. Reflecting on how our erotic drives fit into the grander scheme of life, Miriam DeCosta-Willis celebrates eroticism as the life force linking us with the wider universe:

> Eroticism: The powerful life force within us from which
> spring desire and creativity and our deepest knowledge of the
> universe. The life force that flows like an inscrutable tide
> through all things, linking man to woman, man to man,
> woman to woman, bird to flower, and flesh to spirit. Our
> ancestors taught us this in their songs of love, their myths of
> creation, their celebrations of birth, and their rituals of ini
> tiation. Desire. Pleasure. Wholeness.[1]

Sexuality infuses personal life with passion and vitality. It gives the body a sense of aliveness. This powerful life force is generated internally within our individual biology. Yet it directs us outward to connect with others. For this reason, sexuality expresses itself at the elusive juncture where physiological excitation meets the social construction of desire. The vitality, passion, and desire associated with sexuality are fully embodied—meaning that they are simultaneously biological and cultural.

Religious creativity flows naturally from our erotic energies.[2] Our religious reconstructions of life express and celebrate the life force flowing within us. Erotic desire expresses itself in our quest for self-abandonment. It guides our religious quest for passionate connection with an ideally romanticized "other." And it provides the power propelling quests to transform our mortal natures in the direction of immortality. The somatics of sexuality are thus a partial key to understanding the impulses that generate our creative religious thought and feeling.

The Biology of Desire

Biological evolution operates according to a very simple formula. Natural selection favors those organisms that are most reproductively fit. Evolution is single-minded in this regard. All it really cares about is whether organisms can reproduce and raise their offspring to the point of biological viability. Evolution selects for attributes that enhance the reproductive transmission of gene pools and selects against those that impede this process. Hence, the various traits that distinguish any given species (e.g., digestive systems, immune systems, ability to communicate, etc.) exist by virtue of their contribution to the overall task of transmitting the genetic codes of life.

Evolutionary psychology argues that our brains consist of distinct "mental modules" that were shaped by natural selection to ensure our species' survival. One of the most important of these modules concerns the activity of "mate selection" that guides humans' choice of sexual partners.[3] It seems, for example, that natural selection favored conditions in which males compete with one another for sexual access to females because females risk so much of their reproductive potential with each copulation, while males risk little. It also seems probable that early in our evolutionary history, males used food to lure females, beginning the evolutionary tendency of males to control females (and especially their sexual behaviors). Males are inclined to seek out as many female partners as possible, while females tend to be more discriminating in their choice of partners. Males prefer younger females (who are more likely to be fertile and healthy), while females tend to prefer males who give evidence of being able to provide resources for future parental investment. Natural selection has thus shaped our sexual preferences to ensure that our DNA is successfully transmitted to the next generation.

Human sexuality, then, has deep biological foundations. Among our biologically encoded characteristics is our ability to "fall in love." The capacity for love emerged in our evolutionary history to ensure that we make the kinds of emotional investments that have reproductive consequences.[4] In recent years we have begun to know a lot more about the biology of love. We know, for example, that the core feelings of love are associated with discrete biological systems within human physiology and neuroanatomy.[5] On the basis of recent studies of brain physiology, Helen Fisher theorizes that human love is rooted in three distinct neurological systems.[6] Each system evolved to solve specific mate selection issues and each has its own specialized brain circuitries, hormones, and neurotransmitters. The first neurological component of love has to do with mechanisms that get us aroused, interested, and seeking. The second focuses our attention on one mate. The third forms attachment, or binds us to that mate. Each of these three biologically grounded components of human love produces its own distinct set of motivations and behaviors.

The first biological substrate of human love is what Fisher terms "lust." By lust, Fisher means the craving for sexual gratification that emerged in human biology as a means of motivating our ancestors to seek sexual union with almost any available partner. In both men and women, the hormone testosterone has an excitatory role in stimulating the areas of the brain responsible for lust. Elevated levels of testosterone arouse the sex drive (including frequency and intensity of sexual fantasies, masturbation, and overt courting behavior), declining levels dampen it. The release of testosterone in the body can be influenced by a number of factors. Women, for example, have naturally heightened levels of testosterone around ovulation. Men's levels of testosterone are naturally highest in their early twenties and tend to diminish with age. Increased levels of the neurotransmitter dopamine can also stimulate the release of testosterone. Thus, many intoxicants not only weaken socially constructed inhibitions concerning sexual behavior but also trigger a flow of chemicals that increase sexual desire. Drugs as diverse as caffeine, alcohol, nicotine, marijuana, and cocaine—though having very different neurochemical effects—all produce a sharp increase in levels of dopamine (and, therefore, testosterone). There is at least some chance that eating may increase lust, too—though perhaps owing more to visual and physiological cues than altering levels of testosterone per se. Eating increases blood pressure and the pulse rate, raises body temperature, and sometimes makes us sweat. These physiological changes also occur during sex. Eating also brings potential partners into close physical proximity, advertising availability. This link between eating and heightened levels of biological lust is undoubtedly why men and women have long associated different foods with sexual excitement.[7]

A second biological substrate of human love is what Fisher terms "romantic love." Romantic love pertains to the elation and obsession of "being in love." Romantic love affects perception and cognition in ways that enable persons to focus their courtship affections on a single individual at a time, thereby conserving precious mating time and energy. Romantic love is directly linked with the neurotransmitter dopamine (the link between dopamine and lust is indirect, rising principally from dopamine's ability to stimulate the release of testosterone) and perhaps norepinephrine and serotonin. Dopamine is a natural stimulant, thus administering a reward for behaviors that release it into the nervous system.

Using a functional magnetic resonance imaging machine, Fisher has been able to demonstrate how romantic love is triggered by increased activity in the caudate nucleus. This C-shaped region near the center of the brain is part of the brain's "reward system," responsible for general arousal, sensations of pleasure, and the motivation to acquire rewards. Another neuroanatomical center whose activity can be linked with romantic love is the ventral tegmental area, also a central part of the brain's reward circuitry. Importantly, the ventral tegmental area of the brain is laden with dopamine-making cells. As the ventral tegmental system begins to flood the brain with dopamine, perception and cognition are altered in ways that mobilize us for romantic love.[8] Among the most prominent of these changes in perception, attention, and cognition are:

1. A shift in the configuration of experience, giving "special meaning" to the surrounding world wherein the object of love becomes seen as novel, unique, important.
2. Focused attention on the object of love in ways that make this person becomes central to one's overall configuration of experience.
3. Aggrandizing the beloved.
4. Intrusive thinking whereby the beloved object continues to return to awareness and dominate waking thought.
5. Intense energy and emotional fire.
6. Weakening of boundaries between ego and object; a yearning for emotional union.
7. Jealousy and concern for sexual exclusiveness.
8. Sense of being governed by external forces; thoughts and actions appear involuntary, beyond one's personal control.
9. Intense feelings of elation, well-being, and euphoria.

Romantic love is more distinctively human than lust. It channels our biological urge for reproduction in ways that are more likely to produce long-term relationships conducive to rearing infants (a biological task that extends over many years for humans). We might additionally note that romantic love also appears to be stimulated by the perception of mystery or novelty in the beloved object. Mystery and novelty trigger the brain's reward circuits, releasing dopamine—the neurotransmitter of romantic love.

All of these attributes of this second biological mechanism of love, romantic love, are of special interest for the study of religion. One of religion's most important cultural functions is channeling lust into socially sanctioned forms of behavior. In part, this suggests that many religious ceremonies surrounding the onset of puberty or marriage are undoubtedly designed to direct biological lust into forms of romantic love. We might, however, also remind ourselves that religion is such a powerful cultural force because it co-opts our biological capacities by redirecting them to achieve a wide variety of needs and interests that are really not biological per se. Religion has proven especially capable of "piggybacking" on our biological capacities for romantic love and redirecting them to satisfy a broad spectrum of uniquely human needs. Take, for example, our biologically based need for attachment (the well-known psychological theories of attachment are quite distinct from Fisher's use of this term for describing the third biological substrate of love, which will be described in the second paragraph below). The study of attachment originated in both psychoanalytic and ethological observations of how relationships between infants and caregivers (usually the mother) have long-lasting effects on a person's psychological development. John Bowlby extended attachment theory by amassing an impressive array of data confirming that our early interactions with caregivers provide the cognitive and emotional building blocks from which close relationships are constructed throughout life.[9] Researchers today believe that the "attachment system" evolved in humans and other primates to maintain proximity between infants and their attachment figures (i.e., primary caregivers). Even in adulthood, humans continue to need safe, dependable attachment to some highly regarded "other" if they are to feel sufficiently secure to venture outward into expanding social relationships. Feelings of insecurity activate the attachment system, motivating persons either to seek out new or accustomed attachment figures (or, in some cases, to develop defense mechanisms for coping with the absence of an attachment figure). Many of our emotional programs are directly connected with activating these attachment behaviors. As Bowlby explained, "Many of the most intense emotions arise during the formation, the maintenance, the disruption and the renewal of attachment relationships. The formation of a bond is described as falling in love, maintaining a bond as loving someone, and losing a partner as grieving over someone."[10] What Fisher describes as romantic love, then, simultaneously functions to procure emotionally significant attachment relationships.

It should not be surprising that many come to "fall in love" with God in ways that compensate for unmet attachment needs. Religious devotees demonstrate virtually every perceptual and cognitive trait that Fisher associates with romantic love. That is, they come to aggrandize their beloved god, they believe their chosen god gives special meaning to their lives, they put extraordinary energy into their relationship with this god, and so on. It is, furthermore, patently obvious that certain forms of repetitive prayer, ritual, and worship are sufficient to arouse sexually charged desire to unite with a god. What seems also to be the case is that formal religious practices arouse such lust, only to redirect it toward forms of romantic love through which persons form deep and lasting attachments to their culture's loftiest ideals. Feelings of romantic love in relationship to a supernatural being undoubtedly reinforces—or compensates for—attachment relationships in our everyday lives. Emotional programs prompt us to seek out attachment to valued "others." Religion meets this need. Not only do habitual attachment patterns predict persons' devotional styles, but evidence suggests that individuals with insecure attachment patterns are most likely to undergo sudden religious conversion and rapturously fall in love with God.[11] A perfect example of this will be discussed in a following section of this chapter in connection with a young Christian convert, Sarah. Thus, while religion is not itself a biological adaptation, it certainly builds upon various adaptations that evolved in our early evolutionary history and redirects these biological programs to meet a wide variety of human needs or interests. The biology of romantic love is one of the mechanisms that facilitates these "redirections."

Returning to Fisher's tripartite model of sexuality, the third biological substrate of human love is what she refers to as "attachment" (again, not to be confused with the more general meaning of the term in contemporary attachment theory). For Fisher, attachment refers to the feelings of calm and security that accompany union with a long-term partner. The brain circuitry for male-female attachment developed to ensure that our ancestors lived with a single mate long enough to rear a child through infancy. To accomplish such long-term bonding, nature needed to evolve ways to produce feelings of affection for a mate, children, family, and friends. Evidence suggests that the hormones oxytocin and vasopressin are implicated in producing the feelings of reassurance and security that accompany male-female attachment. This is, of course, one of religion's principal tasks: inducing individuals to sacrifice their selfish interests for the well-being of the larger social group. By forging romantic attachment to gods and goddesses, religion mobilizes the somatic energies that induce worshippers to wholly and completely identify with their culture's ultimate symbol of moral virtue.

Nature is conservative. When nature has a good design, it sticks with it, expanding its uses to suit many situations. The biological imperative behind all three systems of human love is to ensure the production of offspring who are raised to the point of biological viability. Yet, the embedded nature of human lust and love is such that biology alone can not properly regulate human behavior. Hence, as David Schmitt summarizes, "Love must, to some degree, be a socially constructed experience and reflect the time and place within which it occurs."[12] The biology of desire blends imperceptibly with the social construction of desire. And it is at this amorphous intersection of biology and culture that sexuality blends imperceptibly with a variety of cultural phenomena—including religion.

Religion, like sexuality, is fundamentally rooted in individuals' desire to move beyond their individuality toward union with something more than themselves, a divine other. It seems likely that cultures, in their efforts to induce us to sacrifice our individuality to the larger social good, have learned to make efficient use of our biological programs. Theistic religion frequently emphasizes the loving nature of our gods and goddesses. They attract us, arouse our interest, and elicit our desire for connection. They also evoke romantic attachment to a particular god, goddess, or spiritual being who becomes the central focus of our devotion. Indeed, devotees of such diverse theological systems as devotional Hinduism or evangelical Protestantism report nearly every change in perception, attention, and cognition occasioned by the neurological programs of romantic love: a shift in the configuration of experience, giving "special meaning" to the surrounding world wherein the object of love becomes seen as novel, unique, important; aggrandizing the beloved; intrusive thinking whereby the beloved object continues to return to awareness and dominate waking thought; intense energy and emotional fire; weakening of boundaries between ego and object; a yearning for emotional union; jealousy and concern for an exclusive relationship; sense of being governed by external forces; thoughts and actions appear involuntary, beyond one's personal control; and intense feelings of elation, well-being, and euphoria. And, finally, theistic religion also builds upon desire and romantic love to form longer-lasting attachment to the cultural values associated with a chosen deity. The biology of love provides a motivational impetus with which religions induce individuals to adhere to culturally sanctioned moral codes.

It thus seems that culture, like nature, is conservative. When culture has a good design that proves capable of solving its most basic tasks, it sticks with it, expanding its uses to suit many situations. We need to be alert, then, to the many ways that cultural designs aiming to forge long-term attachments to social codes build squarely on the biological substrates of human sexuality. Here, where the biology of desire blends imperceptibly with the cultural construction of desire, sexuality often becomes a central motivating factor in many forms of the religious quest.

The Multivalent Nature of Eroticism

To understand the connection between religion and sexuality we must be able to conceptualize humanity's sexual functions in their broadest range.[13] The most important steps toward connecting religion and sexuality were undoubtedly those taken by Sigmund Freud nearly one hundred years ago. Freud's medical education immersed him in the Darwinian revolution in biological thought. His basic approach to sexuality and its centrality in human motivation was thus exceptionally modern even by today's standards.[14] Freud postulated that the "libido" is the primary motivational force in human personality. The libido, for Freud, is the biological drive that ensures the propagation of the species. In his view, however, the libido impels us towards pleasurable activities that go beyond genital sexuality per se. He further proposed that sexuality unfolds along a developmental process that, depending on a variety of cultural variables, leads us to express our sexuality in differing ways.[15] Although Freud viewed heterosexual intercourse as the normal outcome of sexual development, his theory explains how sexuality might potentially lead to many different expressions and behaviors. He asserted, for example, that the sexual instinct is made up of components, combining a multiplicity of erotogenic zones and aims. He further emphasized the role of culture in "sublimating" the sexual drive toward a wide variety of nonsexual activities (that are nonetheless then charged with sexual drive, release, and satisfaction). Freud's theory of sexuality thus suggests that libidinal drives lead us to activities well beyond genital intercourse, a suggestion that has important implications for discerning the sexual underpinnings of a wide variety of religious phenomena that might not appear "sexual" to the casual observer.

Freud adopted a moderate biological view of sexuality. Although he believed that the libido was an essentially biological drive, he acknowledged the important role that culture has in channeling this libido to different objects and in regulating the release or repression of this fundamental drive. This feature of his thought places him in the mainstream of current thought about human nature, making his insights amenable to all but those who adhere to extreme versions of either biologism or cultural constructivism. What further distinguishes Freud's view of human sexuality is his largely unexamined set of assumptions about how libidinal drives fit into a larger ontological understanding of humanity's place in the greater scheme of things. Freud continuously referred to libido with metaphors that essentially likened sexual drive to the operation of steam in a closed hydraulic system. He assumed that our bodies generate libido much in the way that a boiler generates steam. As this energy is produced, pressure gradually builds in the system. At some point the pressure becomes so intense that it pushes for release, seeking almost any available path of escape. In Freud's view, pleasure is the subjective experience that accompanies the discharge of built-up sexual tensions. Libido represents the body's fundamental drive to discharge accumulated pressure and return to a state of quiescence. Thus, in Freud's view, one of culture's most important tasks is controlling the release of libido. It is culture's role to channel libidinal discharge to socially acceptable outlets (e.g., heterosexual genital copulation within the confines of marriage). Variations in how libidinal energies are released—though wholly understandable within this hydraulic metaphor—violate cultural norms and are thus labeled perversions of either a psychological or moral nature.

Many contemporary theorists understandably take exception to Freud's characterization of libido. Freud, perhaps structuring his thought on the basis of male rather than female orgasms, thought of eroticism primarily as seeking the release of individual forces. He had a basically atomistic view of the place of the individual in the universe. He envisioned libido in terms of transmitting biological life, but did so without any broader teleological considerations of the place of humans in the grander cosmic scheme of things. This is a philosophically defensible position, but only one out of many philosophically defensible approaches to human sexuality. It is also possible, for example, that eroticism is the biological expression of a grander élan vital whereby an immanent spiritual force stimulates matter into ongoing evolutionary development. Might our sexual drives be seeking not to release individual forces but instead to weave otherwise separate entities into a greater whole? In this view, sexuality is seen to be operating in the service of a larger cosmic movement toward beauty, truth, or wholeness. The desire for sexual expression could then be viewed as an expression of a finite being's desire to complete itself through union with the infinite. Carter Heywood argued almost twenty years ago that there is no distinction between erotic desire and the creative power of God. Once we see God as the immanent drive to connect or relate creation together, sexuality can be seen as a "sacred power" and an "empowering spark."

> As we come to experience the erotic as sacred, we begin to know ourselves as holy and to imagine ourselves sharing in the creation of one another and of our common well-being. As we recognize the faces of the Holy in the faces of our lovers and friends, as well as in our own, we begin to feel at ease in our bodyselves—sensual, connected, and empowered. We become resources with one another of a wisdom and a pleasure in which heretofore we have not dared

believe. . . . the erotic crosses over among us, moving us to change the ways we are living in relation. Touched by this sacred power, we are never the same again.[16]

The point here is that the final meaning of human sexuality cannot be determined by pointing to any one set of "facts." Meaning pertains to the relationship between a part and a greater whole. Every ontological system, by delineating its own distinct vision of the universe, generates a distinct range of possible meanings we might ascribe to the facts of human sexuality.

It was precisely on this point that Carl Jung made a decisive break with his former mentor and colleague, Sigmund Freud. Jung rejected the atomistic and mechanistic ontology that Freud brought to his psychological observations. Jung viewed humans in more extensive terms. He gradually articulated an alternative world view that envisions an innate connection between every individual and a universal essence he termed the collective unconscious. For this reason Jung located libido in a much different ontological context than had Freud.[17] Whereas for Freud the term "libido" had the connotations of lust, appetite, or amoral passion, for Jung it referred to a desire that excites eagerness, longing, pleasure, willingness. In Jung's ontology, libido stirs us to move toward an object and, in so doing, prompts us to stretch beyond ourselves in such a way that we can unite with an independent subject. Libido thereby becomes the motivational force behind personal growth and self-transcendence. The quest to unite is essentially a religious quest. Libidinal desires represent the voice of God luring us to connect with the whole of reality.[18] Sexual desire can thus also be viewed as a permutation of a larger cosmic drive longing to connect finite beings with a transcendent reality. Once the sexual drive is understood in this ontological context, the biology of sexual desire symbolizes the human drive to reunite with God.

There are, of course, innumerable other ways to understand the meaning of our erotic natures. The French philosopher George Bataille described eroticism as "an exuberance of life" that "unlike simple sexual activity, is a psychological quest independent of the natural goal: reproduction."[19] Bataille was thus separating eroticism as a psychological quest from its biological underpinnings. What most fascinated Bataille was eroticism's socially transgressive nature. Cultures have as one of their major tasks the regulation of sexuality. Eroticism, according to Bataille, expresses our urge to be free from such repressive constraints. "Eroticism always entails a breaking down of established patterns, the patterns, I repeat, of the regulated social order basic to our discontinuous mode of existence as defined and separate individuals."[20] This is, moreover, why Bataille finds religious mysticism and eroticism to be so intertwined. They are both rooted in the individual's desire to be set free from order and constraint. They are both rooted in the individual's desire to move past separation to union and continuity. The experience of the sacred and sexual union are both often experienced as personal dissolution into a cosmic continuity. Bataille extends this observation by pointing out the aptness of sexual union to symbolize a higher union, noting that the language of sexuality is similar to the language of experiences of divine love. For Bataille, then, both the desire for sexual union and the experience itself are powerful bodily substrates of religious desire and experience.

Sexual Transgression and Cultural Deconstruction

Bataille's observation about the socially transgressive nature of sexuality is important. Modern social structures are in many ways an extension of early humanity's concern with controlling access to sexual partners. Cultures are intensely interested in defining our sexual identities. They define who is related to whom, who has power over whom, who can sexually penetrate whom. Religions often take the lead in performing these cultural functions. It is, after all, the principal function of religion to ensure that individuals subjugate their individual desires to the greater good of community stability. This task often leads them to a general wariness of the body and its desires. No better example exists than Paul's admonishment in his New Testament letter to the Romans that "to be carnally minded is death; but to be spiritually minded is life and peace. Because the carnal mind is enmity against God for it is not subject to the law of God, neither indeed can be. So then they that are in the flesh cannot please God."[21] Or, as he put it a few verses earlier, "Let not sin therefore reign in your mortal body, that ye should obey it in the lusts thereof."[22] These passages should be sufficient to remind us how concerned religion often is with controlling sexuality, especially the sexual behavior of women. Indeed, a principal cultural function of religion seems to be that of channeling sexuality in ways that are consistent with a society's established lineage or inheritance patterns.

Religious studies scholar Jeffrey Kripal observes that religion's role in restraining sexual drives explains why sexuality so often becomes implicated in dramatic attempts to question or even overturn cultural order. Sexuality exudes a charismatic power. This makes sexuality a likely source of desires to transform human religious and social structures, either temporarily or permanently. As Kripal notes, "Human sexuality, both because of its ecstatic, emotionally 'dissolving' capacities and its dramatic powers to express, violate, or affirm intimate social meanings, is a uniquely powerful site for the realization of [cultural] deconstructions and reconstructions."[23]

American religious history provides an abundance of examples illustrating how sexuality can become a powerful site for engineering social change. Three nineteenth-century religious movements—the Shakers, the Latter-day Saints, and the Oneida Community—believed that we cannot implement a divine order on earth until we first thoroughly reorder our sexual lives. All three were theologically conservative. Yet all three believed that their conservative religious outlook carried with it an imperative for radical social change. And all three proposed new cultural arrangements emphasizing novel ideas about human sexuality that ran counter to their era's notions of middle-class decency.

Historian Lawrence Foster provides a detailed analysis of both how and why these three movements generated innovative conceptions of the relationship between religion and sexuality.[24] Foster notes that the Shakers, the Latter-day Saints, and the Oneida Community emerged out of nineteenth-century Protestant revivalism. Revival camp meetings often lasted an entire week. Impassioned preachers called upon their audiences to repent of their sins and to respond to the redemptive grace of God. Emotions soared. So did bodily passions. Many fell to the ground, convulsed with physical spasms, danced wildly, cried out in emotional ecstasy, or fell into trance-like states. The release of bodily inhibitions went hand in hand with the temporary loosening of social inhibitions. Most of those who gathered were used to living in sparsely populated regions of the frontier. These intense religious gatherings generated exciting opportunities for camaraderie. Many behaved in ways that were downright raucous, leading some to observe that more souls were begot than saved. All in all, then, revivalism encouraged persons to cast off inhibitions and freely express their deepest passions. Those attracted to upstart movements such as the Shakers, Latter-Saints, or Oneida Community were well aware that they were driven by bodily urges requiring new and innovative cultural regulation. Ironically, in all three instances, these powerful biological forces gave rise to authoritarian church structures designed to align individuals' desires with the needs of the group.

The sexual substrate of the Shaker experience is the most transparent. The movement's foundress, Ann Lee, suffered four painful deliveries and each of her children died before reaching adolescence. Like many women who had such difficult experiences with childbearing, Ann became increasingly terrified of all sexual intercourse. It is, therefore, not difficult to understand why she became what Lawrence Foster describes as "increasingly ambivalent about her impulses."[25] A few years later she came to identify lust as the root of all evil and corruption in the world, not only in religious matters, but in economic, social, and political affairs as well. The conservative religious community she founded consequently required total celibacy. They strove to organize their bodies according to heavenly rather than earthly precepts. Ann Lee's followers desired bodies that would be free of pain and sorrow. They yearned for celestial bodies free of carnal corruption.

The reason that Ann Lee's followers were called Shakers is that their ecstatic worship set loose a range of physical quivering, quaking, and shaking. One of the movement's earliest leaders, Calvin Green, reveals how their ritually induced ecstasy sublimated sexual impulses into pleasures seemingly not of the flesh:

> There is evidently no labor which so fully absorbs all the faculties of soul and body, as real spiritual devotion & energetic exercise in sacred worship. Therefore there is no operation that has so much effect to mortify & weaken the power of the flesh and energize the soul with the life of the heavenly spirit. . . . [ecstatic worship brings] an enjoyment far superior to any natural recreation, or carnal pleasure— In no earthly pursuit whatever have I ever experienced such delightful feelings or such as would bear any real comparison to what I have felt in sacred devotion.[26]

Providing a devotional outlet for carnal pleasures enabled the Shakers to construct a communal order predicated upon enforced celibacy. Attachment to group cultural and moral codes—not lust—prevailed. It is interesting to note how communal celibacy both fueled a viable economy and engineered a revolutionary social order in which women enjoyed near-equality with men. As Foster observes, "Shaker celibacy, with its subordination of individual sexual life to the larger interests of the community, made possible an equalization of male and female participation in the ecclesiastical system. In addition, celibacy contributed to the success of a communistic system of economic organization in which the good of the individual was subordinated to that of the collectivity."[27] Sexuality, it seems, proved a powerful site for social and religious reconstruction.

If the Shakers stepped outside middle-class norms by suppressing sexuality, the Latter-day Saints did so by blatantly overturning one of its most cherished ideals—monogamy. By the time the Church of Jesus Christ of Latter-day Saints had gathered in Nauvoo, Illinois, members had already learned of the special powers made possible by marriage. Their founder, Joseph Smith, had been led by the Angel Moroni to recover the lost testament of Jesus Christ, the Book of Mormon. The Book of Mormon and subsequent revelations delivered directly to Joseph Smith indicated that marriage plays a vital role in a soul's progress toward spiritual perfection. Yet, few members of the Mormon faith were prepared for Joseph Smith's announcement that God was reinstating the ancient biblical custom of males having more than one wife. True, all Mormons considered the activities of everyday life to have significance for their overall spiritual progress. All knew that marriage extended beyond this lifetime into eternity. All believed that sexuality and marriage are not just worldly activities, but serve long-term spiritual goals. And all were aware the Bible contains numerous precedents for the practice of polygamy. Most however, were unprepared for this flagrant deconstruction of the era's social order.

It is not clear what all precipitated Joseph Smith's decision to make public this revelation concerning polygamy. Joseph was fully aware of his own strong sexual impulses and it is likely he concluded that because they persisted, they must be holy. It is not completely clear how we are to regard the many allegations about Smith's improprieties (after all, the leaders of many newly emerging religious groups have been charged with sexual transgressions). He is said, for example, to have had a relationship with a seventeen-year-old girl, Fannie Alger, whom Smith's wife had brought into their home. Even more scandalous are the charges that he attempted to seduce his close associate Sidney Rigdon's daughter, Nancy. It is fairly certain that Joseph was eventually married to more than fifty women. Yet just how many of those he had sexual relations with is a matter of heated dispute.[28] The possibility that Joseph Smith's religious charisma was grounded in the power of sexual charisma needs to be taken seriously, especially in the light of the many instances in which well-known Protestant clergy whose religious vitality seems closely linked with their ability to wield sexual power over female parishioners (e.g., Jim Bakker, Jimmy Swaggart, Jesse Jackson, Ralph Abernathy, Martin Luther King Jr.)

The Mormons, like the Shakers, gradually erected an authoritarian church structure in which sexuality became a site of important social reconstruction. At a theological level, Joseph Smith taught that a Mormon's duty is to provide fleshly tabernacles for waiting spirits who need to come to earth to further their spiritual growth. Plural marriage enables one to fulfill this duty more completely. Smith also recognized that there were many more females than males in the Mormon community, rendering them vulnerable in the harsh frontier world. Plural marriage actually desexualized the family structure and bound men and women together in loyalty to the long-term purposes of the gathered community of saints. The revelation of plural marriage—though scandalous to the outside world and even many of the Saints themselves—pointed to a new form of kinship ties that would strengthen the fledgling community's social bonds.[29]

Far more transgressive than either Ann Lee's enforced celibacy or Joseph Smith's sanctioned polygamy was John Humphrey Noyes' advocacy of both "complex marriage" and "male continence." John Humphrey Noyes, a law student and son of a wealthy congressman, attended a revivalist meeting and decided to dedicate his life "to the service and ministry of God."[30] Noyes prepared for the ministry at both Andover Seminar and Yale Divinity School before gathering a small group in Putney, Vermont, for the purpose of creating an experimental religious community. Noyes declared that just as "the revivalists had for their great idea the regeneration of the soul," he would put into actual practice his own plan for "the regeneration of society, which is the soul's environment."[31]

Noyes had previously observed how revivalist religion released what he termed "amative tendencies." He saw a natural connection between sexual expression and ecstatic spirituality. Yet Noyes believed that traditional monogamous marriages masked a very non-Christian egotism and possessiveness. Traditional American attitudes toward sex and marriage struck him as symptoms of the disruptive and antisocial egotism rampant in capitalist culture. Noyes envisioned a new spiritual community in which all believers might replace the "I-spirit" with a "we-spirit." Because typical marriage practices are predicated on possessive love, Noyes was determined to institute new sexual and marriage practices that would yield a utopian society. As he put it, "In a holy community there is no more reason why sexual intercourse should be restrained by law than why eating and drinking should be and there is as little occasion for shame in the one case as in the other."[32]

Noyes's community put into operation his theory of complex marriage in which both men and women married into the group as a whole. In this system, "each man is both the husband and brother of all the women, just as each woman is the wife and sister of all the men."[33] Traditional marriage treats women as a form of property, and thus perpetuates possessive forms of love. Noyes believed that existing forms of marriage are a perversion of the nonpossessive love God intended humans to practice. "All experience," he wrote, "testifies that sexual love is not naturally restricted to pairs. . . . the secret history of the human heart will bear out the assertion that it is capable of loving any number of times and any number of persons, and that the more it loves the more it can love.[34]

Noyes elaborated on the need to devise social forms that conform more closely to the facts of human sexuality:

> The law of marriage "worketh wrath." It provokes to secret adultery, actual or of the heart. It ties together unmatched natures. It sunders matched natures. It gives to sexual appetite only a scanty and monotonous allowance, and so produces the natural vices of poverty,

contraction of taste and stinginess or jealousy. It makes no provi-
sion for the sexual appetite at the very time when that appetite is
strongest. . . . This law of society bears hardest on females, because
they have less opportunity of choosing their time of marriage than
men. This discrepancy between the marriage system and nature is
one of the principal sources of peculiar diseases of women, of pros-
titution, masturbation, and licentiousness in general.[35]

The local citizens accused Noyes and his followers of committing adultery
and of extreme licentiousness. They soon drove the community out of Putney,
forcing them to move to upstate New York where they reorganized as the
Oneida Community. Here, Noyes developed new practices known as "mutual
criticism" and "male continence" that were designed to ensure that complex
marriage promoted spiritual progress rather than simple carnal pleasure.
Mutual criticism—the forerunner of modern group therapy—gave institutional
form to the community's need for continuous self-scrutiny and correction of
aberrant behavior. Male continence refers to the fact that Noyes counseled
males to refrain from ejaculating during intercourse.

I conceived the idea that the sexual organs have a social function
which is distinct from the propagative function, and that these
functions may be separated practically. I experimented on this idea
and found that the self control which it requires is not difficult;
also that my enjoyment was increased; also that my wife's experience
was very satisfactory, as it had never been before.
    The discharge of the semen, instead of being the main act
of sexual intercourse, properly so called, is really the sequel and
termination of it.[36]

Noyes's point was that sexual intercourse without male orgasm becomes a
spiritual activity. As Nik Douglas observes, "Whether or not Noyes knew it, he
had discovered the ancient Tantric technique that was practiced centuries be-
forehand."[37] Noyes went so far as to suggest that his sexual techniques were on
the vanguard of a new amative science: "As propagation will become a science,
so amative intercourse will have place among the 'fine arts.' Indeed, it will take
rank above music, painting, sculpture, etc.; for it combines the charms and
benefits of them all. There is a much room for cultivation of taste and skill in
this department as any."[38]
    The Oneida Community existed for more than twenty-five years as a
spiritually and economically prosperous society. Under extreme pressure from
its critics, the community finally abandoned the practice of complex marriage

and soon thereafter disbanded. Yet in the entire history of religion in North America, the Oneida Community is one of the clearest examples of what Kripal had in mind when he explained that human sexuality, both because of its ecstatic, emotionally "dissolving" capacities and its dramatic powers to violate meanings, is a uniquely powerful site for the realization of [cultural] deconstructions and reconstructions.

As Bataille alerted us, our erotic natures often lead to the breaking down of established patterns. Erotic subjectivity has the potential to flow outward into new social patterns, patterns that express our desire for union and connectedness rather than separation or discontinuity. There are, however, other ways that sexuality and religion intertwine. Indeed, the biology of sexual desire and religion share the quest for union with a highly desired other. The somatics of lust often form the experiential template around which we experience passionate union with God.

The Somatics of Religious Passion

Devotional love injects religion with emotional intensity. Devotees are asked to have more than a contractual relationship with their lord. They must love their god or goddess with all their heart. In traditions as culturally diverse as *bhakti* in India or evangelical Protestantism in the United States, the faithful enter into rapturous loving relationships with their savior. Such love is felt deeply. The joy that comes from loving god is more intense than any purely human relationship might inspire. Even when, in Hinduism, the quest for salvation might lead to union with an impersonal divine force (Brahaman) rather than a personal deity, the resultant bliss is charged with elements of romantic love.

Yet, just as in nonreligious manifestations of romantic love, the presence of sexual lust is never far removed. Romantic love (elation and affection focused on a single individual) and lust (craving for union) may have distinct neurological substrates, but they evolved together to direct humans to satisfying relationships with the world. Lust is the boiler which fuels human passion. Romantic love directs this passion toward appropriate cultural objects. For this reason the biology of sexual desire illuminates religious devotion in a manner similar to how knowledge of the chemistry of ecstasy informs our understanding of metaphysical illumination. Anthropologist Felicitas Goodman studied the role of altered states of consciousness in eliciting experiences of an alternate reality. She found that "religious communities that use drugs to [induce ecstasy] teach their members how to switch from intoxication to religious trance."[39] Similarly, it seems that religious communities teach their members how to switch first from lust to romantic devotion, and finally from devotionalism to long-term attachment to cultural ideals.

As Bataille alerted us, the bliss of sexual union and the bliss of religious mysticism are intimately connected. It is fascinating in this regard to consider that the Hindu term for mystical bliss, *ananda*, is etymologically connected with the bliss of orgasmic rapture. Patrick Olivelle explains that *ananda* is the traditional Indian term associated with the intense feeling of joy that devotees experience in meditative trance or in selfless service to god. *Ananda* is the state of bliss associated with the achievement of the union of *atman* (individual soul) and *Brahman* (the world soul or godhead). A careful study of *ananda*'s etymology reveals its origins in the experience of orgasmic rapture. Olivelle found that "*ananda* refers to the orgasmic thrill that makes one lose one's consciousness."[40] In the Vedic commentaries known as the Brahmanas, he discovered clear links between Indic notions of sexual union and meditative union with the divine: "As here when one reaches the climax of human sexual intercourse one becomes in some way unconscious, so there he becomes in some way unconscious, for that is the divine sexual intercourse, for that is the highest *ananda*."[41]

The commingling of lust and romantic love is similarly present in Western religious traditions. Among the first academic psychologists to investigate this connection was James Leuba. In *The Psychology of Religious Mysticism*, Leuba advanced the provocative hypothesis that mystical practices "induce some activity of the sexual organs." Leuba observes that, at root, religion is the human enterprise aimed at maintaining and enhancing life. It is for this reason "invariably connected with sexuality." Central to Leuba's argument is his observation that sexual sensations—including full orgasms in some instances—can take place even in the absence of any appreciable external physical stimulation. By this, Leuba meant that "the sex organs may be aroused to a considerable degree without the person becoming aware of their participation."[42] He cites numerous examples of patients who exhibit highly pleasurable auto-erotic experiences, often quite innocent of any knowledge of the erotic character of the experience. Leuba maintained that affectionate love of god have a similarly sexual character even when the devotee is quite unaware of its erotic basis. He points out that personal deities such as Jesus symbolize a bodily presence capable of touching our inner lives and eliciting bodily response. He cites, for example, the experience of St. Theresa, who seems to have undergone a mystical orgasm when visited by an angel who seemed "all on fire."

Santa Theresa relates that she wrote her Memoirs against her inclination, at the direction of her ecclesiastical superiors. How much she and they suppressed is not known. There remains, however, enough to indicate, it seems to us, the participation of the organs of sex in the extraordinary enjoyment of union with the heavenly Bridegroom. On several occasions she had the vision of an angel who "held in his hands a long golden dart, tipped with fire." She relates that "from time to time he would plunge it through my heart, and push it down into my bowels. As he withdrew the dart, it seemed as if the bowels would be torn away with it; and this would leave me aflame with divine love. . . . It was not a bodily, but a spiritual pain, although the body participated in it to a high degree. There takes place, then, between the soul and God such a sweet love-transaction that it is impossible for me to describe what passes."[43]

We will never know for certain whether auto-erotic phenomena produced this mystical experience, or whether Theresa simply chose the somatics of desire as metaphors for describing the sweet love-transaction she desires between her soul and God. But we do know that this account reveals the close parallel between the attractive, yet threatening, power of sexual passion and the terrific, yet terrifying, power of the sacred. Theresa seems clear that her body played a crucial role in her quest to become "aflame with divine love." The commingling of sexual lust and romantic love in her narrative strongly suggests the existence of a powerful desire to have sexual union with a sacred body—a desire taking diverse forms throughout world history as humans have imagined sex with goddesses, gods, angels, and even extraterrestrials.[44]

We need to consider, too, the rapturous experience of the Pentecostal evangelist Aimee Semple McPherson (1890–1944). McPherson developed into the most famous female preacher of her day, eventually founding the International Church of the Foursquare Gospel. She recounts her first intimate encounter with Christ on an early morning in 1908 following a long night of prayer. It seems that when she finally became quiet and receptive, the holy presence of the Lord descended upon her:

Without effort on my part I began to say: "Glory to Jesus! Glory to Jesus! GLORY TO JESUS!!!" Each time that I said "Glory to Jesus!" it seemed to come from a deeper place in my being than the last, and in a deeper voice, until great waves of "Glory to Jesus" were rolling from my toes up; such adoration and praise I had never known possible.

All at once my hands and arms began to shake, gently at first, then violently, until my whole body was shaking . . . .

. . . and there was the Third Person of the Trinity coming into my body in all His fullness . . .

How happy I was, Oh how happy! Happy just to feel His wonderful power taking control of my being . . . .

Almost without notice my body slipped gently to the floor, and
I was lying stretched out under the power of God, but felt as though
caught up and floating upon the billowy clouds of glory . . . .

My lungs began to fill and heave under the Power as the Comforter came in. The cords of my throat began to twitch and my chin
began to quiver and then to shake violently, but Oh, so sweetly! My
tongue began to move up and down and sideways in my
mouth. . . . Then, suddenly, out of my innermost being flowed rivers
of praise in other tongues as the Spirit gave utterance (Acts 2:4) . . . .

I shouted and sang and laughed and talked in tongues until it
seemed that I was too full to hold another bit of blessing lest I should
burst with glory.[45]

McPherson referred to no less than seven parts of her body in this account.
She likened the Holy Spirit to an electric current, a current that caused her to
quiver, her tongue to move spontaneously, joy to rise out of her innermost
being, her lungs to heave, and great waves of glory to emerge from the innermost of her being before rolling in waves across her body (now suddenly lying
on the floor). Religious studies scholar Peter Gardella has cautioned that reducing this reception of the spirit to mere sexuality would do violence to the full
context of McPherson's Pentecostal experience. Yet "any interpretation should
at least note this physical dimension, and admit the parallels between this
conversion and the descriptions of orgasm provided by modern medicine."[46]

Experiencing religious ecstasy, like experiencing sexual pleasure, requires
first abandoning self-consciousness and self-restraint. Neither rapturous union
with Christ nor female orgasm come to the inhibited. Once McPherson relin-
quished control, simple repetitive action ("Glory to Jesus!") brought her to a state
of excitement that affected her whole body ("rolling from my toes up"). Gardella
astutely observes that "this was the spiritual analogue of the condition physi-
ologists have named the plateau: a preorgasmic stage most reliably reached
through simple, repetitive stimulation, which builds up a critical amount of
tension without bringing about release."[47] Scientific research of females in the
"plateau" phase of sexual arousal will experience strong contractions in and
around the uterus ("it seemed to come from a deeper place") as well as spasmodic tightening of muscles throughout the central body ("great waves of 'Glory
to Jesus' were rolling").[48]

Female orgasm is most successfully reached when males enter during the
plateau. In McPherson's case, "the Comforter came in" after she had reached

this state of overall arousal. As McPherson put it, the spirit of God "was coming into [her] body in all His fullness." Gardella pays particular attention to how "McPherson's feelings mounted and, filled to repletion, she released bodily tension in spasmodic, uncontrollable muscular contractions. Her lungs, vocal cords, and tongue all participated in the release."[49] Muscular contractions during orgasm expel blood from tissue and tension from nerves. McPherson's religious rapture expelled "rivers of praise in other tongues." Both passionate union with the Lord and sexual orgasm are stimulating experiences. Both cause people to think that they have been undergone an extraordinary experience wherein they abandoned their normal sense of self and found union with a source of seemingly infinite pleasure or well-being.

We will never know with complete certainty whether sexual stimulation accompanied McPherson's baptism into Jesus' glory or whether acquired knowledge of sexual delight provided her with apt metaphors of a wholly spiritual event. Yet, even if erotic sensations didn't transport McPherson to devotional ecstasy, we can at least be certain that she used erotic desire to bring her audiences into loving union with Christ. Males no doubt found themselves aroused by her striking beauty and became eager to follow her into a sensuous world of physical/spiritual excitement. Females, too, easily identified with this charismatic woman and surely yearned to have their own intimate experiences of loving connection with Christ. McPherson's provocative physical appearance and suggestive theological imagery were sexually charged. Her narratives and movements across the stage combined to arouse first lust, then romantic love. Importantly, however, her message eventually coaxed those who sought union with Christ to commit themselves permanently to the cultural values that Christ has come to embody. The erotics of desire, then, stimulated worshippers first to embrace, then to attach, and finally to forge long-lasting affiliations with an idealized other. The somatics of human sexuality thereby bestow the reward of internal pleasure to those submitting their individuality to the good of the group.

It is tempting to speculate that McPherson's personal sexuality and her erotic descriptions of surrendering to Christ also played a part in her success as a Pentecostal faith healer. Her stage movements and suggestive narratives stimulated the release of testosterone or dopamine in ways that immediately elevated worshippers' immediate sense of well-being. The biology of desire, then, may have been an integral part of Sister Aimee's "faith healing" ministry. As Sister Aimee induced attendees to surrender themselves in love to Christ, the most suggestible among them would surely have felt a surge of energy and well-being triggered by a pleasurable flood of bodily chemicals. To this extent, the biology of love produced temporary sensations of rejuvenation and restoration to wholeness—all tangible signs that the spirit of Christ had indeed entered worshippers' bodies in all His fullness.

A final example of the sexual nature of religious passion is afforded by the conversion experience narrated by a young woman living in a Christian commune during the early 1970s. Sarah was twenty-four years old. Her loose-fitting apparel and long, "teased" hair gave her a tactile, sensual appearance. She had been living in San Francisco where she "sold dope for a living" before giving birth to a daughter out of wedlock. She realized that her life wasn't working. She was put off by Christianity, believing the Bible to be a myth similar to the myths of other world cultures. But then, by chance, she was invited to visit a Christian commune currently home to about one hundred thirty young people. One night in front of a roaring fire, Sarah asked Jesus to enter her life. And, apparently, he did. In an interview for public television, Sarah explained:

> It really was a physical thing. I mean I felt it physically, in that
> there was a change in my body and I felt something going into
> me. I felt it. I knew it. Like it was from the tips of my toes to the top of
> my head. I could feel it just tingling inside of me. And it was the
> presence of the Lord. And it came into me like it was poured into my
> heart. And I felt it start in the center of me and just go out. It was very
> real. It wasn't just—okay, the Bible says I am saved—but I know
> it! I felt it also.[50]

Sarah's account is striking in many respects. Her sudden act of falling in love with God appears to be an obvious instance where an individual's insecure attachment history activates emotional programs aimed to procure a warm, secure attachment to a valued other. Feelings of insecurity activate emotional systems designed by evolution to bring us into closer proximity with attachment figures. In this commune, the Lord was the most valued and available figure with whom she might restore her fundamental sense of security. There is no question, however, that something more fully somatic motivated her romantic attachment to the Lord. As with McPherson, her passionate union with Jesus caused her to feel definite changes in her body. She felt "something going into" herself. It started "in the center" and she could "feel it just tingling inside." The presence of the Lord was felt inside her, causing sensations "from the tips of [her] toes to the top of [her] head." Sarah seems to have accepted Jesus not just into her soul, but into her body as well. Jesus entered her, causing her to feel as though some form of spiritual fluid was "pouring" into the center of her.

What is of further interest is that over time Sarah's relationship with Jesus came to be characterized less by physical excitement than by single-minded devotion. Sarah reports that thoughts of Jesus continuously thrust their way into her consciousness. She feels close to Jesus, feeling a need to talk with him and to express her love. In a personal prayer to Jesus, Sarah speaks with all the passion of a young woman who has found her perfect mate: "Thank you for being with me Jesus. Let me have my hand in yours, my eyes on you."[51]

It appears that Christian symbolism transformed Sarah's aroused passion into a form of romantic love. Her narration evidences almost every perceptual and cognitive trait that Helen Fisher identifies with passionate love focused on one particular person or valued cultural object. Sarah has now forsaken other forms of connectedness with the world and instead entered into an exclusive relationship based on affection singly focused on Jesus. Thoughts of Jesus intrude constantly into her thoughts. Jesus's love and abilities are clearly aggrandized ("He took me into his hands and lifted up my burdens"[52]). Jesus has, at least for a period of time, become the focal point of her attention and is considered central to her overall awareness and her overall configuration of experience. She invests "special meaning" to this relationship, seeing the object of her devotion as novel, unique, and supremely important. Focusing love on one being energizes her life, moving all other problems or concerns to the periphery of her sense of well-being. She is, furthermore, under the sway of a new spiritual influence. Her new love for Jesus seems to be moving her life forward in ways that seem involuntary, as though she is now governed by forces beyond her own individual personality.

Sarah's conversion provides important clues about the relationship between religious passion and our biologically grounded networks for mating and reproduction. Lust, while important for motivating humans to seek sexual union, cannot alone motivate humans to raise their newborn to the state of full biological viability. As Fisher's research indicates, evolution also favored the human capacities for romantic love and attachment. Love and attachment alter cognition in ways that are likely to keep us emotionally invested in a single individual long enough to form a stable relationship suitable to raising young children. Religion, by providing symbols of an ideal partner, elicits the desire for bodily gratification even as it channels such desire toward longer-term cultural commitments. It does so by building upon the body's innate reward systems (dopamine and the neurochemical stimulation of the caudate nucleus) to flood our thoughts and feelings with an emotionally charged obsession for our culture's idealized "person" (i.e., Christ, saints, the Buddha, Krishna, Shiva, etc.). Religion, in turn, builds upon the somatics of passion by bringing delight, security, and comfort to those who surrender their individuality in heart-felt devotion to a loving God.

These insights into the "somatics of religious devotion" gleaned from the experiences of Sarah, Saint Therese, and Aimee Semple McPherson are all heterosexual. More specifically, they are all examples of a female experiencing bodily penetration from a supernatural male. There is, however, also reason to think that there is a similar somatic structure in male mystical and devotional experience. It is important to note that most images of god in Western culture are male. For this reason, male spirituality in the West tends to have homo-erotic underpinnings. Jeffrey Kripal examined precisely this phenomenon in his *Roads of Excess, Palaces of Wisdom: Eroticism and Reflexivity in the Study of Mysticism.* By "homoerotic," Kripal does not mean to suggest that male reli-gious desire is necessarily connected with the desire for physical homosexual encounters. He simply means that a Western male's desire to unite with a same-sex God is structured by historically and culturally developed symbols that, at root, have homoerotic elements.[53] This is patently obvious, Kripal notes, if we reflect on such simple matters as how accustomed we are to an all-male priesthood who live together in same-sex communities, who engage in ritual cross-dressing, and who receive Christ's body into their mouths as a means of sacramental union. Perhaps too much can be made of the homo-erotic nature of such male religious piety. But it would be odd if we completely ignored the male-to-male symbolic structure through which half the popula-tion seeks union with God. Many questions about the embodied nature of passionate religious experience are yet to be asked.

American Tantra: Sexuality and Spiritual Transformation

In his study of eroticism and the mystical quest, Jeffrey Kripal draws attention to an anthropologist's observation that "erotic subjectivity *does* things."[54] The previous section examined one of the things that erotic subjectivity "does": it fuels the fires of religious passion. Religious devotion is animated by a lustful desire to achieve supreme gratification. Acts of religious devotion arouse and channel the body's desire for union with the "beloved" other. Erotic subjec-tivity, however, does more than impel us toward intimate union. It can also lead to the temporary obliteration of self-consciousness. Such temporary dis-solutions of the self produce sensations of transcendence, not unlike those found in various forms of religious mysticism. Sexuality's ability to transform our personal boundaries has formed the core of a historical tradition that might be called "American Tantra"—a loosely connected lineage of "sexual yoga" that has persisted in American culture for nearly a century and a half.

What is commonly called "Tantrism" refers to a diverse array of esoteric practices originating in Asia (mostly India) in about the sixth century CE.[55] Virtually any description of trantrism is problematic, since scholars are in complete disagreement about whether Tantrism is a central element of almost all Indian-born religion or whether it is purely a construct of Western scholars. The term derives from the Sanskrit root *tan-*, "to extend, stretch, expand." "Tantra" can thus mean "succession," "unfolding," "continuous process," or "extension."[56] Certain texts in the Hindu tradition are labeled Tantras ("scriptures by which knowledge is spread"), though not all these texts contain the distinctive themes ordinarily associated with the concept of Tantrism. Neither these texts nor the practices they describe constitute a unified tradition. It is possible, however, to discern in these texts certain characteristics that are commonly associated with the broad concept of Tantrism. The most important features would seem to be (1) its origin outside of the orthodox Vedic tradition, hence representing itself as "newly revealed" and boldly rebellious; (2) its positive attitude toward the body, hence in opposition to the renunciatory and ascetic strains in Indic thought; (3) its use of radical and transgressive methods to produce enlightenment, often utilizing such controversial or antinomian practices as the ritual use of alcohol, aphrodisiacs, meat-eating, and sexual intercourse; (4) its understanding that the body, as microcosm, replicates all the powers or energies of the entire universe or macrocosm; and (5) its conception of the "subtle body" and "subtle energies" residing in a mystical physiology that includes energy centers or chakras capable of radiating tremendous cosmic power that can bring about immediate and total spiritual transformation.[57]

Throughout history, most Hindus and Buddhists have viewed Tantric practices as aberrations at the far periphery of their religious traditions. When Westerners first "discovered" Trantrism about two hundred years ago, it became a virtual symbol of all that Europeans and Americans found abhorrent about foreign religions. Yet, alternative spiritual traditions have always existed at the periphery of Western religion, too. Various forms of Western gnosticism, magic, and hermeticism all embraced the possibility that the body contains mystical powers that can be activated for the purpose of spiritual transformation.[58]

Among the first Americans to synthesize these alternative spiritual practices into a system of "sexual magic" was Paschal Beverly Randolf (1825–1875).[59] The son of a wealthy Virginia father and a slave from Madagascar, Randolph was raised a free black in New York City where he was first introduced to such esoteric philosophies as Rosicrucianism, spiritualism, and mesmerism. Randolph came to the conclusion that the sexual drive is the most fundamental power in the universe. Sex, he explained, consists of the natural attraction between positive and negative energies. He taught that on the physical plane, male genitals are positive and female genitals are negative; conversely, on the mental plane the female mind is positive and the male mind is negative. He reasoned that sexual intercourse brings these opposing forces together into a higher union, affording humans an immediate connection with the spiritual energies of the cosmos: "At the instant of intense mutual orgasm the souls of the partners are opened to the powers of the cosmos and anything then truly willed is accomplished."[60] Randolph therefore believed that sexual climax not only produces spiritual transformation, but it also aligns us with energies that can be harnessed for such mundane goals as physical health, financial success, or controlling the affections of potential sexual partners.

Even more interesting than Randolph's sex magic was the founding of the "Trantrik Order in America" by the enigmatic Pierre Bernard (1875–1955). We know almost nothing about Bernard's early life, since the biographical information he furnished was deliberately falsified to conceal everything about his personal past. Bernard was most likely born to a middle-class family in California. It seems that he left home in his teens to work his way to India to study the "ancient Sanskrit writings and methods of curing diseases of body and mind."[61] He later claimed to have studied Tantra in Kashmir and Bengal, eventually earning the title of "Shastri," or spiritual adept.[62] By 1904, Bernard had returned to the United States and opened a clinic, known as the "Bacchante Academy," in San Francisco, where he taught classes on a myriad of metaphysical topics. The San Francisco earthquake of 1906, combined with hints of sexual scandal, prompted Bernard to move his academy to New York City, where it reopened in 1909 as the Biophile Club. While in New York, Bernard taught classes in Sanskrit and Hatha Yoga, and even initiated select pupils into Tantric practices. Scandal once again erupted as Bernard was charged with kidnapping one of his young female students, Zella Hopp. Charges were eventually dropped, but in the meantime, the general public learned that Bernard had mysterious powers over his female followers. We will never know what all transpired between Bernard and his female students. A reporter later wrote that upon entering his school he heard "wild Oriental music and women's cries, but not those of distress." Yet Bernard's followers attested to his sincerity and spiritual scruples and for the most part students seemed to attend classes to become better acquainted with "a highly successful health-system of Tantrism, embodying Hatha Yoga, dancing, and psychophysical education."[63]

By 1918, Bernard—or "the Omnipotent Oom" as the press frequently referred to him—moved out to a seventy-two-acre estate in Nyack, New York, where he attracted an extremely wealthy and fashionable clientele. Hugh Urban suggests that Bernard's Tantric teachings were surrounded with a tantalizing aura of secrecy, described as teachings so profound that they must be reserved for the initiated few. Thus, on the first floor of Bernard's retreat could be found students doing exercises designed to promote their physical culture.

Yet, upstairs, higher-level initiates were engaged in more esoteric rites pro-
tected by a veil of secrecy. Bernard's publications described the human body as
the most perfect place of worship—a truly embodied, sensual worship that
doesn't require the outer trappings of organized religion: "The trained imagination no longer worships before the shrines of churches, pagoda, and
mosques or there would be blaspheming the greatest, grandest and most
sublime temple in the universe, the miracle of miracles, the human body."[64] In
an article on Tantrik worship, Bernard further explained: "The animating
impulse of all organic life is the sexual instinct. It is that which underlies the
struggle for existence in the animal world and is the source of all human
endeavor. . . . That affinity which draws the two sexes together . . . is the most
powerful factor in the human race and has ever been the cause of man's most
exalted thought."[65]

The popular press charged Bernard with running a love cult. They accused
his Tantric rites as being "grossly licentious," though noting with a bit of envy
that in these rites, skilled couples were "able to make love hour after hour
without diminution of male potency and female desire."[66] His sexual teachings
generated such scandal that he was eventually forced to discontinue his public
promulgation of Tantrism. Yet by this time Bernard had succeeded in making
lasting contributions to the history of American alternative spirituality.[67] First,
Bernard was a pioneer in the early transmission of Tantra to America, where it
became increasingly fused with Western traditions of sexual magic. And second, like many other Americans to embrace Tantra, Bernard generated intense
scandal and slander from the surrounding society, foreshadowing Tantra's role
in the American imagination as something wonderfully seductive and deli-
ciously transgressive.

Another important phase in the development of American Tantra was "the
somatic movement" in psychotherapy and alternative medical treatments. The
most important teacher in this field was Wilhelm Reich (1897–1957). Reich
began his career working with Sigmund Freud in the field of psychoanalysis.
Reich extended Freud's notion of libido into a new concept of bodily energy he
called "orgone"—a term he derived from the words "organism" and "orgasm"
to convey the sexual nature of this life-enhancing energy. For Reich, orgone
was more than a biological energy. He believed that orgone is a cosmic energy
found everywhere, especially in the atmosphere. As long as orgone flows freely
throughout the body, we will enjoy perfect health and happiness. Yet, muscular rigidities—usually created by emotional complexes and neuroses—block
the free flow of orgone and cause our systems to falter. Reich argued that his
patients' bodies physically mirrored these blockages. Reich believed that sexual
orgasms are able to restore us to physical and spiritual vitality. Orgasms, he

explained, break down the muscular blockages that restrict the free flow of orgone and thereby restore full mental and physical health. For this reason, he advocated "full surrender to the sensations of pleasure during sexual embrace."[68]

Reich gradually concluded that psychotherapy alone could not break down the psychosomatic blockages responsible for human malaise. Therapy needed to include work on the body itself. This meant more than simple massage. Eliminating muscle tensions served the higher purpose of restoring the flow of orgone energy. Reich eventually identified seven segments, or "rings," of the body armor, all arranged along the spinal column along which orgone flows. As Jeffrey Kripal astutely points out, Reich's system recapitulated the major tenets of Asian Tantra.[69] Tantra is predicated on the existence of a mystical physiology and a variety of subtle energies: *sakti*, the "occult energy" that streams through the aspirant's body during initiations and spiritual ecstasy; the serpentine energy *kundalini* that can be awakened through various physical postures and meditative techniques; the seven *chakras*, or "energy circles," located along the spinal column; and the ancient yogic concept of *prana* that refers to "breath" or "life energy." Reich's system, though developed in a Western context, was similarly predicated on the existence of a blissful cosmic energy residing in the body that needs to be released through sexual orgasm or physical manipulation, the loosening of seven rings or circles located along the central spinal column, and the intimate relationship between breath and bio-energy.

Concurrent with Reich's "discovery" of the body's hidden sexual energies was the career of Ida Rolf (1896–1975). Rolf was first introduced to the concept of subtle body energies during a visit to an osteopathic physician soon after her graduation from Barnard College. Osteopathic medicine grew out of mesmerism and other metaphysical healing systems and consequently the existence of a spiritual energy that flows throughout the human body. Osteopathic treatments were initially designed to remove anatomical impediments to the free flow of this metaphysical energy. To pursue her interest in manipulating deep tissue in the effort to restore physical vitality, Rolf earned a Ph.D. in biochemistry from Columbia University.

The most formative influence on Rolf's understanding of "body work" was her study with the Omnipotent Oom, Pierre Bernard. It was undoubtedly Barnard who first taught her about the *chakras*, or energy centers, located along the spinal column, yoga exercises, and Tantra. Jeffrey Kripal points out that the young Rolf was deeply influenced by Bernard's Tantric yoga and extended his teachings into her own system that synthesized his esoteric metaphysics with her previous osteopathic and chiropractic training.[70] "Rolfing" utilized deep massage to produce a kind of cosmic mysticism. One of Rolf's students recounts that Rolf was fundamentally concerned with "initiating people into harmonious spiritual consciousness, which in her view coincides with having vertically aligned body segments."[71] By the 1950s, Rolfing had already become a well-established discipline of body work with a loyal—but small—following. Fate, however, was to intervene, bringing Ida Rolf to the one spot in America that would ensure that her vision of body-based therapy would be disseminated into the nation's growing enthusiasm for massage, alternative healing, body-based psychotherapy, and Asian Tantrism.

When Michael Murphy and Richard Price founded the Esalen Institute in 1962, there was at long last a central location where those interested in the body and its neglected energies might gather. And gather they have. For more than forty-five years now, Esalen has served as a New Age growth center devoted to humanity's physical, psychological, and spiritual transformation.[72] Located on the cliffs of Big Sur, California, Esalen occupies the most spectacularly beautiful piece of land in the United States. Hot mineral springs feed Esalen's famed baths with 120-degree water, creating the focal gathering point where naked bodies come to regenerate. Around these baths are a number of massage tables where even to this day "body workers" trained in a lineage linking them directly with Wilhelm Reich and Ida Rolf remove the muscular blockages impeding our innate drive to spiritual consciousness.

Murphy and Price founded Esalen to further what they believed would be the next step forward in humanity's evolutionary development. They were convinced that humanity is on the edge of a tremendous religious and cultural breakthrough. Inspired by Eastern mystical philosophy, particularly that of Sri Aurobindo, they believed that humans are beginning to discover their innate potentials for growth and transformation. The forces driving us toward this next step of human evolution come both from "above" and from "below." God, understood as Absolute Spirit, is continuously emanating causal energies into our universe—energies best received if we learn to cultivate states of inner quietude. What we think of as "matter" is itself just another permutation of Absolute Spirit. The material world—including our body and its subtle energies—embodies an immanent spiritual force driving ever-upward toward higher levels of organization and consciousness. Humanity's spiritual transformation was thus understood to be caused both from "pulls from above" and "pushes from below." As Esalen's co-founder Michael Murphy explained, "What Aurbodindo called yoga, what Abe Maslow called self-actualization, what Fritz Perls called organismic integrity, Assagioli called psychosynthesis. All these share basically the same idea—that there is a natural tendency toward development, toward unfoldment, that pervades the universe as well as the human sphere, and that our job is to get behind that and make it conscious."[73]

Now well into its fifth decade, Esalen's mission has been to bring together the people and ideas needed to accomplish this job—the job of getting behind the process of human transformation. Toward that goal, the institute invited Ida Rolf to take up residence at Esalen and host ongoing discussions of the theory and practice of what might be called the "somatics" of spiritual transformation. Esalen soon became synonymous with massage. Fritz Perls, Harvey Cox, and Sam Keen are among the many psychological and theological teachers whose Esalen massages proved important in their own personal transformations. But Esalen also reached out to many other teachings and practices that now comprise the American Tantric tradition. Yoga and other Asian spiritual practices continue to be taught regularly in Esalen's week-long classes. Body-based psychotherapy, encounter groups, alternative healing systems, parapsychology, psychedelics, and even martial arts have all made their way into Esalen's ongoing concern with understanding what Murphy described as the natural tendency toward development that pervades the human sphere. Even a short listing of those who have offered classes at Esalen reveals something about its role in disseminating all things Tantric throughout American culture: Abraham Maslow, Fritz Perls, Roberto Assagioli, Aldous Huxley, Joseph Campbell, Paul Tillich, Carl Rogers, J. B. Rhine, Carlos Castenada, Rollo May, Alan Watts, Timothy Leary, Stanislov Grof, and Ken Wilber.

Not all of these individuals left Esalen to transmit messages explicitly extolling sexuality as the key to spiritual transformation. But all contributed in some way to a spiritual vision that (1) was outside the orthodox biblical tradition, hence representing itself as newly revealed and boldly rebellious; (2) embraced a positive attitude toward the body, hence denouncing the prudish tendencies of biblical religion; (3) advocated use of radical and transgressive methods to produce enlightenment, often utilizing such controversial or antinomian practices as the ritual use of alcohol, psychedelics, and sexual intercourse; (4) understood the body as a microcosm replicates all the powers or energies of the entire universe or macrocosm; and (5) affirmed the presence of the "subtle body" and "subtle energies" residing in a mystical physiology. Esalen, in short, played a pivotal role as a clearinghouse for the Tantric-leaning components of alternative American spirituality.

One of Esalen's earliest contributors, Alan Watts, illustrates how Esalen-inspired interests gradually became diffused in popular American culture. In 1971, he published *Erotic Spirituality* to familiarize reading audiences with basic Tantric principles. In his presentation, Tantra becomes an almost orthodox variant of standard Yoga, utilizing breathing exercises and repetition of mantras to purify the mind. He explains that "the actual discipline of Yoga consists of various *upaya* or 'devices' to bring about the temporary cessation of conceptualization."[74] Watts further explains that erotic tension and sexual orgasm are among the most effective of these time-honored *upaya*. Sex transports us to nonverbal levels of experience, ushering us beyond the world of personal ego to the vast *sunyata* (no-thingness) of love.

In a similar vein, Buddhist scholar Jeffrey Hopkins wrote a popular work titled *Sex, Orgasm, and the Mind of Clear Light*. Although Hopkins has no ties to Esalen, his book reveals how fully sexual mysticism has filtered into Americans' quest for alternative spiritual practices. The book was inspired in part by his desire to provide a gay counterpart to Gedun Chopel's *Tibetan Arts of Love* that popularized Tantric principles among heterosexual spiritual seekers. His principal message is that both Hindu and Buddhist traditions proclaim that the essential nature of human mind is "clear light"—luminous and knowing. The mind of clear light is our true nature, though ignored by most of us. To rediscover our true nature, we need to strip the mind of its distractions and superficial concern. Spiritual transformation requires us to penetrate to the more subtle levels of consciousness where we will once again make connection with clear light. Orgasmic pleasure—heterosexual or homosexual—involves the cessation of grosser levels of consciousness and thereby manifests the more subtle levels of mind. In this way, orgasm reveals our true nature as vehicles for the expression of clear light: "When the sense of pleasure is powerful, consciousness is totally involved with that pleasure and thus is completely withdrawn; the subtler levels of consciousness can manifest themselves, at which point the nature of the mind can be apprehended ... The aim of sexual yoga is not mere repetition of an attractive state but revelation of the basic reality of bliss and emptiness underlying appearances."[75]

Though Watts and Hopkins both approached Tantra and spiritual sex with the benefit of broad scholarly backgrounds, most of their readers did not. Many in the general reading public are frankly eclectic in their approach to religious philosophy and mingle Tantrism with other New Age interests such as Sufi dance, T'ai Ch'i, Native American lore, self-help psychology, and Western occultism. More recent books on Tantra intended for popular audiences include *The Art of Sexual Ecstasy*, *Sex Magic, Tantra and Tarot*, and *Tantric Secrets of Sex and Spirit*.[76] Tantra is now also promulgated over the Internet, with several hundred Web sites devoted to the subject, bearing names such as "Oceanic Tantra," "Ceremonial Sensual Pleasuring," "Sacred Sex: Karessa, Tantra, and Sex Magic."[77] As Hugh Urban comments, such manifestations of contemporary American Tantra remind us that the tradition is "a densely tangled web of intersecting threads, both Eastern and Western, ancient and modern, woven through the intricate cross-cultural interplay of scholarly and popular imaginations, and creatively reimagined in each new historical era."[78]

The human body is an instrument finely tuned by evolution to seek the pleasures that come from somatic gratification. Erotic drives prompt us to abandon self-control and seek union with others in the quest for such pleasure (and to ensure the transmission of life). And, as we have seen, erotic subjectivity "does" things. Its ecstatic, emotionally "dissolving" capacities and its dramatic powers to express, violate, or affirm intimate social meanings makes it a uniquely powerful site for cultural innovation. And, too, its ego-dissolving effects on the self and its boundaries provide vivid experiences of self-transformation. As long as humans continue to yearn to reorient their lives through union with "higher powers," the somatics of desire will also fuel the quest for spiritual transformation.

6

Pain, Healing, and Spiritual Renewal

Bodily Sources of Religious Innovation

The brain is not a passive organ. It actively shapes sensory data into forms that are likely to satisfy our personal needs and interests. Many of these needs and interests are purely biological in nature. Yet we are also cultural beings. Many of our needs and interests therefore arise from the fact that our lives unfold through social and historical networks. This explains why the health of the body is a reliable index of the health of our culture (and vice versa). Our bodies register cultural dysfunction. When culture thwarts our vital needs and interests, the infliction often manifests itself in bodily dis-ease. The body's quest to eliminate sources of somatic distress is thus frequently also a quest for a new and more sanative cultural orientation to life.

The intimate connection between the body and culture has important implications for the study of religion. Because the body registers the dysfunctional elements of a cultural system, it can also become the originating source of cultural reconstruction. Pain and illness often provide the impetus for some of the most innovative expressions of human religiosity. Even the most radical impulses in cultural reconstruction are rooted paradoxically in the private experience of the body and its afflictions.[1]

Pain: The Intersection of Biology and Culture

Pain is one of the least understood aspects of human existence. One reason for this is undoubtedly western civilization's long adherence to Cartesian dualism. Our habitual tendency to view the mind and body as separate entities obscures the subtle ways that thought and somatic tissue are parts of the same organic whole. Research indicates that pain is not simply a mental representation of an otherwise purely physical stimulus. As Patrick Wall explains, it has become increasingly clear that "the word pain is used to group together a class of combined sensory-emotional events."[2] Pain is always accompanied by emotion and meaning, which—among other things—means that pain is always unique to the person who suffers.

Damage to our bodily tissue triggers a complex sequence of events in which sensory nerves and brain activity "feed back" upon one another.

> The spinal cord is informed of tissue damage by way of sensory nerves. Cells in the spinal cord react immediately to the input, but the amount of their output depends on small cells that can enhance or diminish the output message. . . . The cord cells signal to many parts of the brain that injury exists. Many parts of the brain then feed back onto the cord cells and amplify or reduce their output messages.[3]

Pain thus emerges as part of a complex syndrome. This syndrome joins together a connected group of bodily activities. For this reason, pain is never an isolated sensation. Tissue damage initiates signals that arouse the nervous system. These signals initiate a startle response that in turn evokes emotional programs ranging from fear and depression to expectation and interest. Differences in our emotional sensibilities make pain a highly idiosyncratic phenomenon, revealing how fully pain links nerve signals with personal biography. Not only do we develop our own idiosyncratic strategies for labeling and responding to sensory signals, but we do so in part by filtering such signals through cultural meanings about the source and significance of pain. Almost every culture provides its members with ideal patterns of responding to sensory trauma. Deities and other cultural heroes typically bear pain without being personally diminished. Greek legends about the courageous Spartans, cinematic action heroes such as Rambo or James Bond, and religious imagery of Christ's crucifixion are all examples of cultural patterns for how we might optimally interpret and respond to sensory signals that alert us to tissue damage. Cultural understandings of pain vary by ethnic group, and may also provide different templates for persons according to age, gender, or social status. Pain, as we shall see, can even be glorified as a prerequisite to profound personal transformations whereby the self melds with a transcendent deity.

The fact that pain is a complex interaction of nerve signals, emotions, and personal/cultural meanings has many implications for understanding its connection with religion. As an emotion-laden phenomenon, pain has a pronounced motivational effect upon cognitive structures such as attention, orientation, exploration, and muscular response. Pain also triggers the brain's modules for identifying the causal source of threat or causal forces that might bring cure. Efforts to detect causal agency bring culturally acquired belief systems to bear on the interpretation of current experience (and— if necessary—making adaptive changes in these belief systems). When pain becomes chronic, we become particularly motivated to utilize culturally acquired belief systems concerning superheroes or deities who are somehow immune to debilitating sensations and who somehow reside "above" physical disability. Superheroes and deities provide patterns for deflecting attention away from debilitating pain and toward normative sets of behavior. Suffering persons learn to imitate and identify with cultural icons and thereby internalize response patterns that can profoundly alter the significance of nerve signals emanating from damaged tissue.

Religion also ameliorates pain by inducing muscle relaxation. Almost any activity that produces muscle relaxation will have at least some therapeutic value. Both religious belief in supernatural agents and religious rituals divert attention, thereby mitigating our tendency to respond to threat by assuming rigid, defensive postures. Of further importance is the fact that rituals initiate types of bodily action that can significantly alter pain signals. Our bodies are wired to respond to nerve sensations through coordinated muscular action. For example, we alleviate the painful sensations accompanying hunger or thirst by engaging in a series of "consummatory actions" aimed at alleviating bodily deprivation. Any series of actions aiming to satisfy hunger or thirst will at least temporarily assuage bodily pain. Similarly, ritual actions such as prayer, yoga, or ecstatic dancing constitute consummatory behaviors so far as they are believed to be appropriate ways of availing ourselves of remedial power. And, too, we know that many ritual activities are capable of producing neurotransmitters that can affect pain signals.[4] Serotonin and norepinephrine, for example, seem to decrease pain by causing nocicepetors to release endorphins, which act as natural pain-relievers. Many aerobic activities can stimulate the release of endorphins, thus possibly explaining why many religious rituals and mystical practices have been accorded healing power in a wide variety of religious cultures. Pain-driven persons are thus motivated to value any religious practice affecting the "chemistry of consciousness."

There are, then, numerous connections between bodily pain and religious constructions of reality. One of the first scholars to investigate these connections was Elaine Scarry. Scarry was primarily interested in how experiences of pain provide a unique portal through which we might glimpse the imaginative ways that humans make, and unmake, their worlds. Scarry argues that pain immediately and forcefully "unmakes" our world. By this she means that pain causes our world to collapse. For the person in pain, there is no reality besides pain. Scarry writes that "physical pain does not simply resist language but actually destroys it, bringing about an immediate reversion to a state anterior to language, to the sounds and cries a human being made before language is learned."[5] Prolonged pain consequently unmakes our world, stripping us of accustomed relationships to persons or objects beyond our skin. This is, in turn, why pain ultimately triggers the human imagination. Pain requires the imagination to link sentient experience with an intentional state and an intentional object. Our imagination makes it possible for us to move past being wholly passive and helpless recipients of experience and instead become active agents capable of modifying ourselves and our worlds. In this way, sentient experience such as pain signals the process whereby humans imaginatively and creatively make new worlds.

Scarry makes an important contribution to the study of spirituality in the flesh by showing us how pain drives the imagination to modify our constructions of both self and world. She deftly alerts us to the fact that pain constitutes a "framing event" that in turn structures all of our other perceptual, somatic, and emotional processes. A potentially limiting aspect of Scarry's analysis of pain is her repeated evocation of a number of dubious ontological and psychological assumptions. She insists, for example, that pain never has "referential content" and that imagination is always devoid of activity, felt-occurrences, or experienceable conditions. Neither side of this assertion squares with the biological, psychological, or philosophical study of embodied experience. Few human experiences—and surely not pain—are either wholly subjective or wholly objective in the ways she proposes. The important point, however, is that Scarry alerts us to the fact that bodily sensations drive the imagination to create concepts of the self and world that will alleviate threats to our well-being. Her study of the role of pain in making worlds amplifies the basic thesis of this chapter: some of the most radical impulses in cultural reconstruction are paradoxically rooted in the private experience of the body and its afflictions.

Pain: From Absence to Sacred Presence

The phenomenon of ritualized pain is a paradigmatic example of how bodily suffering motivates efforts to construct, and reconstruct, our worlds. Throughout the course of history, religious individuals have deliberately hurt their bodies for the sake of their souls. Self-flagellation, barefoot pilgrimages, body piercing, walking on hot coals, and even self-immolation have all been celebrated as acts of religious piety. Just why, we might ask, do religions sanction rituals of self-hurting? Why do religions often develop elaborate theologies that glorify pain?

The key to understanding ritualized pain resides in the embodied nature of all experiences, including the experience of pain. Bodily pain signals more than organic tissue damage. It is also a signal of the breakdown of the body's capacity to pursue meanings or goals. This is what David Bakan had in mind when he described pain as "the psychic manifestation of telic decentralization."[6] Humans strive towards purposes; pain registers the severing of such telic striving almost as frequently as it does the severing of tissue.

Ariel Glucklich helps us understand the often-bizarre instances of ritualized pain by showing their relationship to telic striving. Ritualized pain, he shows, reorganizes the self in ways that make it possible for us to strive for wholly spiritual meanings and goals. Glucklich explains that pain produces very specific kinds of cognitive-emotional changes. These changes in our thought and feelings necessitate an immediate change in our sense of self, our priorities, and our motivations. To this extent, pain initiates a host of physiological and psychological changes that might be characterized as a death-rebirth process. Pain destroys our former sense of self and goal orientation. In so doing, it simultaneously makes it possible for religion to step in and reconfigure our sense of self in ways that connect us with a "higher" reality. By ritualizing pain, religions help transform the destructive or disintegrative effects of pain into a positive religious-psychological mechanism. "Sacred pain" reintegrates persons with a larger community or a more fundamental state of being. As Glucklich puts it, ritualized pain facilitates "the act of subserving a lower telos in favor a higher one."[7]

Pain affects the neuropsychological processes that create our sense of self and agency. The more irritation applied to our body, the less the central nervous system is able to generate signals that construct a stable sense of self. "Modulated pain weakens the individual's feeling of being a discrete agent; it makes the 'body-self' transparent and facilitates the emergence of a new identity. Metaphorically, pain creates an embodied 'absence' and makes way for a new and greater 'presence.' "[8] Even deliberate self-hurting can therefore function in the service of important cultural goals.

Glucklich astutely observes that the connection between bodily pain and theological constructions exists in "that fuzzy area where culture meets biology. This is the place where sensation becomes representation, and conversely consciousness is experienced somatically—in the body."[9] Exploring this fuzzy area requires scholarly adeptness. It requires, for example, that we steer a middle course between the opposing disciplinary perspectives of pure biology and pure cultural constructivism. The cultural constructivists are surely right that we don't have access to pain. We only have access to discourse *about* pain, and this discourse is socially and culturally constructed. Yet experience is grounded in biological activity, and our scientific culture has a great deal of information about this bedrock foundation of how sensation becomes representation and how consciousness is experienced somatically. For this reason, Glucklich concludes that "embodied experience, including pain and its representation, are a mix of biological facts and cultural consciousness (metaphors, emotions, attitudes). The problem . . . is precisely how this mix works, and how scholarship may combine objective description with subjective experience."[10] Getting this mix right—or even nearly right—is the ultimate goal of a spirituality in the flesh.

The Language of the Body

Bodily pain is a peculiar mix of biological facts and cultural consciousness. It arises at the fuzzy area where sensation becomes representation, and, conversely, consciousness is experienced in the body. The body responds to damaged tissue and threatened goal orientations by improvising adaptive strategies. The body creatively expresses these adaptive strategies in its own language—a language of emotions, bodily postures, and metaphorical conceptions. A spirituality in the flesh must be attentive to the language of the body and appreciate the adaptive desires this language communicates.

Concern with "body language" brings us back to the work of Wilhelm Reich, whose speculations about sexuality appeared in the previous chapter. Reich distinguished himself in early psychoanalytic circles by his emphasis on mind/body interaction. Like most psychoanalysts, Reich was interested in the way we protect ourselves by devising defense mechanisms. Reich referred to defense mechanisms as "character armor."[11] He observed that defense mechanisms serve as protective armor; they protect us from both external threats and from desires or urges that potentially threaten us from within. Believing that the body and mind work together as one whole, he reasoned that all of our physical expressions reveal something about our personality. Our posture, glances, or even our gait all convey our characteristic personality traits. Thus, for example, persons with chronically stooped shoulders might be keeping their face and eyes hidden as a way of protecting themselves from hurtful contact with others. Reich's point was that defense mechanisms express themselves not only psychologically but also through specific body gestures and muscular tensions. The body's methods of muscular "armoring" is a language that expresses the organism's strategies for protecting itself against painful or threatening experiences (or from its own internal urges).

Reich concluded that if psychotherapy is to be successful, it must pay attention to the body and its expressive language. He gradually developed therapeutic techniques aimed at releasing built-up muscular tensions and restoring a more natural flow of bodily energy which he called "orgone" energy. Much as Freud had described the flow of libido in essentially hydraulic terms, Reich reasoned that our interactions with the surrounding world are driven by the flow of orgone. And, again paralleling Freud, he suggested that orgone tends to follow a natural sequence of escalating tension, release, and relaxation.

Reich's theories have been almost wholly dismissed by academically trained psychologists (he died in prison serving a term after the Food and Drug Administration had declared his therapeutic practices to be fraudulent). Yet his writings nonetheless emboldened a good many psychotherapists to follow his lead in viewing humans as a psychosomatic unity and to pay close clinical attention to the language of the body. Gestalt therapy, bioenergetics, rolfing therapy, primal scream therapy, and sundry massage therapies all follow Reich in emphasizing the need to include "body work" in any comprehensive therapeutic system. Thus, even though Reich and his theories have long since been relegated to the far fringe of clinical psychology, his work has inspired others to recognize the importance of body language as a symptom of significant themes or issues in our personalities.

One of Reich's followers, Alexander Lowen, reformulated the basic principles of orgonomics in his own theory of bioenergetics. Bioenergetics, he explained, is predicated on "the premise that we are the life of our bodies. The primary nature of every human being is to be open to life and love. Naturally, we reach out to what we think will be pleasurable, but I maintain that the act of reaching out is itself the basis of the experience of pleasure. It represents an expansion of the total organism, a flow of feeling and energy to the periphery of the organism and the world.... We can define the feeling of pleasure as the perception of an expansive movement in the body—opening up, reaching out, making contact."[12] Lowen consequently views health in terms of our capacity to make pleasurable responses to the environment. Unfortunately, however, we are often forced to protect ourselves against hurt by developing defensive armor. Therapists must therefore pay attention to the subtle forms of nonverbal communication that convey an individual's defensive postures toward life. Bodily gestures convey a great deal of information about a person's deepest strategies.

Body-oriented therapies such as bioenergetics alert us to the body's own expressive language. The position and movement of the body communicate the organism's overall connection with the world. Lowen postulates that the healthy organism seeks to make pleasurable contact with the surrounding world. He reasons that an optimal approach to life "entails a flow of feeling, excitation or energy from the core or heart of the person to the peripheral structures and organs."[13] Bodily gestures are thus significant in that they reveal the extent to which a person spontaneously connects with the outer world. A person's way of moving, subjective sense of either vitality or sluggishness, posture, tone of voice, or facial expressions reveal whether past experiences have forced her or him to adopt defensive armoring. The therapist tries to help clients understand how and why their characteristic defenses developed, and what life would be like if they could release these defensive postures and restore a more freely flowing connection to the world. Various exercises or body work help clients release muscular tension, thereby increasing their energy levels and restoring their capacity for pleasure, spontaneity, and joy.

Lowen identifies six major areas of contact with the external world: the face (including the sensory organs located in the face), the two hands, the genital apparatus, and the two feet. These six contact areas (plus the core, or heart) are simultaneously the principal sites of expressive communication revealing how freely the self reaches out to the world. Lowen suggests that these critical areas of the body are not only expressed through physical gestures but reflected in language as well. He asks us to consider the vast array of verbal expressions connected with proprioceptive sensations related to these regions: having an open heart, having a broken heart, being tight-fisted, standing on our own two feet, being balanced, keeping in touch, having a taste for life, losing face, approaching with our eyes wide open, and so on. Bodily metaphors express a person's current capacity—or desire—to make pleasurable contact with the surrounding world. For this reason, bodily metaphors imaginatively shape our language for reconstructing ourselves and the world in a more functional way.

Lowen and other psychotherapists who emphasize body work join a host of philosophers who share their interest in how bodily metaphors structure human cognition. Mark Johnson and George Lakoff are perhaps the best known of those who have explored the vast extent to which meaning, imagination, and reason are patterned by bodily experience.[14] They note that most thinking is metaphorical. Metaphors "fund" experience. They sort raw sensory data and categorize them into patterns connected with our bodily orientation to the world. Furthermore, metaphors give experience a rich inferential structure, helping us form judgments and make expectations. Importantly, most of our metaphors are drawn from our bodies and their physical relationship to the world. Thus, for example, we come to view difficulties as physical blockages or burdens (e.g., "Concern for my family is weighing upon me"). More of something is viewed as "up" (e.g., "Prices are up") while less of something is viewed as "down." Intimacy is often conceptualized as proximity or closeness (e.g., "We have been close for years, but are now drifting apart"). The cause of something is understood in terms of physical forces ("She pushed her ideas on the rest of us"). Change is thought of in terms of motion ("I started moving in the right direction").

Further hints about how bodily metaphors shape cognition have been provided by body-oriented psychotherapies. Lowen, for example, points out that the force of gravity and the weight of objects affect how we conceptualize other impediments to our movement through life ("Family problems are weighing me down"; "Jesus lifted up my burdens"). Experiences of sinking or falling fund other situations in which we come up against resistance ("I am falling behind at work"; "I am drowning in sorrow"). Bodily sensations of imbalance provide a template for precarious relationships with sources of nurturance or well-being ("I am slipping into . . ."; "Our marriage is teetering"). Conversely, metaphors connected with being "touched," "balanced," "raised," or "lifted up" indicate expectation of overcoming impediments and excitement at the prospects of free-flowing connection with the world.

Attention to body language draws renewed attention to that fuzzy area where culture meets biology. Muscular tensions, defensive postures, and proprioceptive metaphors all arise at the place where sensation becomes representation, and conversely consciousness is experienced somatically—in the body. Religions are frameworks of orientation to life and, for this reason, we should expect them to be rich in the expressive language of the body. The language of religious innovation is thus often rife with bodily metaphors. Pain and illness not only register dysfunction, they also fund experience with images that express the desire for new, more functional postures toward life.

Bodily Pain and Cultural Reconstruction

Almost thirty years ago, William McLoughlin proposed that major innovations in American religious history can best be understood as episodes of cultural renewal. McLoughlin interpreted these episodes of renewal as examples of what anthropologist Anthony Wallace terms "revitalization movements."[15] Revitalization movements typically emerge during periods of rapid social change. Inherited belief systems no longer provide effective guidance. Disorientation ensues. The result is a "period of individual stress" when, one by one, people start to lose their bearings on life. People respond to this stress by becoming psychologically or physically ill. Many begin to engage in acts of deviant behavior. Over time, they come to realize that their problems are not wholly personal but are instead due to breakdowns in the wider culture. They realize that their doctors no longer cure, their police and courts do not maintain social order, and their churches don't offer spiritual comfort.

Some persons endure stress or strain even in the healthiest of societies. When cultures are functioning well, they provide resources that can assuage these stresses and strains. There come times, however, that—at least for some segments of society—culture is no longer functional. Too many persons suffer from jarring disjunctions between traditional values and the realities of their everyday lives. The conditions are ripe for the emergence of a new cultural authority. Just as periods of ecological crisis create conditions under which genetic mutations are more likely to be "selected for" by natural selection, periods of cultural distortion provide fertile ground for the emergence of new leaders or new movements that introduce new and more socially viable cultural norms. Spokespersons for new cultural patterns have often themselves suffered acutely from the breakdown of traditional cultural patterns. As psychologist Erik Erikson has said of Martin Luther, these cultural innovators eventually learn "to lift their individual patienthood to the level of a universal one and try to solve for all what they could not solve for themselves alone."[16] Put differently, private experiences of pain or illness are often the nucleus of even the most radical attempts at cultural reconstruction.

McLoughlin observed that revitalization movements typically invoke the imagery of an immanent and hence accessible deity. God's apparent absence from existing religious institutions is compensated for by a renewed sense of God's presence in nature. Instead of seeking God in traditional churches, people instead learn to seek God deep within themselves. "The spiritual and physical worlds intermingle. God can be discerned as easily in a flower, a blade of grass, or a child as in a church."[17] Once persons learn to connect with God in their immediate experience, they are once again prepared to enter into productive relationships with the wider world. Thus, whereas stable societies more typically emphasize God as a transcendent Lord or Judge to whose will we must submit, in periods of cultural stress the theological pendulum invariably swings to a renewed interest in theological immanence.

The premise of both McLoughlin's and Wallace's theories of cultural revitalization is that religion is a principal source of ideology; that is, religion provides a comprehensive philosophy that gives meaning and order to the lives of people in their pursuit of a meaningful life. When personal and social stress become so acute that they manifest themselves in pain or illness, conditions become ripe for the dismantling of older ideological formulations and the emergence of new, more adaptive ones. There is, then, an intimate connection between the private sufferings of the body and episodes of religious innovation. By paying attention to the body's pain and illness, we can learn a great deal about the religious strategies that seek to reconstruct culture in more fully functional ways.

Physical Bodies, Metaphysical Energies

The thirty years following the Civil War witnessed a great deal of disruption in Americans' inherited way of life. Massive immigration, rapid urbanization, and unprecedented industrialization drastically altered the nature of everyday life. It would be no exaggeration to say that the "glue" that had previously bonded American society together had either evaporated or simply decomposed. Churchman Washington Gladden lamented that American society had splintered into "scattered, diverse, alienated, antipathetic groups." In his view the social and economic forces that were reshaping the nation were simultaneously eroding the very basis of community feeling.

> It is not very many years since society in this country was quite homogeneous; the economical distinction between capitalist and laborer was not clearly marked.... But our national process has given full scope to the principle of differentiation.... Anyone can see that progress, under a system like ours, must tend to the separation of men, and to the creation of a great many diverse and apparently unrelated elements. Under this process men tend to become unsympathetic, jealous, antagonistic; the social bond is weakened.[18]

American culture was losing its organicity. Social roles and status came to reflect little more than the separation of individuals into groups possessing more and less. Warmth and immediacy in human relationships gave way to contractual role expectations. The public sphere of life operated according to impersonal rules which did little to kindle a cohesive cultural bond. Few Americans believed theirs to a society built upon what Victor Turner calls "communitas." That is, the "essential and genuine human bond, without which there could be no society" appeared to many urban dwellers to be at low ebb.[19] Growing numbers—especially those belonging to the white, Anglo-Saxon, Protestant group that had come to enjoy a sense of ownership in the nation—found themselves confused, bewildered, and beleaguered. They no longer believed they possessed the resources which would make them or their world whole and of a piece.

Rampant culture dis-ease took its toll on the stability of personal life. Dr. George Beard, a New York neurologist of the 1870s and 1880s, gave succinct definition to what many had already begun to fear. American character was beset with "nervous exhaustion."[20] The symptoms were many: hysteria, headaches, insomnia, inebriety, cerebral irritation, premature baldness, hopelessness, fear of being alone, fear of society, fear of fears. Beard discounted theories attributing neurasthenic ailments to characterological imbalances or organic disorders. American nervousness was strictly a deficiency or lack of nerve force; it was a condition of nervous bankruptcy.

Beard had no trouble identifying the root cause of American nervousness. Modern civilization was robbing its citizens of all their mental energy. No other period in world history had ever required so many mental tasks as did American modernity. Railway travel, the periodical press, the telegraph, religious liberties, the mental activity of women, religious excitements associated with Protestantism, loud noises, the specialization of labor, social conventions that suppress emotional expression, and the chaotic flux of new ideas were all sapping individuals of their mental strength. The human brain just wasn't equipped to handle so many functions. Beard found that urban dwellers and those in brain-working families in the eastern portions of the United States were suffering the most. He reasoned that the lifestyle demanded of "civilized, refined, and educated" persons rendered them tragically susceptible to this psychological impotency.

Beard illustrated both the etiology and symptoms of nervous exhaustion with an analogy to Edison's recently discovered electric light. The human nervous system, like an electrical circuit, can supply only a limited quantity of energy.

[When] new functions are interposed in the circuit, as modern civilization is constantly requiring us to do, there comes a period, sooner or later, varying in different individuals, and at different times of life, when the amount of force is insufficient to keep all the lamps burning; those that are weakest go out entirely, or as more frequently happens, burn faint and feebly—they do not expire; but give an insufficient and unstable light—this is the philosophy of modern nervousness.[21]

"Insufficient and unstable light" translates to psychosomatic illness. And, as Beard observed, this was an ever-more-frequently recurring phenomenon. The prognosis for American nervous disorders wasn't good at all. Beard predicted that there would be an increasing incidence of nervous exhaustion for at least the next quarter century. Modern civilization was not likely to stop advancing, and the human brain just wouldn't be up to the task. Any substantial improvements would have to await the evolutionary development of sturdier neural equipment. In the meantime, his contemporaries would just have to learn to cope with faint and feebly flowing minds.

Beard's diagnosis implicitly indicted American culture with inefficiently channeling the human energies at its disposal. The high incidence of American nervousness attested to the rigorous demand that a pluralistic society places on its members. Individuals were constantly being forced back on their own resources. Diligence and redoubled effort only overtaxed, not replenished, precious human energies. Debilitated individuals by definition lack the inner resources to bring about a full recovery. Help would have to come from without. But where were these extrapersonal energies to be found? Who would point the way?

Sadly, neither the nation's churches nor its medical doctors were of much help. Intellectual secularism and social pluralism undermined confidence in biblical religion. And the materialistic assumptions underlying the era's scientific medicine made it difficult for physicians to recognize the true nature of American nervousness. The first breakthrough in the treatment of nervous exhaustion came from an unlikely source: a backwoods clockmaker, Phineas P. Quimby (1802–1866).[22] After attending a demonstration of Franz Anton Mesmer's "science of animal magnetism," Quimby devoted himself to both the theory and practice of this unusual medical system. Mesmer believed he had detected the existence of a superfine energy he called "animal magnetism," owing to its presence in all living organisms and its response to magnetic influence. Animal magnetism, Mesmer explained, is the universal energy imparting life or vitality to all living organisms. So long as animal magnetism flows freely into the human body (and then flows evenly to all parts of the body), we will enjoy perfect health. If, however, an individual's supply of animal magnetism is for any reason thrown out of equilibrium, one or more bodily organs will consequently be deprived of sufficient amounts of this vital fore and begin to falter. Since there is only one cause of illness, it follows that there is only one truly effective mode of healing—restoring the body's supply of animal magnetism. Simply put, Mesmer believed he had reduced medical science to the art of placing patients in sleep-like states of consciousness which would render them especially receptive to the influence of this life-giving energy.

Quimby experimented with a variety of mesmerist practices aimed at quickening the flow of animal magnetism into his clients. There was only one problem: these practices didn't always work. True, his treatments usually brought instantaneous relief from physical ailments that had previously seemed incurable. But all too often the symptoms reappeared a few days later. It dawned on Quimby that the patient's illnesses might have more to do with their beliefs than with the flow of animal magnetism. He moved mesmerism one step closer to modern psychiatry by specifically identifying dysfunctional attitudes—not magnetic fluids—as the root cause of American nervousness. Or, in Quimby's words, "all sickness is in the mind of belief... to cure the disease is to correct the error, destroy the cause, and the effect will cease."[23]

Quimby continued to innovate. Eventually, he developed a healing philosophy that was variously termed Mind Cure Science, New Thought, and even Christian Science. His gospel of mental cure had a beautiful simplicity about it. Right beliefs channel health, happiness, and wisdom out of the cosmic ethers and into our mental atmospheres. By controlling our beliefs, we control the shunting valve connecting us with the subtle energy responsible for health and vitality. The key element, Quimby counseled, was to identify ourselves in terms of internal rather than external reference points. So long as persons believe that their well-being depends solely on the external environment, they will obscure their inner-connection with spiritual energy and power. As Quimby explained, "There are two sciences, one of this world, and the other of a spiritual world, or two effects produced upon the mind by two directions."[24]

In his own backwoods way, Quimby was more attuned to the pains and ailments of his contemporaries than the scientifically educated George Beard. Quimby intuitively realized that his patients' problems were not those of deficient neural equipment. It was their outmoded ideas about human nature which rendered them so psychologically vulnerable. Ironically, the more tenaciously they held to their moral and religious beliefs, the worse off their psyches became. He concluded that the surest antidote to American nervousness was to reprogram a patient's maladaptive worldview. Quimby's genius was that he recognized that the science of animal magnetism could be adapted to reconstruct the body's orientation to cultural experience.

Quimby was one of many nineteenth-century Americans who puzzled at the "controlling force" behind sickness and health. The causal origins (and hence, cure) of what Beard called "American nervousness" defied easy identification. Quimby was, however, quick to see how the concept of animal magnetism offered a viable solution. By imbuing Mesmer's mysterious fluid with language that resonated with Christian belief in the Holy Spirit, Quimby fashioned a notion of more-than-natural agency that straddled a thin line between science and theology. It also made belief in supernatural agency palatable to those eager to abandon scriptural religion.

Much as Ariel Glucklich explained about ritual pain, Quimby's healing system transformed the disintegrative effects of pain into a positive religious-psychological mechanism. Pain or illness, in Quimby's system, provided the motivation to connect find God within. Quimby helped his clients learn to recognize God as "invisible wisdom which fills all space, and whose attributes are all light, all wisdom, all guidance and love."[25] He further taught that no mediator is needed to effect this spiritual transformation. Nor was it necessary to confess guilt or renounce self-love. Quimby believed that if his Mind Cure Science could just show people "that a man's happiness is in his belief, and his misery in the effort of his belief," then he would have done what never had been done before. Quimby concluded, "Establish this and man rises to a higher state of wisdom, not of this world, but of that World of Science . . . the Wisdom of Science is Life Eternal."[26]

It is estimated that during his twenty-five-year career, nearly twelve thousand patients made a pilgrimage to Quimby's door. Most came out of sheer desperation only after medical physicians had given up hope of cure. His records show that his patients had been previously diagnosed with nearly every possible illness: consumption; smallpox; cancer; lameness; diphtheria; and, of course, the many symptoms of American nervousness (problems with sleeping, digestive disorders, irritability, headaches, eye strain, exhaustion). Quimby never let the small problem that he knew nothing about human physiology deter him from attempting cure. Instead, he went right to work correcting their false beliefs and instructing them about how they might improve their ongoing connection with the spiritual source of vital living. A typical instance is the testimony given by a woman who sought out Quimby:

> Six years of great suffering, and as a last resort, after all other
> methods of cure had utterly failed to bring relief. . . . It was like being

turned from death to life, and from ignorance of the laws that governed me to the light of truth, in so far as I could understand the
meaning of his explanations. . . . The general effect of these quiet
sittings with him was to light up the mind, so that one came in time
to understand the troublesome experiences and problems of the past
in light of his clear and convincing explanations. I remember one
day especially, when a panorama of past experience came before me,
and I saw just how my trouble had been made; how I had been kept
in bondage and enslaved by the doctors and the false opinions that
had been given me. From that day the connection was broken
with these painful experiences and . . . I lived in a larger and freer
world of thought.[27]

Cures of this kind abounded. Healing was accompanied by a host of bodily
sensations, all of which provided metaphors for understanding the ultimate
cause of health and happiness. As the testimony above indicates, formerly
ailing bodies were freed from bondage. Restrictions to the free flow of their
personal energies were broken. Lives were turned toward truth. Pain was
banished. Connections with pain were broken and wider panoramas of sight
came into view. Change was experienced as motion: motion toward truth and
light. These bodily metaphors of movement toward health and vitality eventually shaped a great deal of the New Thought philosophy that, in turn, put an
indelible stamp upon any number of twentieth-century New Age spiritualities.
    Quimby's students carried his healing practices to an ever-widening au-
dience. One student, Mary Baker Eddy, founded one of the five largest religious
denominations to emerge in American history (physical healing was also
central to the formation of the Seventh-day Adventist movement and played a
significant role, too, in the popular appeal of both the Jehovah's Witnesses and
Pentecostalism—thus implicating pain and illness in the origins of four of
these American sectarian successes). Eddy arrived at Quimby's doorstep in
1862 a helpless physical and mental wreck. The mesmeric healer cured her
afflicted body and, in the process, filled her receptive mind with new ideas.
Once healed, Mrs. Eddy resolved that she, too, would take up a career in mental
healing. Until her death in 1910, Mrs. Eddy worked incessantly at giving literary, theological, and institutional expression to the science of mental healing.[28] Other students of Quimby (notably Warren Felt Evans, Anetta Dresser,
and Julian Dresser) spearheaded what is variously referred to as the Mind Cure
of New Thought movement. The quest for health motivated millions of late-
nineteenth-century Americans to adopt this version of the "aesthetic" strand of
American spirituality promising that physical health, mental serenity, and even

worldly prosperity flow automatically once we have established inner-rapport with the subtle energies guiding the cosmos.[29] It seems, then, that thousands of nineteenth-century Americans suffered from pain and bodily limitation only to reconstruct their world in ways that seemed more capable of supporting active engagement with the world. A key to this regenerative process was formulating new notions of more-than-worldly agency, but notions devoid of the theistic or human-like attributes so commonly associated with Christian concepts of god.

No less a member of "highbrow" American society than William James attributed his own healing and subsequent outlook on life to the practices and worldview spawned by the mind-curists. Throughout his life, James suffered from a variety of ailments that were in all likelihood psychosomatic rather than organic: angina, insomnia, backaches, intermittently poor eyesight, fatigue, and depression.[30] He described the melancholia often brought on by these chronic afflictions in particularly vivid terms. Paralyzing depression often "fell upon me without any warning, just as if it came out of the darkness"; "it as if something hitherto solid within my breast gave way entirely, and I became a mass of quivering fear"; and he was often overtaken by "a horrible dread at the pit of my stomach, and with a sense of the insecurity of life."[31] Unable to sustain vital connections with life, James yearned for a new vision of life that would illuminate the path toward health.

What James came to believe was that each of us, via the unconscious layers of the mind, "is conterminous and continuous with more of the same quality, which is operative in the universe outside of him, and which he can keep in working touch with, and in a fashion get on board of and save himself when all his lower being has gone to pieces in the wreck."[32] Our body, James opined, is more extensive than the secularist imagines. Just as the mind-curists taught, "we inhabit an invisible spiritual environment from which help comes."[33]

James had long before rejected traditional Christian beliefs about God and salvation. His psychological background provided him ample evidence of how the human mind naturally and spontaneously constructs the kind of god-ideas described by contemporary cognitive science. That is, he knew full well that uncertain or ambiguous situations prompt humans to envision "quasi-sensible" beings capable of exerting casual control over worldly events. He concluded that "such is the human ontological imagination, and such is the convincingness of what it brings to birth. Unpicturable beings are realized, and realized with an intensity almost like that of an hallucination."[34] James's commitment to scientific rationality had, however, trained his mind to reject many of the conceptions of human-like features that our innate mental modules would usually use to construct notions of more-than-worldly agency. This had, however, left him without a spiritual outlook on life.

It was, ironically, James's own private experience of the body and its afflictions that impelled him to find religion once again especially relevant and
set him in search for new and more culturally viable ways of identifying a
metaphysical "controlling force" capable of influencing health and well-being.
Turning from monotheism to pantheism, James found comfort in the belief
that he was inwardly connected with a metaphysical MORE. When pressed to
identify what palpable effects come from such receptivity to the MORE, James
repeatedly insisted that we experience the inflow of a spiritual energy that
"actually exerts an influence, raises our centre of personal energy."[35] Bodily
metaphors permeated James's metaphysical constructions. Contact with metaphysical energies gave James "extended sight" to see a wider universe. The
MORE "lifted" his center of personal energy. It allowed him to "get on board" a
place of security and to "keep in working touch" with restorative powers. Pain
and enduring illness provided the imaginative core around which James re-
constructed the world in a manner more befitting life in a modern, pluralistic
setting. In the process he became the leading spokesperson for an identifiable
form of unchurched religion—an orientation that continues to appeal to the
approximately 20 percent of all adult Americans who consider themselves
"spiritual, but not religious."

This interest in the connection between our physical bodies and metaphysical energies has become an enduring theme in recent "alternative" spirituality.[36] Physical and metaphysical modes of thinking come together in
Theosophy with its theories of *chakras* and astral planes, chiropractic medicine
with its methods for restoring the flow of *Innate*, Therapeutic Touch with its
work inducing *prana* into the physical body, acupuncture's system for im-
proving the movement of chi, and sundry color or crystal healing systems that
diffuse divine white light into our bodies.[37] All proclaim that contact with an
uncanny energy restores the body's free-flowing engagement with life. And all
believe that contact with subtle energies provides empirical support for various
alternative spiritual philosophies that are at considerable variance with the
nation's dominant churches. Metaphysical religion views spirituality as a
journey, not a destination. It values all religious traditions and all sacred
scriptures, but doesn't believe that any one of them has a monopoly on truth.
Metaphysical religion thus encourages exploration into Eastern religions,
mystical practices, altered states of consciousness, and various occult traditions
all in the hope of enhancing one's personal capacity to establish harmony with
the "invisible spiritual environment" from which rejuvenating energies come.
Metaphysical spiritualities define God not as a transcendent person but rather
as an immanent energy available to all living beings without need for an external mediator (whether viewed as a savior or an ecclesiastical organization).

And, finally, most metaphysical spiritualities teach Tantric-like doctrines concerning the existence of "subtle bodies" and "subtle energies" that are potential sources of tremendous cosmic power.

It is interesting to speculate just why some medical systems become linked with essentially biblical theologies while others become linked with metaphysical spirituality. Virtually all scholarship on this topic has focused on historical and cultural factors. However, we might at least speculate as to whether there might also be factors connected with the biological rather than cultural pole of our embodied nature. The body itself may incline us to certain kinds of religious metaphors. As Lakoff and Johnson point out, our conceptions of the world are largely structured by the specifics of our body's sensorimotor experience. Metaphysical healing brings healers and patients in close physical contact. Massage or other forms of tissue manipulation are typically involved. We can thus safely assume that metaphysical healing induces increased blood flow and other forms of somatic excitation that patients readily interpret as an influx of subtle energy.

Other kinds of bodily experience specific to metaphysical healing also generate metaphors that permeate alternative spirituality. Consider, for example, Lakoff's and Johnson's observation that we typically describe our experience of intimacy in terms of physical closeness or proximity.[38] Intimate contact with the healer and with subtle energies makes certain kinds of metaphysical language more likely than others (e.g., "We are conterminous with the MORE," or "The currents of Universal Being circulate through me"). Difficulties are routinely conceptualized in terms of blockages or burdens (e.g., "I had been kept in bondage," or "My chakras were blocked, but they are now open and the flow of spiritual energy is restored"). We typically think of quantity in terms of the physical direction of up. Hence the experience of restored bodily vitality lead to certain kinds of metaphysical imagery (e.g., "My center of energy was raised," or "I am now connected with higher spiritual dimensions"). Change is usually conceptualized as motion (e.g., "I turned from death to life" or "I am now on a spiritual journey").

Not surprisingly, those whose lives have been changed by energy-based healing systems frequently define God in terms of energetic motion such as "force" or "power" rather than more static personal imagery of Father, Son, and so on. Experiences of tingling or other forms of physical excitation provide an experiential template for believing in the existence of subtle spiritual energies. Another bodily experience attributed to the inflow of subtle spiritual energies is warmth, which of course is a common body-based metaphor for intimate relationship. Renewed hope is metaphorically experienced as the opening of new vistas (seeing auras or unseen spiritual dimensions). Increased physical activity is metaphorically experienced as expanding into a wider world (inhabiting a wider spiritual universe). Metaphysical spirituality would thus seem to express a very particular range of bodily experiences.

The vocabulary of metaphysical religion would thus appear to be traceable to a distinct set of bodily experiences. We are far from being able to distinguish the biological and cultural dimensions of human embodiment with any specificity (if even such a distinction could ever be made), but it would surely seem that certain kinds of body language translate better into some modes of theological construction than others. The language of metaphysical spirituality reflects the body language of those for whom pain and illness broke down earlier theological constructions based on distance, tradition, obedience, and discipline. The language of metaphysical spirituality is instead rife with metaphors rooted in bodily experiences of intimacy, change, increased vitality, and spontaneity.

In sum, many of our alternative healing systems are rooted in very specific kinds of bodily experiences. These experiences dispose people toward specific ranges of religious vocabulary. Alternative healing systems thereby help translate the private afflictions of the body into agendas for personal and cultural renewal.

Pain, Illness, and Initiatory Rites

From a cross-cultural perspective, it is clear that healing systems often serve as initiatory rites. Healers utilize techniques that bring patients into direct contact with what a given culture believes to be the highest or most effective power available to human beings. In premodern societies, healing rituals reenact cosmological dramas. Shamans are both healers and mystagogues; they not only heal but also establish new and more vital connections between the natural and supernatural realms of existence. In early Christianity, healing was thought to be a sign of Jesus' divine nature and his ability to mediate between earth and heaven. For this reason, Christianity has for two thousand years considered healing to be a principal form of Christian proclamation and ministry.[39] In more recent times, medicine has divorced itself from a sacred context, introducing patients only to the powers of scientific technology. Given the gradual separation of physical healing from the ordinary activities of institutional religion, it is understandable that the most fascinating examples of healing-centered spirituality frequently arise at the far fringes of cultural orthodoxy. Metaphysical healing systems, precisely because they are located in cultural territory somewhere between science and religion, have proven uniquely capable of rediscovering the initiatory powers of medical cure.

The religious studies scholar Mircea Eliade examined initiatory rites and the methods they use to elicit direct encounters with a sacred realm. He observed that nearly all initiatory rites utilize some form of death/rebirth symbolism. The death/rebirth experience enables initiates to discard dysfunctional identities and discover a new, "higher" self. Participants are helped to believe that the rite "involves their entire life" and renders them "a being open to the life of the spirit."[40] Persons suffering from pain or illness are, of course, already disposed toward such spiritual transformation. Their telic striving toward worldly goals has been curtailed, leaving them void of their normal sense of purpose or direction. And thus, as Ariel Glucklich shows, their pain initiates a host of physiological and psychological changes leading to felt-connection with "a more fundamental state of being." Glucklich notes how, at a biological level, "pain weakens the individual's feeling of being a discrete agent; it makes the 'body-self' transparent and facilitates the emergence of a new identity. Metaphorically, pain creates an embodied 'absence' and makes way for a new and greater 'presence.' "[41]

That our metaphysical healing systems often facilitate the experience of such a "greater presence" (outside any formal connection with a religious institution) should therefore not be a surprise. Their healing practices effectively serve as initiatory rituals, inducing persons to reconstruct their worlds in ways that are both physically and spiritually regenerative. As with rituals generally, healing practices evoke profound emotions (e.g., hope, wonder, and expectation) and arouse patients' cognitive efforts to identify causal agencies capable of effecting cure. Healing practices are, moreover, especially likely to induce experiential states similar to those that Hamer, Newberg, and d'Aquili claim make persons especially prone to mystical awareness. Pain and illness have thus rendered a significant subculture of modern Americans susceptible to ritually induced emotions and experiential states well-designed to initiate them into the world of metaphysical religion.

Understanding spirituality in the flesh helps us appreciate why illness and healing so often serve as initiatory rites. Precisely understanding how bodily sensations give rise to specific theological constructs will, however, undoubtedly prove difficult. Drawing a line between bodily sensation and cultural representation requires judgments that fall short of conclusive demonstration. Nonetheless, greater attention to body language and to the embodied nature of theological metaphors is likely to illuminate a great deal about the process whereby persons discard former identities and adopt new strategies for engaging the many worlds that surround them.

7

Spirituality In/Of the Flesh

Our brains receive input from the rest of our bodies. A complex series of neurophysiological events organizes this input into conscious thought. Our thoughts necessarily bear the impress of what our bodies are like and how they function in the world. As cognitive scientist George Lakoff reminds us, "We cannot think just anything—only what our embodied brains permit."[1]

My goal in this book has been to show how knowledge of what our bodies are like gives us a deeper understanding of religion. Although some readers might find this a fairly obvious point, it is one that many scholars in the humanities have not quite grasped. Even though humanists often profess interest in the "body," most are only concerned with cultural images of the body. Philosophers, historians, and theologians have adopted the "constructivist" assumptions of postmodernism and are consequently interested only in how culture shapes discourse about the body. Rarely do humanities scholars avail themselves of what other disciplines have learned about the biological substrates of thought and experience. The result has been scholarship that is neither interdisciplinary nor anywhere near conversant with the explosion of knowledge in an era marked by the successful mapping of the human genome.

Preceding chapters have demonstrated how a spirituality in the flesh provides new critical categories for studying and evaluating religion. We have seen, for example, that emotions exert powerful influences on attention, memory, perception, and cognition. We cannot think just anything—only what our emotional programs selectively motivate our brains to think. Our brains, furthermore, operate on the basis of fragile neurochemical activities. Even the slightest alterations in the chemistry of the brain significantly alter the nature of consciousness. Reproductive biology also provides categories for understanding religion. The tripartite mechanisms regulating lust, romantic love, and long-term attachment factor significantly in our urge to unite with what seems desirably "other" than ourselves. And finally, physical pain motivates us to reconstruct our worlds in more functional, life-affirming ways. Discrete emotions, altered neurochemistry, the biology of love, and the motivational effects of pain all suggest themselves as critical concepts that help explain why we form—and commit ourselves—to specific kinds of religious ideas.

The topics covered in this book barely scratch the surface of contemporary research into the biological foundations of religious thought and experience. They are meant to be suggestive, not exhaustive. The biological sciences are capable of generating dozens of other critical categories for studying religion. For example, we can surely benefit from recent studies that examine the causal relationship between physical movement and higher cognitive operations.[2] Emerging knowledge in this field promises to shed new light on how ritual behavior transmits religious concepts (e.g., understanding how physical experiences such as kneeling, getting small, or putting one's face on the ground help structure religious notions such as submission or humility).

Biological studies of our sensory modalities would also seem to provide a promising approach to otherwise perplexing religious phenomena. Consider, for example, the fact that humans possess a vast array of taste buds, shaped through natural selection to ensure our pursuit of fitness-enhancing foods. Even as infants, we are naturally rewarded for seeking out the slightly sweet breast milk that provides us with vitamins and helps fight off infection. How fascinating, then, that milk is considered a sacred beverage in many societies.[3] The book of Exodus provides a perfect example of this when it describes Israel as "a land of milk and honey." There are, of course, cultural explanations of why milk is revered, especially since it provides nutrition without killing animals. Yet we should not overlook the biological reasons that milk is venerated as a pure, even paradisiacal, beverage. Envisioning a future paradise replete with sweet, pure milk is quite likely one more way that culture has redirected biological reward mechanisms into the service of tribal needs. Our olfactory sensibilities might provide yet another critical category for investigating religion. Smell alerts us to opportunities and dangers in the surrounding environment. Objects that might harm or contaminate us come to be thought of as "foul smelling" or "stinky." Conversely, "fresh smelling" is an experientially based metaphor for food or objects likely to serve our adaptive needs. We would expect, therefore, that our olfactory connection with the world frequently influences religious conceptions of purity/taboo, beliefs about the sacred, or ritual activity. Ritual and worship frequently include pronounced olfactory dimensions. Incense, camphor, flowers, and foods fund religious activity with sensory clues for discriminating between the sacred and profane. Our bodily senses of taste and smell are thus further examples of the many promising research agendas opened up by the study of spirituality in the flesh.

Bodily Metaphor and the Religious Imagination

The fact that our brains receive their input from the rest of our bodies has considerable implications for understanding human thought. Our bodies structure this input in particular ways, molding thought into forms that serve the body's needs and purposes. George Lakoff and Mark Johnson remind us that human thought is "shaped crucially by the peculiarities of our human bodies, by the remarkable details of the neural structure of our brains, and by the specifics of our everyday functioning in the world."[4] For this reason, thought is not purely literal. It is also metaphorical and imaginative. Thought is metaphorical in that the specifics of our body's connection with the world provide a template through which sensory input is filtered. Thought is also imaginative in that its basic purpose is to construct models of the world that might best lead to satisfactory relations with the surrounding world.

Religious thought is no exception. It, too, is both metaphorical and imaginative. Religious thought arises in the middle loop of brain activity whereby the input received through our bodies is translated into imaginative constructions guiding us to bodily response. As the study of both sexuality and pain revealed, our bodies are frequently the source of the metaphors that guide our religious constructions. Insofar as metaphors fund experience with meaning and inferential patterns, they perform basic epistemological functions. Consider how our bodily orientation to the surrounding environment exerts leverage on our thoughts about such things as being healthy, being happy, or being in control.[5] For example, bodily metaphors often cause us to associate illness with specific kinds of change in spatial reference. After all, serious illness forces us to lie down; when we are healthy we are fully upright. We therefore think that we fall ill, drop dead, or decline in health. Conversely, we conceptualize health in terms of "upward" spatial changes. We are at the peak of health, or we hope to rise from the dead. Meanwhile, happiness and sadness are also associated with specific body postures. Depression causes our posture to droop, while a positive emotional state enables us to stand erect. We therefore come to think in terms of our spirits sinking, our feelings being down, or falling into a state of depression. Or, we think of being in high spirits, getting up for an important event, and being boosted by a recent success. Finally, being in control or being helpless is also understood in bodily terms. Victors in a fight or those strong enough to lift a heavy object are typically on top while those with less strength find themselves on the bottom. Thus we come to think of having control over someone, being on top of a situation or being at the height of our power. Conversely, we think of falling from power, being *low* man on the totem pole, or being under someone else's command.

Our bodies, then, provide metaphorical patterns for understanding ourselves and the world we live in. This explains the ubiquity of body-based metaphors in religious thought. The testimony of Sarah whose conversion to Christianity was described in chapter 5 provides a ready illustration of how metaphors of our spatial orientation to life shape religious representations.[6] Sarah recounts how she arrived at a Christian commune at a low moment in her life. She was a single mother with little control over her life. Her life seems empty, falling apart, and in decline. Then Jesus poured into her heart. "[Jesus] *took* me into his *hands* and lifted *up* my burdens." Belief in Jesus has helped her believe she now has the resources to gain control of her life. Sarah feels that her burdens are being lifted; she feels support from outside herself and thinks her fortunes are reversing. Sarah now proclaims, "My life is *in his hands*," and that she is "a disciple of the most *high* God." It is fascinating to observe how readily Sarah interprets her improved functioning with metaphors of upward ascent or of physical gestures of support. In infancy we learn to grasp a desired object. Parents hold our hands to keep us safe. Taking pleasure-giving objects into our hand is thus becomes a primary metaphor of human thought and desire. Meanwhile, burdens cause us to stoop or fall. Sarah was struggling with the burden of parenting a child on her own. The community of Christians that she recently joined have helped her with this burden, allowing her to relax her strenuous effort ("I *fell* into the family"). Someone very powerful—hence existing on high—is now in control of her life. She is in his hands. She yearns for a sustained relationship with this source of this support, an extended loving relationship with her desired other ("Thank you for *being with* me Jesus. . . . Let me have *my hand in* yours, *my eyes on* you"). As Sarah's conversion illustrates, religious thought is rife with bodily metaphors. These metaphors represent our spatial orientation to life and impart inferences about how we might adjust ourselves to meet life's adaptive challenges.

Human thought is more than representational. It is also imaginative. We are biologically programmed to live, to seek pleasure, and to avoid pain. Our bodies function in pursuit of these biological purposes. We construct models of the world that will seemingly make the world actable and responsive to our biological desires. William James envisioned the mind's imaginative activities as transpiring in what he called the "middle loop" that connects sensory input coming from the surrounding world and action that engages the surrounding world. The strategic models we imaginatively construct are hypotheses. They mold perceptions into categories that guide appropriate action, leading us to behaviors that appear likely to yield satisfaction. Some of these hypothetical models take on religious features. We imaginatively construct models of the world that extend and transcend the limits otherwise imposed upon our existence. Religious constructions of experience imaginatively envision a world that contains supernatural resources (i.e., ultimate or metaphysical causal powers) or ultimate meanings for our lives.

What our bodies are like and how they function motivate the human religious imagination. As Freud speculated more than eighty years ago, the precariousness of biological existence sets us in search of causal agents whose power is not limited to the constraints of finitude.[7] It is interesting in this regard that our gods typically possess bodies that are exempt from human frailties. Gods and other supernatural agents fill an imaginatively constructed universe with the resources needed to accomplish our bodies' adaptive tasks. Although supernatural beings seem utterly fanciful, they are imaginative reconstructions built on quite ordinary bodily experiences. For example, vivid dreams of deceased acquaintances provide experiential templates for envisioning a realm populated with not-quite-physical "bodies." And, too, ordinary cognitive operations make it seem likely that we have some kind of mind or soul separate from the body (e.g., "observing" our own thinking process or "observing" how we control our body parts much in the way we control physical objects).[8]

To note that religion arises as an embodied experience, then, is to realize that it serves the biological purpose of constructing models of the world conducive to our bodily needs and aspirations. Religious thought, both in its metaphorical and imaginative aspects, can be interpreted in terms of the bodily activities it serves. Just how extensively religious thought can be understood from this perspective remains to be seen. For although knowledge of how the body functions already tells us a great deal about the religious imagination, we still have much to learn.

Spirituality In the Flesh: Reconsidering Religion
from a Biological Perspective

The preceding chapters have been an extended reflection on E. O. Wilson's bold suggestion that "we have come to the crucial stage in the history of biology when religion itself is subject to the explanations of the natural sciences."[9] Emotion, neurochemistry, pain, and sexuality have proven to be useful categories for understanding religion as an embodied experience; that is, an experience that is a mix of biological and cultural factors. It is tempting, then, to offer a few concluding comments about rendering religion subject to the explanations of the natural sciences.

Religious beliefs emerge in the middle loop of experience. Our brains imaginatively construct images of the world that seem amenable to a wide range of objective and subjective interests. In virtually every known culture, humans have hypothesized the existence of more-than-worldly agents who pose either promise or threat. Stewart Guthrie, Pascal Boyer, Scott Atran, and Todd Tremlin are among those who have written at length about the brain's tendency to see humanlike "agency" in natural phenomena—even when no such agency in fact exists.[10] In their view, religious belief can be wholly explained by the fact that natural selection shaped brains predisposing us to the "overdetection" of agency. They understandably conclude that religion represents a magical (prescientific) view of the world predicated on faulty conceptions of causality. No wonder, then, that scientific theorists like Guthrie, Boyer, Atran, and Richard Dawkins arrive at almost wholly negative assessments of religion. Because they equate religion with belief in the palpably untrue, they believe that religion inevitably leads to misguided, and potentially harmful, conduct. Biologically trained scholars concede that the architecture of the brain makes religious belief an understandable and nearly universal part of the human condition. Their point, however, is that our continued survival as a species demands that we abandon these patently false conceptions of the universe.

Biological theorists have already gone a long way toward subjecting religion to the explanations of the natural sciences. Yet, so far they fall short in at least two ways. First, religious constructions of experience do not necessarily entail humanlike agents. Theravada Buddhist conceptions of Nirvana, Chinese reflection on the impersonal nature of the Dao, and Western Deism are all examples of imaginative constructions of reality that do not hypothesize humanlike entities. All three are examples of humanity's effort to hypothesize some more-than-sensory, more-than-physical source of meaning and power. But they do not entail conceptions of personal, human-like agency. Religious thinking, therefore, is not necessarily synonymous with belief in palpably unreal, human-like causal agents. Put differently, religious thought is inherently nonrational (i.e., it is imaginative and hypothetical rather than based on sensory-based inductive reasoning), but it is not inherently irrational.

A second shortcoming of biologically oriented explanations of religion is that they fail to note the limit-nature of many of humanity's recurring developmental challenges. That is, the course of human development from life to death is fraught with experiences that cannot be successfully resolved through means-end reasoning alone. Virtually every human being confronts developmental challenges that require them to consider the limits of a strictly sensory or rational approach to life. Embodied experience thus includes situations that theologian David Tracy aptly describes as having a "limit dimension" or "limit character." According to Tracy, what distinguishes thought as religious is not that it evokes images of supernatural agents but that it acknowledges a horizon that is inherently insusceptible of sensory-based formulation. Experience becomes distinctively religious at those points an individual recognizes "a certain ultimate limit or horizon to his or her existence."[11] Some limit-experiences arise in moments when we realize that we do not possess the resources within ourselves to affect wholeness, and we are thus confronted with the final limits of our finitude. Examples of such moments might be recognizing missed opportunities or realizing that we have a terminal illness. Other kinds of limit-experiences are typically encountered in midlife when otherwise routine tasks prompt us to ponder such matters as: With the years that I have left, what should I do with my life? Why be moral? Why is there a universe? Is death the termination of my existence? Humans, it seems, do find their vital interests connected with questions concerning the first or ultimate cause of life. It is true that such questions point us beyond the limits of what natural selection shaped our brains to contemplate, but it is also true that these questions bear directly on humanity's pursuit of wholeness and fulfillment.

The common element in limit-experiences is that they disclose the profound limitations of a purely sensory or rational approach to life. All carry with them the conviction that *if* we are to resolve this challenge successfully, *then* we must in some way acknowledge and accommodate ourselves to a reality that is in some fundamental way more-than-sensory, more-than-physical. Humans might respond to limit-experiences in wholly nonreligious ways. There is surely dignity in stoically resigning oneself to life's physical limitations. But a purely humanist approach to life entails accepting the limitations of finite experience rather than trying to overcome them through specifically religious cognitive and behavioral strategies. Put differently, humans might surely respond to limit-experiences in nonreligious ways, but doing so means restraining rather than stimulating the body's natural urge toward satisfaction. Any comprehensive understanding of the human condition must acknowledge that many of our most profound adaptive challenges encourage us to adopt world images that include some notion of life's limit-dimension.

These two considerations help refine our understanding of religion from a biological perspective. Religion is an adaptive response, motivated by the body's quest for fulfillment and wholeness. What distinguishes an adaptive response as religious is that it constructs images of the world that first hypothesizes, and then helps us accommodate to, some metaphysical (i.e., beyond the limits of our physical senses) source of meaning or power. This metaphysical source of meaning or power will be conceptualized the same way we form any other abstract idea. We fashion hypothetical constructs on the basis of bodily metaphors and cultural images. It is true that these hypothetical constructions usually do utilize ready-at-hand images of human-like agents. Yet what distinguishes them as religious is the fact that they imaginatively envision metaphysical sources of meaning and power that are relevant to our adaptive needs (whether personal or not; whether exerting causal influence in our physical universe or not). In sum, religion emerges as a form of embodied hope.

Understanding religion as embodied hope provides certain measures or criteria for assessing its value. At least in theory, biological assessments of religion should be neither easier nor more difficult than evaluating any other brain-born constructions of the world. Their basic task is to deem religion good or desirable insofar as it promotes our overall well-being, and undesirable when it thwarts our adaptive tasks.

In practice, however, attempts to subject religion to the evaluative criteria of the natural sciences prove complex and imprecise. This is due in part to the fact that our bodies quest for the satisfaction of both objective (i.e., pertaining to physical survival and reproduction) and subjective interests. As the philosopher Alfred North Whitehead put it, living beings exhibit a threefold urge to live, to live well, and to acquire an increase in satisfaction.[12] The evaluative measures needed to assess religion's role in enabling humans "to live" are very different that those entailed in considering how we might optimally "live well" or "acquire an increase in satisfaction."

The actual conditions that promote the urge of beings to live are potentially discernable through empirical investigation. Such fields as evolutionary biology, ecology, developmental psychology, and various subdisciplines of economics or sociology all shed light on the optimal conditions necessary for the ongoing support of life. We might consider, for example, how the natural sciences help us evaluate the ubiquitous phenomenon of religiously based violence. The natural sciences, by furnishing the critical category of tribalism, clarify how religion repeatedly fosters the most pernicious kinds of tribalism (i.e., the formation of social units predicated on the clear demarcation of in-group and out-group members). Tribalism has been critical to the survival of social groups throughout the course of human history. Rendering religion subject to the explanatory categories of biology therefore helps us understand that religious tribalism does indeed serve important survival functions. This survival, however, has always been at the expense of other social groups. Biological evaluations of religious tribalism must therefore also consider the costs of violence over time and across populations. Today, religious violence threatens not only the survival of some select, isolated social groups but the whole of life on this planet. It would thus seem that regardless of how valuable tribalism may have been in humanity's earlier evolutionary history, it is now a major threat to the future of this planet.[13] One of religion's primary functions—inducing individuals to subordinate their selfish interests to the good of the larger social group—may now be one of the most pernicious obstacles to world stability. As this example illustrates, the natural sciences furnish critical categories that bring clarity and focus to the evaluation of religion. These categories generate criteria for assessing the functions religion performs in our personal and communal lives. In this case, it seems that religion constitutes an impediment to humanity's long-term prospects for survival.

Determining what it means "to live well" or "to acquire an increase in satisfaction" is less amenable to empirical analysis and therefore far more susceptible to multiple interpretations. Here we move beyond considering those interests directly related to biological survival and focus instead on subjective interests such as creativity, play, meaning, or purpose. All of these activities are possible only because natural selection favored brains that delight in higher-order cognition such as seeking novelty, detecting patterns, considering the possible, and so on. Yet these activities, while grounded in mental modules acquired through natural selection, are substantially free from biological determinism. Pursuing these subjective interests yields the most distinctively human forms of happiness and fulfillment. We might also note that efforts to live well and to increase our range of satisfactions predictably bring us into vivid realization of the limit-character of human existence, inviting us to consider the relevance of specifically religious images of the world. It follows that criteria appropriate to evaluating religion's value to reproductive fitness are largely irrelevant to evaluating its value to our subjective needs and interests. Biology, then, is too restricted in scope to answer many of the questions we might have about the significance of religion in modern life.

These cautions are relevant to the contemporary intellectual scene. Those wanting to interpret religion from the perspective of the biological sciences must be careful to distinguish between their analyses of religion's effect on humanity's drive to live and its effect on our drives to live well or gain an increase in satisfaction. Subjecting religion to the evaluative criteria of the natural sciences is appropriate if such evaluations are restricted to issues of how religion affects our objective interests and if they proceed according to criteria explicitly drawn from an evolutionary-adaptive framework. Unfortunately, however, many contemporary scientific accounts of religion slide imperceptibly into full-blown manifestos on how humans ought optimally to live. Scientific interpreters of religion don't seem to recognize that biology per se has little to stipulate in the way of appropriate evaluative criteria when it comes to humanity's pursuit of interests that don't bear directly on survival or reproductive fitness. As a consequence, many of the negative assessments of religion that have appeared in recent publications have born the stamp of ideology, not science. This is a problem that most contemporary scientific writers have not fully avoided. Few critics of religion acknowledge subtle differences in religious attestations to the existence of an ultimate or metaphysical source of meaning and power (i.e., they don't consistently distinguish between belief in unseen supernatural causal agents and other kinds of thoughts about more-than-physical principles of meaning or power). Even fewer acknowledge that many of life's most perplexing challenges cannot be successfully resolved through means-end reasoning and can therefore make it intellectually justifiable to adopt certain kinds of religious postures toward life.[14] And fewer still consistently differentiate between criteria appropriate to assessing religion's effect on humanity's biological needs and criteria appropriate to assessing religion's effect on humanity's nonbiological needs or interests.

There are many valid criticisms that need to be made about religion from a scientific perspective. But efforts must be made to avoid sweeping pronouncements to the effect that religion is detrimental to our pursuit of all interests. Again, such arguments are too often a statement of ideology, not science. There is much still to explain about religion from the perspective of the natural sciences, but these explanations must be careful about specifying just how we proceed from explanation to evaluation.

Spirituality Of the Flesh—Reconsidering the Body from a Religious Perspective

This book has been an effort to demonstrate how scientific information about the body helps explain religion. It has done so by suggesting that truly interdisciplinary efforts to understand religion can and must avail themselves of what is now known about our bodies, the neural structure of our brains, and the genetic basis of our perceptual and cognitive interactions with the world. Yet, as I have argued throughout, drawing attention to the "leverage" that the body has on religion by no means ignores the role of culture in human experience. Our embodiment is very much a cultural mode of embodiment. As Ariel Glucklich noted in *Sacred Pain*, "Embodied experience, including pain and its representation, are a mix of biological facts and cultural consciousness (metaphors, emotions, attitudes). The problem... is precisely how this mix works, and how scholarship may combine objective description with subjective experience."[15] This book has suggested several ways of trying to get this mix right, yet recognizes that we are still a long way from discerning the complexities of embodied experience. One thing is clear, however: interpretations of religion that fail to engage in serious interdisciplinary reflection on "biological facts" will from now on appear hopelessly irrelevant to the wider academic world.

Many scholars understandably fear that drawing attention to the leverages that our bodies have on religion inevitably desacralizes the universe. There is a realistic possibility that scientific studies of religion will become so reductionistic (i.e., insinuating that religion is "nothing but" genes, emotions, the misfiring of neurochemical activities, etc.) that they obscure what is more-than-biological about human thought or action. Yet this need not be the case. The body can, in fact, be made the locus of serious theological reflection. Paula Cooey, Sallie McFague, James Nelson, Lisa Isherwood, Elizabeth Stuart, Carter Heywood, and Riane Eisler are among those who have examined the constructive possibilities of what might be called "body theology."[16] Their attempts at body theology have, however, not been based on serious interdisciplinary investigation of the biological substrates of human nature. As a result, their body theologies have focused more on cultural discourse about the body than upon what we biologically know about the body and how it functions in the world.

Studying spirituality in the flesh does not necessarily denude our world of sacred meanings. It very well might, in fact, lead to an inspiring resacralization of our universe. Many years ago, Peter Berger concluded his sociological study of religion by suggesting that his discipline's critical actually open up new possibilities for thinking religiously in a scientific era. Sociological theory, he notes, must in and of itself view religion in strictly worldly terms. The social sciences have nothing to say about what religion claims to reveal—something that is "more" than worldly. Berger explains that "sociological theory must, by its own logic, view religion as a human projection, and by the same logic can have nothing to say about the possibility that this projection may refer to something other than the being of its projector."[17] Yet, saying that religion is a human projection does not logically preclude the possibility that the projected meanings may actually disclose something about a more-than-physical reality. If we posit a religious view of the world, it follows that the "stuff" out of which we project religious meanings can itself be traced back to a religious source.

> Put simply, this would imply that humans project ultimate mean-
> ings into reality because that reality is, indeed, ultimately meaning-
> ful, and because our own being (the empirical ground of these
> projections) contains and intends these same ultimate meanings.[18]

This is a radical hypothesis. It implies that the material universe is itself teeming with ultimacy. The material universe creates conceptions of the sacred because it is, at root, sacred itself. As Berger went on to demonstrate in later books, this radical hypothesis also implies that scientific understandings of the human condition can provide the raw material for religious reflection.[19] Descriptions of how humans project ultimate meaning can be traced back to the ontological source of all life and activity in the universe. Berger is thus inviting us to reflect religiously on scientific knowledge about the activities through which organisms seek to live, to live well, and to gain an increase in satisfaction. Reflection of this sort in no way undermines the scientific or intellectual credibility of the knowledge itself. It does, however, suggest that it is permissible to interpret scientific knowledge in ways that go beyond the methodology that first generated it. We can surely pose the speculative question whether the "efficient" causes of human thought or action depicted by the sciences might be mechanisms through which the First Cause of the universe operates. If human existence is grounded in ultimate reality, then various human traits—particularly those that suggest they defy entropy and actually increase life and order in the universe—might be seen as "traces" or this ultimate reality in our everyday experience.

Berger's radical suggestion turns traditional methods of interpreting religion on their head. Instead of "reducing" religion to causal activities in the material world, this approach considers the possibility that causal activities in the material world are themselves manifestations of a larger cosmic reality. What we view as a "push" from one perspective might become a "pull" when viewed from another perspective. This provides a fascinating way of understanding biologically based insights into human thought and action. Perhaps our bodies construct sacred worlds because they are themselves inherently sacred. After all, something doesn't come from nothing. You can't get anything out of cosmic evolution unless it was in some way there all along. The human body is composed of star dust. Every atom of our bodies can be traced back to the cosmic explosion from which the universe itself came into being. It follows that everything our bodies do or create can in some way be considered re-arrangements of the cosmic stuff set into motion by the Big Bang. If material organisms such as ourselves manifest consciousness, is in not probable that consciousness must have in some way been in the "material" universe all along?

My point is this: This book has explored spirituality *in* the flesh. It has described some of the biological processes that cause humans to think or act religiously. But none of this philosophically precludes the possibility that humans think and behave religiously because our biological natures are sub-stantively spiritual—that is, they embody the creative purposes of the final or ultimate cause of the universe. When viewed this way, a spirituality *in* the flesh readily gives way to a spirituality *of* the flesh. After all, we find ourselves alive and aware in a universe we did not create. Life, in all its biological diversity and splendor, is a gift. It is sacred. Life is the one ultimate we as embodied crea-tures can positively know. And, of course, we can only know it in ways struc-tured by what our bodies are like and how they function in the world.

The religious person differs from the nonreligious person by proclaiming that all is not vanity. To the nonreligious, life has no ultimate meaning or purpose—entropy will ultimately prevail as energy and organization finally dissipate and life as we know it disappears. In contrast, the religious individual believes that something of ultimate significance is expressing itself through embodied existence. Religion counters the scientific perspective by proposing that we do not live in a closed physical universe; unlike science, religion pro-claims that entropy is not the final principle governing life. Humans project these beliefs because they are embodied agents of life. We are, after all, carriers of an impulse to live, to live well, and to gain an increase in satisfaction. And in this pursuit, we construct visions of the world that seek to identify an ultimate or final cause operative in the universe. Thinking this way is surely not sci-entific. Religious thought is conjectural; it creatively spins hypothetical models of what might possibly exist. Religious thought is therefore not susceptible to public verification in the way our sciences (which restrict themselves to con-siderations of the efficient cause of events) are. Yet religious thought is wholly consistent with our practical needs as acting individuals. It is a vital function of embodied life.

Just how a spirituality of the flesh might be educed from what we know about the biological substrates of religion depends largely on our own personal over-beliefs. William James introduced the term "over-belief" in the conclu-sion to *The Varieties of Religious Experience*. He conceded that empirical facts or information about human experience don't force us to any one logical

166 SPIRITUALITY IN THE FLESH

conclusion about the ultimate shape of things. We are faced with building this information out into a set of over-beliefs, a set of concepts that promise to lead us to satisfactory relations with life. The function of religious over-beliefs is much like that of any other set of hypotheses generated in the middle loop of thought. Their purpose is to orient individuals to the broadest range of experience, including what experience testifies to be its ultimate context, and to induce the appropriate existential and ethical response.[20] Over-beliefs thus symbolize the relationship we believe exists between natural processes and the ultimate cause (or God) from which reality proceeds. The word "god" here is a symbol for what theologian Gordon Kaufman describes as "a reality, an ultimate tendency or power, which is working itself out in an evolutionary process that has produced not only myriads of living species, but also at least one living form able to shape and transform itself . . . into a being in some measure self-conscious and free."[21] Yet in a spirituality of the flesh, all religious over-beliefs are imaginative constructions drawn from embodied experience. They are not about a God, but about life—about constructing a vision of what might further the expression of life in ways that are ecologically and environmentally sound. For this reason, James cited fellow psychologist James Leuba, who noted that "not God but life, more life, a larger, richer, more satisfying life, is in the last analysis the end of religion. The love of life, at any and every level of development, is the religious impulse."[22]

This book is not about over-beliefs.[23] It goal is descriptive and analytic, not normative. It has tried to review contemporary modern insight into what our bodies are like and how they function in the world, and to demonstrate how such insight illuminates our understanding of religion. However, it is important to conclude by noting that such analysis is not inherently antagonistic to religious understandings of the world. Indeed, it is quite possible that a spirituality in the flesh might lead to a resacralization of the universe and in this way fortify our love of life, at any and every level of development.

Notes

CHAPTER ONE

1. Edward O. Wilson, *Sociobiology: The New Synthesis* (Cambridge, MA: Belknap, 1975), p. 192.

2. Ibid., p. 176.

3. There is as yet no single evolutionary explanation of religion. It is widely agreed that various forms of group cooperation (e.g., kin selection and reciprocal altruism) are adaptations shaped by natural selection. Yet it is important to note that some caution must be exercised in explaining religion in terms of "for the good of the group"—an evolutionary perspective known as "group selection" and rather controversial in contemporary evolutionary thought. In *Adaptation and Natural Selection* (Princeton, NJ: Princeton University Press, 1966), George Williams demonstrated how virtually all adaptations evolve at the individual level and thus, even though between-group selection is theoretically possible, within-group selection is invariably the driving force of natural selection. Richard Dawkins expanded upon this thesis in his highly influential *The Selfish Gene* (New York: Oxford University Press, 1976). Edward O. Wilson and David Sloan Wilson (no relation) have, however, continued to argue that a case can be made that genes can evolve by virtue of benefiting whole groups and despite being selectively disadvantageous within groups. In *Darwin's Cathedral: Evolution, Religion, and the Nature of Society* (Chicago: University of Chicago Press, 2002) and other publications, David Sloan Wilson has maintained that group selection must be evaluated on a case-by-case basis. Proceeding along this route, he argues that religion is primarily a group-level adaptation. David Sloan Wilson further maintains that religious belief is biologically advantageous for its practitioners because its morals,

rituals, and beliefs contribute to group solidarity, thereby bestowing greater survival/ reproductive success upon practitioners. Group selection is a controversial theory in the sciences because it could only work if the differential survival of religious groups is much greater than the disadvantage suffered by individuals within the group (and there are mathematical models that suggest this isn't the case). This debate highlights just how complex evolutionary explanations of phenomena as intricate as religion can be. We should keep in mind, however, that a fully biological (evolutionary) account of religion must finally entail explanations of differences in reproductive fitness. Thus, even though religion surely meets such important human (and bodily) needs as assuaging fear of death, giving persons a sense of meaning or purpose, enhancing self-esteem, and so on, these are not, strictly speaking, biological (evolutionary) explanations unless they translate into explanations of varying degrees of reproductive fitness. A particularly helpful account of how a broadly evolutionary perspective sheds important light on religion can be found in Lee Kilpatrick, *Attachment, Evolution, and the Psychology of Religion* (New York: Guilford, 2005).

4. William LaFleur, "Body," in *Critical Terms for Religious Studies*, ed. Mark C. Taylor (Chicago: University of Chicago Press, 1998), p. 37.

5. George Lakoff and Mark Johnson, *Philosophy in the Flesh: The Embodied Mind and Its Challenge to Western Thought* (New York: Basic Books, 1999), p. 4.

6. Ibid., p. 102.

7. Edward O. Wilson, *Sociobiology*, p. 55.

8. Ariel Glucklich, *Sacred Pain: Hurting the Body for the Sake of the Soul* (New York: Oxford University Press, 2001), p. 12.

9. Ibid., p. 14.

10. Daniel Dennett, *Breaking the Spell: Religion as a Natural Phenomenon* (New York: Viking, 2006), p. 259.

11. Lakoff and Johnson, *Philosophy in the Flesh*, p. 102.

12. Charles Darwin, *The Origin of Species* (New York: Mentor Books, 1958), p 74, emphasis added.

13. Theodosius Dobzhansky, Francisco Ayala, G. Ledyard Stebbins, and James Valentine, *Evolution* (San Francisco: W. H. Freeman, 1977), p. 66.

14. Charles Darwin, cited in Dobzhansky et al., *Evolution*, p. 97.

15. Dobzhansky et al., *Evolution*, p. 31.

16. Edward O. Wilson, *Sociobiology*, p. 3.

17. Dobzhansky et al., *Evolution*, p. 503.

18. George Gaylord Simpson, *The Meaning of Evolution* (New Haven, CT: Yale University Press, 1949), p. 261.

19. Ibid., p. 262.

20. See G. Ledyard Stebbins, *The Basis of Progressive Evolution* (Chapel Hill: University of North Carolina Press, 1969).

21. See Francisco Ayala, "The Concept of Biological Progress," in *Studies in the Philosophy of Biology*, ed. Francisco Ayala and Theodosius Dobzhansky (London: Macmillan, 1974).

22. Konrad Lorenz, *On Aggression* (New York: Harcourt, Brace & World, 1963), p. 265.

23. Edward O. Wilson, *Sociobiology*, p. 550.

24. Simpson, *Meaning of Evolution*, p. 287.

25. Steven Pinker, *How the Mind Works* (New York: W. W. Norton, 1997), p. 21.

26. The functionalist school of thought was the first indigenous expression of American psychology as the discipline first appeared in American universities between 1890 and 1920. Rather than a fixed psychological doctrine, functionalism first emerged as a general outlook, loosely structured around several universities and individuals. William James, James Mark Baldwin, G. Stanley Hall, J. R. Angell, John Dewey, Robert Woodworth, and Harvey Car can all be said to have been a part of the movement. See Duane Schultz, *A History of Modern Psychology* (New York: American, 1957), and Edwin G. Boring, *A History of Experimental Psychology* (New York: D. Appleton-Century, 1929). Boring notes that even though the functionalist school of thought was fairly amorphous, "it was nevertheless in a broad way an expression—the only expression—of the epistemological attitude in American psychology in general" (p. 528).

27. Lakoff and Johnson, *Philosophy in the Flesh*, pp. 9–15

28. See John Dewey, "The Reflex Arc Concept in Psychology," *Psychological Review* 3 (July 1896): 357–70. Dewey credited James with helping him to appreciate the biological nature of mind, but was concerned that James's early psychological writings didn't go far enough to demonstrate that these three functions are not distinct parts but simply distinctions of interpretation unified within experience itself. This charge is probably true of James's early psychological writings, but James corrected this in his later writings in radical empiricism. See the discussion of Dewey's functionalist psychology in Darnell Rucker, *The Chicago Pragmatists* (Minneapolis: University of Minnesota Press, 1969).

29. William James, "Reflex Action and Theism," in *The Will to Believe* (New York: Dover, 1956), pp. 113–14.

30. William James, "Remarks on Spencer's Definition of Mind as Correspondence," in *Collected Essays and Reviews*, ed. Ralph Barton Perry (New York: Longmans, Green, 1911), pp. 52–53.

31. Lakoff and Johnson, *Philosophy in the Flesh*, p. 95.

32. The most widely cited exposition of the cognitive science of religion is Pascal Boyer's *Religion Explained: The Evolutionary Origins of Religious Thought* (New York: Basic Books, 2001). Perhaps the most accessible introduction to the field is Todd Tremlin's *Minds and Gods* (New York: Oxford University Press, 2006). Other important explorations of the cognitive foundations of religious thought are Scott Atran's *In Gods We Trust: The Evolutionary Landscape of Religion* (New York: Oxford University Press, 2002) and Illka Pyysiainen's *How Religion Works: Towards a New Cognitive Science of Religion* (Leiden: Brill, 2001). Although I am in agreement with the basic premise of cognitive theories of religion, I have four reservations about the field as a whole. First, cognitive science utilizes a distinctive vocabulary that masks rather than clarifies the process whereby acting persons distinguish between reliable and

unreliable conceptions of the world. Although cognitive science is surely correct in pointing to the role of innate mental modules in channeling human ideas, cognitive scientists typically pay too little attention to many other important processes that dictate which beliefs are considered intellectually viable or existentially relevant (e.g., imitation, identification, social reinforcement, attachment needs, and experiential results). Second, cognitive science usually pays scant attention to the phenomenology of experiences that actually elicit the construction of—or the gradual "decision" to commit oneself to—religious ideas. The point here is that acting individuals are often conscious of "detecting" and "proving" the existence of more-than-physical causal agents. This would seem to necessitate supplementing standard cognitive science explanations of religion with a more functional (rather than just identifying static cognitive structures) approach to accounting for both the origin and persistence of religious ideas in individuals' lives. Third, cognitive scientists typically rely so heavily on deductive reasoning that they postulate—and reify—cognitive faculties (e.g., folkmechanics, folkbiology, folkpsycholgy) for which the inductively gathered evidence does not support all the claims that are typically made. And fourth, despite their repeated claims that "god ideas" are the universal element in religion, there are in fact many nontheistic ways of conceptualizing more-than-physical causes. Cognitive scientists need to pay more consistent attention to the fact that persons can be socialized into thinking of causal relationships in ways that are not constrained by any particular mental module.

33. Atran, *In Gods We Trust*, p. 57.

34. Ibid., p. 66.

35. Tremlin, *Minds and Gods*, p. 108. In Scott Atran's book this point is stated a bit differently when he observes that "religion has no evolutionary function per se. It is rather that moral sentiments and existential anxieties constitute—by virtue of evolution—ineluctable elements of the human condition, and that the cognitive invention, cultural selection, and historical survival of religious beliefs owes, in part, to success in accommodating these elements" (*In Gods We Trust*, p. 279).

36. See Pascal Boyer, *The Naturalness of Religious Beliefs* (Berkeley: University of California Press, 1994), p. 9.

37. See Scott Atran's discussion of the shortcomings of purely cognitive understandings of religion, *In Gods We Trust*, pp. 13, 264.

38. I have previously examined developmental psychology in an effort to identify critical issues recurring over the course of human life that are optimally resolved by adopting a broadly religious posture. See *Religion and the Life Cycle* (Philadelphia: Fortress, 1988).

39. William James, *The Varieties of Religious Experience: A Study in Human Nature* (1902; Cambridge, MA: Harvard University Press, 1985), p. 382.

40. Ibid., p. 408.

41. Volney Gay, "Passionate about Buddhism: Contesting Theories of Emotion," *Journal of the American Academy of Religion* 71 (September 2003): 606.

42. Ibid., p. 607.

CHAPTER TWO

1. Leda Cosmides and John Tooby, "Evolutionary Psychology and the Emotions," in *Handbook of Emotions*, ed. Michael Lewis and Jeannette Haviland-Jones, 2nd ed. (New York: Guilford, 2000), pp. 91–115.

2. Edward O. Wilson, *Sociobiology*, p. 256.

3. Ibid., p. 565.

4. Garrett Hardin, "Population Skeletons in the Environmental Closet," *Bulletin of the Atomic Scientists*, June 1972, p. 39.

5. Lionel Tiger and Robin Fox, *The Imperial Animal* (New York: Holit, Rinehart & Winston, 1971), p. 22.

6. Michael Ruse, "Darwinism and Determinism," *Zygon* 22 (December 1987): 422.

7. Lorenz, *On Aggression*, p. 265.

8. Robert Plutchik provides an overview of the evolutionary approach to the study of emotions in his essay "The Circumplex as a General Model of the Structures of Emotion and Personality," in *Circumplex Models of Personality and Emotions*, ed. Robert Plutchik and Hope Conte (Washington, DC: American Psychological Association, 1997), pp. 17–46.

9. Carroll Izard, *Human Emotions* (New York: Plenum, 1977), p. 3.

10. Cosmides and Tooby, "Evolutionary Psychology," pp. 103–11.

11. Joseph LeDoux, *The Emotional Brain: The Mysterious Underpinning of Emotional Life* (New York: Simon & Schuster, 1996), p. 16.

12. Ibid.

13. See Richard J. Davidson, Klaus R. Scherer, and H. Hill Goldsmith, eds., *Handbook of Affective Sciences* (New York: Oxford University Press, 2003); Richard Lazarus and Bernice Lazarus, *Passion and Reason: Making Sense of Emotions* (New York: Oxford University Press, 1994); and Lewis and Haviland-Jones, *Handbook of Emotions*.

14. Robert Plutchik, *Emotions and Life: Perspectives from Psychology, Biology, and Evolution* (Washington, DC: American Psychological Association, 2003), p. 73.

15. Aaron Ben-Ze'ev, *The Subtlety of Emotions* (Cambridge, MA: MIT Press, 2000).

16. See James Averill, "Intellectual Emotions," in *The Emotions*, ed. Rom Harré and W. Gerrod Parrott (Thousand Oaks, CA: Sage, 1996), pp. 24–38.

17. See Keith Oatley and Jennifer Jenkins, *Understanding Emotions* (Malden, MA: Blackwell, 1996), p. 125.

18. Plutchik, *Emotions and Life*, p. 322.

19. See the discussion of the physiological, perceptual, and cognitive changes associated with fear in Cosmides and Tooby, "Evolutionary Psychology," pp. 93–94.

20. Carroll Izard and Brian Ackerman, "Motivational, Organizational, and Regulatory Functions of Discrete Emotions," in Lewis and Haviland-Jones, *Handbook of Emotions*, p. 260.

21. Ibid.

22. See Arne Ohman's "Fear and Anxiety: Evolutionary, Cognitive, and Clinical Perspectives," in Lewis and Haviland-Jones, *Handbook of Emotions*, pp. 573–606.

23. Izard and Ackerman, "Functions of Discrete Emotions," p. 259.

24. Plutchik, *Emotions and Life*, p. 329. See also R. W. Novaco, "The Functions and Regulation of the Arousal of Anger," *American Journal of Psychiatry* 133 (1976): 1124–28.

25. Eric Hoffer, *The True Believer* (New York: Harper & Brothers, 1953), p. 89.

26. For a discussion of how anger arises in response to disruptions of moral or cultural order, see "Morality, Domination, and the Emotion of 'Justifiable Anger,'" chapter 6 in Catherine Lutz, *Unnatural Emotions* (Chicago: University of Chicago Press, 1988); and Carol Tavris, *Anger: The Misunderstood Emotion* (New York: Simon & Schuster, 1982). See also Catherine Peyroux's "Gertrude's Furor: Reading Anger in an Early Medieval Saint's Life" and Charlotte Hardman's "Emotions and Ancestors: Understanding Experiences of Lohorung Rai in Nepal," both in *Religion and Emotion*, ed. John Corrigan (New York: Oxford University Press, 2004), pp. 309, 334.

27. Sigmund Freud, *The Future of an Illusion*, trans. W. D. Robson-Scott (1927; Garden City, NY: Anchor Books, 1964), p. 25.

28. Ibid., p. 90.

29. Robert Solomon, *The Passions* (Garden City, NY: Anchor, 1976), p. xviii.

30. This was William James's point in his essay "The Sentiment of Rationality," where he argued that we cannot conceptualize reason as though it occurs somewhere outside the human brain. James elaborated on this point in his famous essay "The Will to Believe," when he wrote that "if any one should thereupon assume that intellectual insight is what remains after wish and will and sentimental preference have taken wing, or that pure reason is what then settles our opinions, he would fly quite as directly in the teeth of the facts" (p. 8). Both essays appear in *The Will to Believe*.

31. A thorough discussion of scholarly attempts to define Western apocalypticism can be found in John J. Collins's *The Apocalyptic Imagination* (New York: Crossroads, 1985). See also such fine studies as Klaus Koch's *The Rediscovery of Apocalyptic* (Naperville, IL: Allenson, 1972), and Paul Hanson's *The Dawn of Apocalyptic* (Philadelphia: Fortress, 1975).

32. David Hellholm, "The Problem of Apocalyptic Genre and the Apocalypse of John," in *Society of Biblical Literature 1982 Seminar Papers*, ed. K. H. Richards (Chico, CA: Scholars, 1982), p. 168.

33. John J. Collins, *Apocalyptic Imagination*, pp. 214–15.

34. My reconstruction of the setting of the book of Daniel follows that found in E. R. Chamberlin, *The Antichrist and the Millennium* (New York: Dutton, 1975). Readers interested in a brief overview of the history and current status of Daniel should consult Shemaryahu Talmon's entry in *The Literary Guide to the Bible*, ed. Robert Alter and Frank Kermode (Cambridge, MA: Belknap, 1987), pp. 343–56.

35. Daniel 7:3, Daniel 7:21, Revised Standard Version.

36. Daniel 7:27.

37. A sound discussion of the controversies surrounding the authorship and date of composition of Revelation can be found in Adela Yabro Collins's *Crisis and Catharsis* (Philadelphia: Westminster, 1984).

38. George Bernard Shaw, cited in Bernard McGinn's essay on the literary study of Revelation, in Alter and Kermode, *The Literary Guide to the Bible*, pp. 523–44.

39. See Adela Yarbro Collins, *The Combat Myth in the Book of Revelation* (Missoula, MT: Scholars, 1976), p. 33.

40. Adela Yarbro Collins, *Combat Myth*, p. 114.

41. Revelation 13:1

42. Adela Yarbro Collins, *Crisis and Catharsis*, p. 160.

43. Ibid., p. 144.

44. Ibid., p. 151.

45. Ibid., p. 162.

46. See my earlier work, *Naming the Antichrist: The History of an American Obsession* (New York: Oxford University Press, 1995).

47. Increase Mather, quoted in Thomas Brown, "The Image of the Beast: Anti-Papal Rhetoric in Colonial America," in *Conspiracy: The Fear of Subversion in American History*, ed. Richard Curry and Thomas Brown (New York: Holt, Rinehart & Winston, 1972), p. 4.

48. Cotton Mather, quoted in Richard Slotkin, *Regeneration through Violence: The Mythology of the American Frontier, 1600–1860* (Middleton, CT: Wesleyan University Press, 1973), p. 120.

49. Martin Marty and R. Scott Appleby, eds., *Fundamentalisms Observed* (Chicago: University of Chicago Press, 1991), p. 820.

50. Glen Shuck, *Marks of the Beast: The Left Behind Novels and the Struggle for Evangelical Identity* (New York: New York University Press, 2005), p. 16.

51. Amy Johnson Frykholm, *Rapture Culture: Left Behind in Evangelical America* (New York: Oxford University Press, 2004), p. 76.

52. Ibid., p. 125.

53. Ibid., p. 179.

54. Ibid., p. 132.

55. Norman Cohn, *The Pursuit of the Millennium* (London: Secker & Warburg, 1957), p. 309. The revised edition of this text wholly omits this analysis and sharply reduces other psychoanalytic interpretations of the meaning and motivations of apocalyptic discourse.

56. Michael Barkun, *Disaster and the Millennium* (New Haven, CT: Yale University Press, 1974), pp. 110–114.

57. David Aberle, "A Note on Relative Deprivation Theory as Applied to Millenarian and Other Cult Movements," in *Millennial Dreams in Action: Studies in Revolutionary Movements*, ed. Sylvia Thrup (New York: Schocken, 1970), p.209.

58. Charles B. Strozier, *Apocalypse: On the Psychology of Fundamentalism in America* (Boston: Beacon, 1994), p. 252.

59. Ibid.

60. William James, "The Moral Philosopher and the Moral Life," in *The Will to Believe*, p. 210.

61. Hardin, "Population Skeletons," p. 39.

62. Paul Pruyser, *A Dynamic Psychology of Religion* (New York: Harper & Row, 1976), p. 159.

63. W. Warren Wagar, *Terminal Visions* (Bloomington: Indiana University Press, 1982), p. 66.

CHAPTER THREE

1. See Catherine Albanese, *Nature Religion in America* (Chicago: University of Chicago Press, 1990).

2. Perry Miller, *Errand into the Wilderness* (Cambridge, MA: Belknap, 1975), p. 185.

3. William Clebsch, *American Religious Thought* (Chicago: University of Chicago Press, 1973), p. xvi.

4. Jonathan Haidt, "The Moral Emotions," in Davidson et al., *Handbook of Affective Sciences*, pp. 852–70. Haidt specifically mentions the affinity between his work and the treatment of emotion in Nico Frijda, *The Emotions* (Cambridge: Cambridge University Press, 1986).

5. Dacher Keltner and Jonathan Haidt, "Approaching Awe, a Moral, Spiritual, and Aesthetic Emotion," *Cognition and Emotion*, 17 (March 2003): 306. See also Michelle Shiota and Dacher Keltner, "The Nature of Awe: Elicitors, Appraisals, and Effects on Self-Concept," *Cognition and Emotion* 21 (August 2007): 944–63.

6. See C. Clark, "Emotions in the Micropolitics of Everyday Life," in *Research Agendas in the Sociology of Emotions*, ed. T. D. Kemper (Albany: State University of New York Press, 1990), pp. 305–34.

7. Keltner and Haidt, "Approaching Awe," p. 312.

8. Haidt, "Moral Emotions," p. 863.

9. Barbara Fredrickson, "What Good Are Positive Emotions?" *Review of General Psychology* 2 (1998): 300–319.

10. Izard and Ackerman, "Functions of Discrete Emotions," in Lewis and Haviland-Jones, *Handbook of Emotions*, p. 257.

11. Richard Dawkins, *Unweaving the Rainbow: Science, Delusion and the Appetite for Wonder* (New York: Houghton Mifflin Company, 1998), p. 264.

12. Atran, *In Gods We Trust*, p. 57.

13. Most of the following summary of the biological, psychological, and philosophical perspectives on wonder can be found in my *Wonder: From Emotion to Spirituality* (Chapel Hill: University of North Carolina Press, 2006).

14. Haidt, "Moral Emotions," p. 863.

15. Lazarus and Lazarus, *Passion and Reason*, p. 136.

16. Don Browning, *The Moral Context of Pastoral Care* (Philadelphia: Westminster, 1976), p. 85.

17. Ibid., p. 87.

18. There are many fine introductions to the work of Jean Piaget. One of the most succinct is the summary provided in Henry Maier's *Three Theories of Child Development* (New York: Harper & Row, 1969). Readers might also wish to consult Richard Evans's *Jean Piaget: The Man and His Ideas* (New York: E. P. Dutton, 1973) or Mary Ann Spencer Pulaski's *Understanding Piaget* (New York: Harper & Row, 1971). Helpful assessments of Piaget's long-term impact on developmental psychology can be found in David Elkind and John Flavell, eds., *Studies in Cognitive Development: Essays in Honor of Jean Piaget* (New York: Oxford University Press, 1969).

19. In celebration of the centennial anniversary of Jean Piaget's birth, *Psychological Science* published a collection of articles assessing his legacy to the field of cognitive psychology. See *Psychological Science* 7 (July 1996): 191–225. That same year, Orlando Lourenco and Armando Machado published "In Defense of Piaget's Theory: A Reply to Ten Common Criticisms," *Psychological Review* 103 (January 1996): 143–64. Patricia Miller also provides a helpful overview of the current status of Piaget's contributions to the field, in *Theories of Developmental Psychology*, 4th ed. (New York: W. H. Freeman, 2001).

20. William Charlesworth, "The Role of Surprise in Cognitive Development," in Elkind and Flavell, *Studies in Cognitive Development*, pp. 300–301.

21. Ibid., p. 308.

22. See the excellent discussion of Piaget and "the world of possibilities" in Paul Harris, "On Not Falling Down to Earth: Children's Metaphysical Thinking," in *Imagining the Impossible: Magical, Scientific, and Religious Thinking in Children*, ed. Karl Rosengren, Carl Johnson, and Paul Harris (Cambridge: Cambridge University Press, 2000), pp. 157–78.

23. See Jean Piaget, The *Language* and *Thought of the Child*. Translated by Marjorie Gabain (New York : Meridian Books , 1955).

24. See Carl Johnson, "Putting Different Things Together: The Development of Metaphysical Thinking," and Paul Harris, "On Not Falling Down," both in Rosengren et al., *Imagining the Impossible*.

25. Jean Piaget, *The Psychology of Intelligence* (London: Routledge & Kegan Paul, 1950), p. 148.

26. Jean Piaget and B. Inhelder, *The Growth of Logical Thinking from Childhood to Adolescence*, cited in Maier, *Three Theories*, p. 149.

27. See the excellent discussion of this issue in Carl Johnson, "Putting Different Things Together," in Rosengren et al., *Imagining the Impossible*, p. 200.

28. This unfortunate slighting of the role of wonder in stimulating metaphysical thought is especially curious given the larger context of Piaget's life and thought. Piaget's godfather introduced the young Piaget to Bergson's descriptions of "creative evolution" and "the elan vital," thereby opened up the budding scientist's sense of wonder. The experience, he recounted, was "a moment of enthusiasm close to ecstatic joy."(Vidal: *Piaget Before Piaget*, p. 52) He was "seized by the demon of reflection" the very moment he entertained the radical and previously unexpected possibility that God can be identified with the whole of life (p. 52). Piaget now had an experiential template for envisioning the whole of life as a dialectical movement toward some

"supreme" or "ideal" reality that in some way lies beyond our observed reality. Thus, in his autobiography, Piaget expressed his personal belief that life has an innate tendency to seek out "the ultimate order of the universe."(p. 193) Although Piaget obviously didn't engage in metaphysics in any traditional sense, the personal meaning or purpose of his life work flowed from the wonder generated by his perception of something intensely powerful, real, and beautiful about the movement of life. See Fernando Vidal's *Piaget Before Piaget* (Cambridge, MA: Harvard University Press, 1994).

29. Robert Kegan, a self-professed follower of Piaget, warns that we must be careful to correct for the tendency of Piagetians to be principally concerned "about *cognition*, to the neglect of *emotion*; the *individual*, to the neglect of the *social*; the *epistemological*, to the neglect of the *ontological* (or concept, to the neglect of being); *stages of meaning-constitution*, to the neglect of *meaning-constitutive process*," See Robert Kegan, "There the Dance Is: Religious Dimensions of a Developmental Framework," in *Toward Moral and Religious Maturity*, ed. Christaine Brusselmans, James A. O'Donohoe, James W. Fowler, and Antoine Vergote (Morristown, NJ: Silver Burdette Company, 1980), p. 406.

30. See the discussion of perception and creativity in Ernest Schactel's *Meta-morphosis: On the Development of Affect, Perception, Attention, and Memory* (New York: Basic Books, 1959). Schactel, a psychoanalyst and student of child psychology, argues that psychologists have devoted far too much attention to the child's acquisition of autocentric perception (i.e., perception that guides utilitarian manipulation of distinct objects in the environment) and not enough to the acquisition of allocentric perception (i.e., perception that goes beyond utilitarian interest and perceives an object "not as isolated from the rest of life but as containing it the *mysterium tremendum* of life, of being.... the relatedness to a particular, very concrete object in fully allocentric perception is also always a relatedness to something more than just an isolated, separate, single object" [p. 183]). He adds, "The main motivation in this development toward allocentric perception is not coercion by reality ... [but] rather an insatiable curiosity and wish to approach and make contact with the surrounding world in a thousand different ways, and the pleasure in these contacts" (p. 147).

31. Martha Nussbaum, *Upheavals of Thought: The Intelligence of Emotions* (Cambridge: Cambridge University Press, 2001), p. 54.

32. Ibid., p. 55.

33. Ibid., p. 321.

34. This overview of John Muir's life and thought is drawn from the third chapter of my *Wonder*. A good place to begin a study of John Muir's life and thought are Frederick Turner's *Rediscovering America: John Muir in His Time and Ours* (New York: Viking, 1985), and Linnie Marsh Wolfe's *Son of the Wilderness: The Life of John Muir* (New York: Knopf, 1951). Michael Cohen's *The Pathless Way: John Muir and American Wilderness* (Madison: University of Wisconsin Press, 1984) is not so much a biography as it is an examination of Muir's spiritual and intellectual development as seen in the context of today's environmentalist debates. Likewise, Stephen Fox's *The American Conservation Movement: John Muir and His Legacy* (Madison:

University of Wisconsin Press, 1985) explores Muir's life and thought within the context of the gradual emergence of American's interest in conservation.

35. John Muir, *The Story of My Boyhood and Youth* (Boston: Houghton Mifflin, 1913), p. 31.

36. Ibid., pp. 65, 75, and 113. Muir's biographical reflections include his memory that he "never tired of listening to the wonderful whip-poor-will" (p. 68), that he regarded his family's hog "a very wonderful beast" (p. 75), and that "the next great flower wonder on which we lavished attention" was the cypripediums (p. 121).

37. Ibid., p. 286.

38. John Muir, *My First Summer in the Sierra* (Boston: Houghton Mifflin, 1979), pp. 125–27.

39. Cited in Cohen, *The Pathless Way*, p. 18.

40. Cohen, *The Pathless Way*, p. 18.

41. Cited in Frederick Turner, *Rediscovering America*, p. 187.

42. Cohen, *The Pathless Way*, p. 259.

43. Fox, *American Conservation Movement*, p. 81. In November of 1875, Muir wrote that "when one comes out of the woods everything is novel.... even our fellow beings are regarded with something of the same keenness and freshness of perception that is brought to a new species of wild animal." Cited in Cohen, *The Pathless Way*, p. 225.

44. Cited in Cohen, *The Pathless Way*, p. 212.

45. Muir, cited in Fox, *American Conservation Movement*, p. 82.

46. See the succinct overview of Muir's contributions to environmentalist thought in Bron Taylor and Jeffrey Kaplan, eds., *The Encyclopedia of Religion and Nature* (New York: Continuum, 2005). Both Michael Cohen and Stephen Fox also provide extended overviews of Muir's relationship to the growth of environmental awareness in North America.

47. This section on Rachel Carson comes from chapter 7 in my *Wonder*. The most thorough biography of Rachel Carson is Linda Lear's *Rachel Carson: Witness for Nature* (New York: Henry Holt, 1997). Paul Brooks also connects Carson's life and thought in his *The House of Life: Rachel Carson at Work* (Boston: Houghton Mifflin, 1972). Stephen Fox sets Carson's work into the larger sweep of modern environmental thought in his *American Conservation Movement*, pp. 292–99.

48. Rachel Carson, cited in Fox, *American Conservation Movement*, p. 293.

49. Rachel Carson, *The Edge of the Sea* (Boston: Houghton Mifflin, 1955), p. 3.

50. Rachel Carson, *Silent Spring* (Boston: Houghton Mifflin, 1962), p. 249.

51. Rachel Carson, from the foreword to the original edition of *Under the Sea-Wind* (New York: Simon & Schuster, 1941).

52. Rachel Carson, from her National Book Award acceptance speech, cited in Brooks, *House of Life*, p. 127. The reversal of figure and ground characteristically produced by the emotion of wonder is exemplified in this observation of Carson's: "Looking out over the cove I felt a strong sense of the interchangeability of land and sea in this marginal world of the shore, and of the links between the life of the two. There was also an awareness of the past and of the continuing flow of time, obliter-

ating much that had gone before, as the sea had that morning washed away the tracks of the bird" (Ibid., p. 170).

53. Rachel Carson, *The Sea Around Us*, cited in Fox, *American Conservation Movement*, p. 416.

54. Carson, *The Edge of the Sea*, 7.

55. Lear, *Rachel Carson*, p. 284.

56. Rachel Carson, "Help Your Child to Wonder," *Woman's Home Companion* (July 1956): 46. See also Lear, *Rachel Carson*, p. 284.

57. Rachel Carson, address to Theta Sigma Phi sorority of women journalists in 1954, included in *Lost Woods: The Discovered Writing of Rachel Carson*, ed. Linda Lear (Boston: Beacon, 1998), p. 163.

58. In *Unweaving the Rainbow*, Richard Dawkins is peculiarly preoccupied with discrediting the frequent association of wonder with religious rather than scientific interpretations of the universe. "It is my thesis," he explains, "that the spirit of wonder which led Blake to Christian mysticism, Keats to Arcadian myth and Yeats to Fenians and fairies, is the very same spirit that moves great scientists, a spirit which, if fed back to poets in scientific guise, might inspire still greater poetry" (p. 27). Dawkins unfortunately never explains to us what the value of poetry for human existence might be, and the general framework of his theory of human nature would seemingly render poetic thought a useless misapplication of thought. Instead, we are told that humans "have an appetite for wonder . . . which real science ought to be feeding" (p. 114). Thus, while Dawkins recognizes the existence of wonder and its role in stimulating novel engagements with the environment, he can find no normative value for the emotion unless it eventuates in scientific rationality.

59. In *How the Mind Works*, MIT psychologist Steven Pinker contends that the cognitive operations to which we give the name "mind" were "shaped by natural selection to solve the problems of the hunting and gathering life led by our ancestors" (p. 21). To Pinker, then, our minds have been designed by natural selection to understand distinct objects within the physical environment rather than to discern philosophical or theological meanings of existence. He concludes that our brains simply lack the equipment to contemplate religious questions productively. Although he readily admits that the natural world evokes wonder in us, he insists that if wonder leads to contemplation of the meaning or purpose of the whole of nature, it is simply engaging us in mental activities that are inherently unproductive. In fact, Pinker decrees, "The meaning of the whole is determined by the meaning of the parts and the meaning of the relations that connect them"—thus casting suspicion on the kinds of cognitive operations triggered by wonder that typically construct images of a possible great whole in terms of which observed phenomena might be related (p. 564). Meanwhile, in his *In Gods We Trust*, Scott Atran focuses on the way that natural selection shaped our minds for "agency detection in the face of uncertainty" (p. 71). Atran's basic point is that when causally opaque situations trigger reactions such as those associated with wonder, the brain generates confused and erroneous concepts (e.g., belief in gods, ghosts, or angels) that only impair our ongoing adaptation to the physical universe.

60. Rachel Carson, letter to Dorothy Freeman, cited in Lear, *Rachel Carson*, p. 311.

61. Rachel Carson, address to Theta Sigma Phi, included in Lear, *Lost Woods*, p. 160.

62. When an elderly fundamentalist accused Rachel Carson of ignoring God and the Bible in her discussions of nature, she took the trouble of responding. "It is true that I accept the theory of evolution as the most logical one that has ever been put forward to explain the development of living creatures on this earth. As far as I am concerned, however, there is absolutely no conflict between a belief in evolution and a belief in God as the creator. Believing as I do in evolution, I merely believe that is the method by which God created, and is still creating, life on earth. And it is a method so marvelously conceived that to study it in detail is to increase—and certainly never to diminish—*one's reverence and awe* both for the Creator and the process" (Brooks, *House of Life*, p. 9, emphasis added).

63. Rachel Carson, *A Sense of Wonder* (New York: Harper & Row, 1956), pp. 42–43.

64. Ibid., p. 88.

65. Carson, *The Edge of the Sea*, p. 250.

66. James, *Varieties of Religious Experience*, p. 23.

67. John E. Smith, *Experience and God* (New York: Oxford University Press, 1998), p. 60.

68. Erich Fromm, *Psychoanalysis and Religion* (New Haven, CT: Yale University Press, 1950), p. 94, emphasis added.

69. See the excellent discussion of this point in Carol Nemeroff and Paul Rozin, "The Makings of the Magical Mind: The Nature and Function of Sympathetic Magical Thinking," in Rosengren et al., *Imagining the Impossible*, pp. 1–34. See also Karl Rosengren and Anne Hickling, "Metamorphosis and Magic: The Development of Children's Thinking About Possible Events and Plausible Mechanisms," ibid., pp. 75–98.

70. Personality theorist Gordon Allport argued that mature religious thought must have a heuristic quality. His point was that "fixed" religious ideas breed intolerance and even combativeness. Mature religiosity, he argued, views beliefs not as a closed system of truths, but as hypotheses toward richer relationships with life. In his view, a heuristic faith has an open, eager, and fresh quality. See Gordon Allport, *The Individual and His Religion* (New York: Macmillan, 1950). Readers might also wish to consider what role wonder plays in a person's transition from forms of religious thinking that James Fowler labels "conventional faith" to what he labels "universalizing faith." See James Fowler, *Stages of Faith: The Psychology of Human Development and the Quest for Meaning* (San Francisco: Harper & Row, 1981).

71. Marjorie Taylor and Stephanie Carlson, "The Influence of Religious Beliefs on Parental Attitudes about Children's Fantasy Behavior," in Rosengren et al., *Imagining the Impossible*, pp. 247–68.

72. Nussbaum, *Upheavals of Thought*, p. 54.

73. Rachel Carson, " The Edge of the Sea," p. 250.

CHAPTER FOUR

1. Dean Hamer, *The God Gene: How Faith is Hardwired into Our Genes* (New York: Doubleday, 2004), p. 139.

2. Ibid., p. 8.

3. Ibid., p. 7.

4. Ibid., p. 215.

5. Hamer devotes a short chapter to a review of studies on twins reared apart conducted both by researchers at the University of Minnesota and researchers affiliated with the Australian Twin Registry. The data gathered in these studies strongly suggest that genes are responsible for roughly half of the variation in religiousness (beliefs, practices, feelings) from one twin to the next. See N. G. Waller, B. A. Kojetin, T. J. Bouchard, D. T. Lykken, and A. Tellegen, "Genetic and Environmental Influences on Religious Interests, Attitudes, and Values: A Study of Twins Reared Apart and Together," *American Psychological Society* 1 (1990): 138–42; D. T. Bouchard, M. McGue, D. Lykken, and A. Tellegen, "Intrinsic and Extrinsic Religiousness: Genetic and Environmental Influences and Personality Correlates," *Twin Res* 2 (1999): 88–98; and B. M. D'Onofrio, L. J. Eaves, L. Murrelle, H. H. Maes, and B. Spilka, "Understanding Biological and Social Influences on Religious Affiliation, Attitudes, and Behaviors: A Behavior Genetic Perspective," *Journal of Personality* 67 (1999): 953–83.

6. Andrew Newberg, Eugene d'Aquili, and Vince Rouse, *Why God Won't Go Away: Brain Science and the Biology of Belief* (New York: Ballantine Books, 2001), p. 6. See also Newberg's and d'Aquili's earlier work, *The Mystical Mind: Probing the Biology of Religious Experience* (Minneapolis, MN: Fortress, 1999).

7. Ibid., p. 80.

8. Ibid., p. 139.

9. Ibid., pp. 122–23. Readers might wish to consult the excellent review essay assessing the relevance of cognitive neuroscience to the study of religion (including *Why God Won't Go Away*) in Kelly Bulkeley's "The Gospel According to Darwin: The Relevance of Cognitive Neuroscience to Religious Studies," *Religious Studies Review* 29 (April 2003): 123–29.

10. Scott Atran, *In God We Trust: The Evolutionary Landscape of Religion* (New York: Oxford University Press, 2002). Atran is particularly interested in how evolution shaped the human brain to seek out "agency" in the face of uncertainty. Religion, he argues, stems from the mind's misguided efforts to identify "supernatural agency"— what he considers to be "the most culturally recurrent, cognitively relevant, and evolutionarily compelling constant in religion" (57).

11. Pascal Boyer, *Religion Explained* (New York: Basic Books, 2001). Boyer brings a cognitive-evolutionary framework to the study of religion. He assumes that the brain is a machine operating according to rules developed through evolution. "Religion is about the existence and causal powers of non-observable entities and agencies" (p. 8), and is made up of "a limited catalogue of possible supernatural beliefs" (p. 11). He maintains that religious representations are particular combinations of mental rep-

resentations that satisfy two conditions: "First, the religious concepts violate certain expectations from ontological categories. Second, they preserve other expectations" (p. 71).

12. Steven Pinker, *How the Mind Works* (New York: W. W. Norton, 1997). Pinker argues that the human brain "was shaped by natural selection to solve the problems of the hunting and gathering life led by our ancestors" (p. 21). Religion, however, is a misapplication of those problem-solving functions to questions or topics that the brain isn't designed to solve. Religion, then, consists of misguided efforts to address questions we aren't capable of answering. The result is that religion "is the common folly of believing in the palpably untrue" (p. 54).

13. Jensine Andresen, ed., *Religion in Mind: Cognitive Perspectives on Religious Belief, Ritual, and Experience* (Cambridge: Cambridge University Press, 2001). The essays in this volume extend empirical research from psychology and anthropology to the analysis of religious belief, ritual, and experience.

14. David Sloan Wilson, *Darwin's Cathedral: Evolution, Religion, and the Nature of Society* (Chicago: University of Chicago Press, 2003). Wilson argues that religions can be understood as distinct organisms (as opposed to collections of organisms). Religions, like organisms, are designed by evolution to survive and reproduce. Religions accomplish these goals by inducing individuals to sacrifice their own interests to those of the group. Religion therefore functions as "a complex regulatory system that binds members into a functional unit" (25).

15. Hamer, *The God Gene*, p. 89. For a more complete description of this experiment and its implication for understanding spirituality in the flesh, see my *Stairways to Heaven: Drugs in American Religious History* (Boulder: CO: Westview, 2000). Much of this chapter comes from the historical narrative presented in that earlier book. Readers might also wish to review Roland Griffiths' study of psilocybin's role in producing mystical experiences, "Psilocybin Can Occasion Mystical-Type Experiences," *Psychopharmacology* 187 (July 2006): 268–83. Using volunteer subjects who had some established spiritual practice, Griffiths found that 60 percent who took psilocybin reported a profound mystical experience compared with fewer than five percent of control subjects.

16. See Richard E. Schultes, "Hallucinogenic Plants of the New World," *Harvard Review* 1 (1963): 18–32; and "Botanical Sources of the New World Narcotics," *Psychedelic Review* 1 (1963): 145–66.

17. See the following by Weston La Barre: "The New World Narcotic Complex" (appendix), in *The Peyote Cult*, 4th ed., (New York: Archon Books, 1975), pp. 263–65; "The Narcotic Complex of the New World," *Diogenes* 48 (1964): 125–38; and "Hallucinogens and the Shamanic Origins of Religion," in *The Flesh of the Gods: The Ritual Use of Hallucinogens*, ed. Peter Furst (New York: Praeger, 1972) p. 261–278.

18. La Barre, "Hallucinogens," p. 272.

19. Weston La Barre, "Old and New World Narcotics: A Statistical Question and an Ethnological Reply," *Economic Botany* 24 (1970): 79.

20. La Barre, "Hallucinogens," p. 276.

182 NOTES TO PAGES 81–88

21. See Ralph Linton, *Use of Tobacco among North American Indians* (Chicago: Field Museum of Natural History, 1924). See also Joseph Epes Brown, ed., *The Sacred Pipe* (Baltimore: Penguin, 1971).

22. For analyses of the physiological effects of nicotine, see D. J. K. Balfour, ed., *Nicotine and the Tobacco Smoking Habit* (New York: Pergamon, 1984).

23. La Barre, "Narcotic Complex," p. 129.

24. See Francis Robicsek, *The Smoking Gods* (Norman: University of Oklahoma Press, 1978). Another work on shamans' use of tobacco is Johannes Wilbert's *Tobacco and Shamanism in South America* (New Haven, CT: Yale University Press, 1987).

25. Paul Radin, *The Winnebago Tribe* (Lincoln: University of Nebraska Press, 1970), p. 97.

26. Willard Park, *Shamanism in Western North America* (Evanston, IL: Northwestern University Press, 1938).

27. Linton, *Use of Tobacco*, p. 25.

28. Joseph Epes Brown, *The Sacred Pipe*, p. 21.

29. Overviews of the pharmacological properties of peyote can be found in La Barre, *The Peyote Cult*, pp. 138–50; and Richard Schultes and Albert Hofmann, *Plants of the Gods: Origins of Hallucinogenic Use* (New York: McGraw-Hill, 1979), 132–43. A more recent and detailed investigation of the psychopharmacology of peyote (focusing on the alkaloids other than mescaline) is Daniel Perrine's "Visions of the Night," *Heffter Review of Psychedelic Research* 2 (2001): 6–52.

30. Ruth Shonle, "Peyote, the Giver of Visions," *American Anthropologist* 27 (1925): 59.

31. More detailed descriptions of peyote rites are to be found in La Barre, *The Peyote Cult*, pp. 43–56; J. S. Slotkin, *The Peyote Religion* (Glencoe, IL: Free Press, 1956), pp. 22–27; and Omer Stewart and David Aberle, *Peyotism in the West* (Salt Lake City: University of Utah Press, 1984).

32. La Barre, *The Peyote Cult*, p. 50.

33. Ibid.

34. Ibid., p. 166.

35. Barbara Myerhoff, "Peyote and the Mystic Vision," in *Art of the Huichol Indians*, ed. Kathleen Berrin (New York: Harry N. Abrams, 1978), p. 56.

36. See my *Spiritual, But Not Religious: Understanding Unchurched America* (New York: Oxford University Press, 2001) for a more detailed description of unchurched American religion and references to pertinent scholarly treatments of related topics.

37. See Robert Ellwood's excellent accounts of the religious counterculture in both the 1950s and 1960s in his *The Fifties Spiritual Marketplace* (New Brunswick, NJ: Rutgers University Press, 1997) and *The Sixties Spiritual Awakening* (New Brunswick, NJ: Rutgers University Press, 1994).

38. A discussion of Blood's nitrous oxide-induced mystical philosophy can be found in Hal Bridges, *American Mysticism* (New York: Harper & Row, 1970), pp. 15–19.

39. James's initial publication on nitrous oxide appeared in *Mind* 7 (1882): 186–208. It also appears in an abridged form as "Subjective Effects of Nitrous Oxide," in Charles Tart, ed., *Altered States of Consciousness* (Garden City, NY: John Wiley & Sons, 1969), pp. 367–70.

40. James, *Varieties of Religious Experience*, p. 307.

41. In addition to my *Stairways to Heaven* and Robert Ellwood's *The Sixties Spiritual Awakening*, other accounts of the role of psychedelics in American religious life include Jay Stevens, *Storming Heaven: LSD and the American Dream* (New York: Harper & Row, 1988); Timothy Leary, *High Priest* (New York: World Publishing, 1968); Robert De Ropp, "Psychedelic Drugs," in *Encyclopedia of Religion*, ed. Mircea Eliade, vol. 12 (New York: Collier Macmillan, 1987), pp. 53–55; and Huston Smith, *Cleansing the Doors of Perception* (New York: Jeremy Tarcher, 2000).

42. See the concluding chapter ("Final Reflections on the Sixties") of Ellwood's *The Sixties Spiritual Awakening*, pp. 326–36.

43. Marlene Dobkin de Rios, *Hallucinogens: Cross-Cultural Perspectives* (Albuquerque: University of New Mexico Press, 1984), p. 203.

44. Magazine and Web poll, reported in *Tricycle: The Buddhist Review* (Fall 1996): 44.

45. Ram Dass, interview in ibid., p. 102.

46. Canadian government's Commission of Inquiry, *The Non-Medical Use of Drugs* (New York: Penguin, 1971), p. 117.

47. Charles Tart, *On Being Stoned: A Psychological Study of Marijuana Intoxication* (Palo Alto, CA: Science & Behavior Books, 1971), p. 212.

48. William Novak, *High Culture: Marijuana in the Lives of Americans* (New York: Alfred A. Knopf, 1980), p. 9.

49. Ibid., p. 12.

50. Ibid., p. 124.

51. Ibid., p. 155.

52. See Bruce D. Johnson, *Marihuana Users and Drug Subcultures* (New York: John Wiley & Sons, 1973).

53. See Charles Tart's statistical tables "Religious Affiliation" and "Effect of Background Factors on Spiritual Experiences," in *On Being Stoned*, pp. 43 and 221.

54. Roland Fischer provided a fascinating explanation of altered states of consciousness in terms of the ratio of sensory-intake versus sensory-processing activities in the brain, in "A Cartography of the Ecstatic and Meditative States," *Science* 174 (November 26, 1971): 897–904. Although Fischer's model minimizes consideration of the cultural and ritual influences on the structuring of consciousness, it does provide a helpful framework for understanding how very specific states of neurological arousal might give rise to specific, state-bound modes of consciousness.

55. Arthur J. Deikman, "Deautomatization and the Mystic Experience," *Psychiatry* 29 (1966): 324–38, reprinted in Tart, *Altered States of Consciousness*, p. 44.

56. Ronald Shor, "Hypnosis and the Concept of the Generalized Reality-Orientation," reprinted in Tart, *Altered States of Consciousness*, p. 236.

57. Felicitas Goodman's *Ecstasy Ritual, and Alternate Reality* (Bloomington: Indiana University Press, 1988), p. 41.

58. A review of the thorny issues entailed in the debate about the "truth status" of drug-induced ecstasy, including a summary of R. C. Zaehner's and Mircea Eliade's vehement attack on what they consider pseudo mysticism, can be found in my *Stairways to Heaven*, pp. 164–77.

59. This is the point argued eloquently by Bertrand Russell in his "Critique of Mysticism," in *Reason and Responsibility* (Belmont, CA: Wadsworth, 1985), p. 85.

60. James, *Varieties of Religious Experience*, p. 21.

CHAPTER FIVE

1. Miriam deCosta-Willis, introduction to *Erotique Noire: Black Erotics*, ed. Miriam deCosta-Willis, Reginald Martin, and Roseann P. Bell (New York: Anchor Books, 1992), xxix. Cited in Dwight Hopkins, "The Construction of the Black Male Body," in *Loving the Body: Black Religious Studies and the Erotic*, ed. Anthony Pinn and Dwight Hopkins (New York: Palgrave, 2005), p. 180.

2. An excellent discussion of the link between eroticism and religious creativity can be found in Jeffrey Kripal's *Roads of Excess, Palaces of Wisdom: Eroticism and Reflexivity in the Study of Mysticism* (Chicago: University of Chicago Press, 2001). Early in the book, Kripal notes that religious creativity flows most naturally from "the primary processes of the mind linked to the pleasure principle and its libidinal energies" (p. 12).

3. This overview of the standard evolutionary portraits of sexual selection is based on Jerome Barkow's *Darwin, Sex, and Status: Biological Approaches to Mind and Culture* (Toronto: University of Toronto Press, 1989), p. 326. See also Geoffrey Miller, "How Mate Choice Shaped Human Nature: A Review of Sexual Selection and Human Evolution," in *Handbook of Evolutionary Psychology*, ed. Charles Crawford and Dennis Krebs (Mahwah, NJ: Lawrence Erlbaum, 1998), pp. 87–130.

4. This discussion of the "biology of love" borrows heavily from David Schmitt, "Evolutionary and Cross-Cultural Perspectives on Love: The Influence of Gender, Personality, and Local Ecology on Emotional Investment in Romantic Relationships," in *The New Psychology of Love*, ed. Robert Sternberg and Karin Wies (New Haven, CT: Yale University Press, 2006), pp. 249–73.

5. See R. Buck, "The Genetics and Biology of True Love: Prosocial Biological Affects and the Left Hemisphere," *Psychological Review* (2002), 109, 739–44; L. M. Diamond, "Emerging Perspectives on Distinctions Between Romantic Love and Sexual Desire," *Current Directions in Psychological Science* 13 (2004): 116–19; and T. R. Insel and L. J. Young, "The Neurobiology of Attachment," *Nature Reviews Neuroscience* 2, (1997) 129–36.

6. Helen Fisher, *Why We Love: The Nature and Chemistry of Romantic Love* (New York: Henry Holt, 2004).

7. Ibid., p. 81.

8. Ibid., p. 55.

9. See John Bowlby, *Attachment and Loss*, 3 vols. (New York: Basic Books, 1969, 1973, 1980). See also I. Bretherton, "Attachment Theory: Retrospect and Prospect," in

"Growing Points in Attachment Theory and Research," ed. I. Bretherton and E. Waters, special issue, *Monographs of the Society for Research in Child Development* 50, nos. 1–2, serial no. 209 (1985): 3–35.

10. Bowlby, *Attachment and Loss*, vol. 3, p. 40.

11. An excellent overview of current attachment theory and the psychological study of religion can be found in Lee Kirkpatrick, *Attachment, Evolution, and the Psychology of Religion* (New York: Guilford, 2005).

12. Schmitt, "Evolutionary and Cross-Cultural Perspectives on Love," in Sternberg and Wies, *New Psychology of Love*, p. 252.

13. Especially helpful in this connection is Jeffrey Kripal's essay "Sexuality," in *Encyclopedia of Religion*, 12:8241–47. Readers might also wish to examine his accompanying article, "Phallus and Vagina," 10:7017–26.

14. See Sigmund Freud, "Three Essays on the Theory of Sexuality," in *The Standard Edition* (London: Hogarth, 1953), 7:130–243; and "The Sexual Life of Human Beings," in *The Complete Introductory Lectures in Psychoanalysis* (London: George Allen & Unwin, 1956), pp. 303–19.

15. See the chapter "How to Do the History of Psychoanalysis: A Reading of Freud's Three Essays on the Theory of Sexuality" in Arnold Davidson's *The Emergence of Sexuality* (Cambridge, MA: Harvard University, 2001) for a more complete examination of Freud's view that the sexual instinct is made up of components and that heterosexual copulation has no privileged connection to the sexual instinct.

16. Carter Heywood, *Touching Our Strength: The Erotic as Power and the Love of God* (San Francisco: Harper & Row, 1989), p. 102. See also Riane Eisler's treatise on how we might construct "a world where pleasure rather than pain can be primary" (p. 12), in *Sacred Pleasure: Sex, Myth, and the Politics of the Body* (San Francisco: HarperSanFrancisco, 1995).

17. For a more complete discussion of the relationship between Freud's and Jung's understandings of libido, see Murray Stein's "From Freud to Jung and Beyond," in *The Fires of Desire: Erotic Energies and the Spiritual Quest*, ed. Frederica Halligan and John Shea (New York: Crossroad, 1992), pp. 27–40

18. See Ann Belford Ulanov, "The Holding Self: Jung and the Desire for Being," in Halligan and Shea, *The Fires of Desire*, pp. 146–70.

19. George Bataille, *Eroticism: Death and Sensuality*, trans. Mary Dalwood (San Francisco: City Lights Books, 1986), p. 11. Bataille's interpretation of sexuality stems from his premise that human beings are discontinuous, that we live life as isolated individuals. Eroticism, he claims, represents the yearning for profound continuity, to go beyond discontinuous modes of living. To this extent, all eroticism has a sacramental character. What is more obscure in Bataille's thought is his further premise that "death means continuity of being" and eroticism thus hints of and aims toward death.

20. Ibid., p. 19

21. Romans 8:6–8. (Revised Standard Version)

22. Romans 6:12.

23. Kripal, "Sexuality," in *Encyclopedia of Religion*, 12:8241–43.

24. Lawrence Foster, *Religion and Sexuality: The Shakers, the Mormons, and Oneida Community* (Urbana: University of Illinois Press, 1984).

25. Ibid., p. 25.

26. Calvin Green, cited in Foster, *Religion and Sexuality*, p. 34.

27. Foster, *Religion and Sexuality*, p. 39.

28. The best book-length study of Joseph Smith and the rise of Mormonism is probably Jan Shipps' *Mormonism: The Story of a New Religious Tradition* (Urbana: University of Illinois Press, 1985). The source containing the most serious allegations concerning Joseph Smith's sexual improprieties is Fawn Brodie's controversial biography *No Man Knows My History: The Life of Joseph Smith, the Mormon Prophet* (New York: Alfred A. Knopf, 1945).

29. Two Mormon scholars, Leonard J. Arrington and Davis Bitton, have estimated that between 1850 and 1890, no more than 5 percent of all Mormon men and 12 percent of all Mormon women entered into plural marriages. See their overview of the entire polygamy issue in *The Mormon Experience: A History of the Latter-day Saints* (New York: Alfred A. Knopf, 1979).

30. In addition to Foster's excellent account of the sexual themes played out in the Oneida Community's history, this overview also relies upon the brief summaries of the movement in Winthrop Hudson, *Religion in America* (New York: Charles Scribner's Sons, 1973), and Nik Douglas, *Spiritual Sex: Secrets of Tantra from the Ice Age to the New Millennium* (New York: Pocket Books, 1997), pp. 177–80.

31. John Humphrey Noyes, cited in Hudson, *Religion in America*, p. 186.

32. Noyes, cited in Foster, *Religion and Sexuality*, p. 73.

33. Noyes, cited in Douglas, *Spiritual Sex*, p. 177.

34. Noyes, cited in Foster, *Religion and Sexuality*, p. 91.

35. Ibid.

36. Noyes, cited in Douglas, *Spiritual Sex*, p. 178.

37. Douglas, *Spiritual Sex*, p. 178.

38. Noyes, cited in Douglas, *Spiritual Sex*, p. 179.

39. Felicitas Goodman, *Ecstasy, Ritual, and Alternate Reality* (Bloomington: Indiana University Press, 1988), p. 41.

40. Patrick Olivelle, "Orgasmic Rapture and Divine Ecstasy: The Semantic History of Ananda," *Journal of Indian Philosophy* 25 (1997): 159.

41. Ibid.

42. James Leuba, *The Psychology of Religious Mysticism* (Boston: Routledge & Kegan Paul, 1925), p. 138. I might note that a phone call made to a local psychiatrist specializing in treatment of sexual dysfunction elicited numerous anecdotes seemingly confirming the ubiquity of cases in which religious devotionalism is associated with auto-erotic stimulation. Dr. Richard Grant shared with me anonymous anecdotes of men and women, who reported strong and lasting erections while praying in church and women who found that intense Bible reading often led to the most pleasurable orgasms they had ever experienced (one woman, incidentally, believed that this was God's way of rewarding her for her piety).

43. Ibid., p. 144.

44. See "Sex with Angels," in Jeffrey Kripal, *Esalen: America and the Religion of No Religion* (Chicago: University of Chicago Press, 2007), pp. 349–52. Kripal reminds us that in Genesis 6:2 (Revised Standard Version), we learn how a host of horny "sons of god" seek and have sex with the "daughters of men." Such "sex with angels" later transformed into the medieval succubi and incubi traditions involving male and female demons that come at night to have sex with humans while they sleep and late medieval witchcraft traditions of having sex with the devil. A more modern twist on these themes entails accounts of sexual liaisons between humans and extraterrestrials who visit earth in UFOs. See Paul Deane, *Sex and the Paranormal: Human Encounters with the Supernatural* (London: Vega, 2003).

45. Aimee Semple McPherson, *This Is That: Personal Experiences, Sermons, and Writings* (Los Angeles: Echo Park Evangelistic Association, 1919), p. 44. This passage from McPherson's autobiography can also be found in William McLoughlin's "Aimee Semple McPherson: Your Sister in the King's Glad Service," *Journal of Popular Culture* 1 (Winter 1967): 193–217.

46. Peter Gardella, *Innocent Ecstasy: How Christianity Gave America an Ethic of Sexual Pleasure* (New York: Oxford University Press, 1985), p. 82.

47. Ibid.

48. See Mary Jane Sherfey, *The Nature and Evolution of Female Sexuality* (New York: Vintage, 1973). Her summary of studies of female sexual response is found at pp. 62–114.

49. Gardella, *Innocent Ecstasy*, p. 83.

50. Transcribed from a documentary titled *Religious America: Lighthouse in Loleta*, produced by Philip Garvin for WCBH, Boston (1972).

51. Ibid.

52. Ibid.

53. Jeffrey Kripal, *Roads of Excess*, pp. 16–18.

54. Ibid., p. 12. Kripal is here citing a phrase found in Don Kulick, "The Sexual Life of Anthropologists: Erotic Subjectivity and Ethnographic Work," introduction to *Taboo: Sex, Identity and Erotic Subjectivity in Anthropological Fieldwork*, ed. Don Kulick and Margaret Willson (Urbana: University of Illinois Press, 1986), p. 5.

55. The best starting points for an introduction to tantrism are David Gordon White's "Tantrism" and Brian K. Smith's "Hindu Tantrism," both in the *Encyclopedia of Religion*, 13:8984–94. Also helpful are Hugh Urban, *Tantra: Sex, Secrecy, and Power in the Study of Religion* (Berkeley: University of California Press, 2003); Ronald Davidson, *Indian Esoteric Buddhism: A Social History of the Tantric Movement* (New York: Columbia University Press, 2002); Bernard Faure, *The Red Thread: Buddhist Approaches to Sexuality* (Princeton, NJ: Princeton University Press, 1998); and David GordonWhite, *Kiss of the Yogini: "Tantric Sex" in Its South Asian Contexts* (Chicago: University of Chicago Press, 2003).

56. Brian K. Smith, "Hindu Trantrism," in *Encyclopedia of Religion*, 13:8987.

57. Adapted from Brian K. Smith, "Hindu Trantrism," in *Encyclopedia of Religion*, 13:8990–93.

58. For an extremely helpful overview of how Western esotericism has fed into contemporary alternative spirituality in the United States, see Wouter Hanegraaff's *New Age Religion and Western Culture: Esotericism in the Mirror of Secular Thought* (Albany: State University of New York Press, 1998), as well as his article "Human Potential before Esalen," in *On the Edge of the Future: Esalen and the Evolution of American Culture*, ed. Jeffrey Kripal and Glenn Shuck (Bloomington: Indiana University Press, 2005), pp. 17–44.

59. See John Patrick Deveney, *Paschal Beverly Randolph: A Nineteenth-Century American Spiritualist, Rosicrucian and Sex Magician* (Albany: State University of New York Press, 1997). Deveney's work informs the helpful overviews of Randolph's career found in Hugh Urban, *Tantra*, pp. 215–18, and Hugh Urban, "Magica Sexualis: Sex, Secrecy and Liberation in Modern Western Esotericism," *Journal of the American Academy of Religion* 72 (September 2004): 700–706.

60. Paschal Beverly Randolph, cited in Deveney, *Paschal Beverly Randolph*, p. 218.

61. See the overviews of Pierre Bernard's life in both Hugh Urban's *Tantra* and "Magica Sexualis," as well as in Nik Douglas, *Spiritual Sex*.

62. There is good reason to believe that Bernard did travel in India, or at the very least acquired extensive knowledge about Yoga and other spiritual disciplines from Hindus he met in California. In California he met Swami Ram Tirath who later wrote, "My friend Pierre Bernatrd (Shastri) . . . has attained the highest office of Vedic learning and is the recipient of the greatest honors a Sanskritist can achieve. He perfectly understands our doctrine both in principle and practice. . . . Dr. Pierre Bernadr compares most admirably with the Brahmanical Trantrik High Priests of India" (Douglas, *Spiritual Sex*, p. 193).

63. Douglas, *Spiritual Sex*, p. 196.

64. Pierre Bernard, cited in Urban, *Tantra*, p. 720.

65. Ibid.

66. Charles Boswell, "The Great Fuss and Fume over the Omnipotent Oom," cited in Urban, *Tantra*, p. 721.

67. Urban, "Magica Sexualis," pp. 721–22.

68. Wilhelm Reich, cited in Douglas, *Spiritual Sex*, p. 215.

69. Jeffrey Kripal, *Esalen: America and the Religion of No Religion* (Chicago: University of Chicago Press, 2007), p. 235.

70. Ibid., p. 236.

71. Rosemary Feitis, "Ida Rolf Talks about Rolfing and Physical Reality," in *Bone, Breath and Gesture*, ed. Don Harlon Johnson (Berkeley: North Atlantic Books, 1995), p. 87.

72. The best histories of Esalen are Walter Anderson's *The Upstart Spring: Esalen and the American Awakening* (Reading, MA: Addison Wesley, 1983) and Jeffrey Kripal's *Esalen*. Also of importance are the essays on Esalen's contributions to American psychology and religion, in Kripal and Schuck, *Edge of the Future*.

73. Michael Murphy, cited in Neal Vahle, "Esalen Celebrates Its Silver Anniversary," *New Realities*, September/October 1987, p. 31. See also my discussion of causal language in Esalen's history, "Esalen and the Cultural Boundaries of Metalanguage," in Kripal and Schuck, *Edge of the Future*, pp. 197–223.

74. Alan Watts and Eliot Elifsofon, *Erotic Spirituality* (New York: Macmillan, 1971), p. 14.

75. Jeffrey Hopkins, *Sex, Orgasm, and the Mind of Clear Light* (Berkeley: North Atlantic Books, 1998), pp. 75, 78.

76. See the overview of Tantrism's implication in "The Cult of Ecstasy," in the final chapter of Hugh Urban's *Tantra*, pp. 263.

77. Ibid.

78. Ibid., p. xiii.

CHAPTER SIX

1. This observation is drawn from an insightful article by Matthew Schneirov and Jonathan David Geczik, "Beyond the Culture Wars: The Politics of Alternative Health" in *The Politics of Healing*, ed. Robert Johnston (New York: Routledge, 2004), pp. 245–58. Their article concludes, "The radical impulse in alternative health toward social reconstruction therefore is rooted paradoxically in the private experience of the body and its afflictions. The body registers the costs of progress and becomes the enduring source of efforts at social reconstruction" (256).

2. Patrick Wall, *Pain: The Science of Suffering* (New York: Columbia University Press, 2000), p. 30.

3. Ibid., p. 46.

4. See "Getting to Know Pain," in *Pain Sourcebook*, ed. Allan R. Cook (Detroit: Omnigraphics, 1998), p. 5. This article originally appeared in a June 1996 supplement to *Mayo Clinic Health Letter*.

5. Elaine Scarry, *The Body in Pain: The Making and Unmaking of the World* (New York: Oxford University Press, 1985), p. 4.

6. David Bakan, *Disease, Pain, and Sacrifice: Toward a Psychology of Suffering* (Chicago: University of Chicago Press, 1968), p. 59.

7. Glucklich, *Sacred Pain*, p. 99.

8. Ibid., p. 207.

9. Ibid., p. 15.

10. Ibid., p. 14.

11. See Wilhelm Reich, *Character-Analysis* (New York: Noonday, 1949).

12. Alexander Lowen, *Bioenergetics* (New York: Coward, McCann & Geoghegan, 1975), p. 138. See also James Kepner, *Body Process* (San Francisco: Jossey-Bass, 1993), in which Kepner describes the self as "the system of contacts or interactions with the environment" and explains that "full and adaptive functioning is dependent on contact functions being fully available to the organism to met the changing requirements of interaction in the environment" (10).

13. Ibid., p. 139.

14. Lakoff and Johnson, *Philosophy in the Flesh*. Of particular importance are their discussions of "primary metaphors," pp. 49–57, and "the anatomy of complex metaphor," pp. 60–73.

15. William McLoughlin, *Revivals, Awakenings, and Reform* (Chicago: University of Chicago Press, 1978). McLoughlin's book was published as part of the University of

Chicago Press's highly regarded Chicago History of American Religion Series and, although generating much debate and criticism, has long been recognized as a classic in the field of American religious historiography. See also Anthony Wallace, "Revitalization Movements," *American Anthropology* 58 (1956): 264–81.

16. Erik Erikson, *Young Man Luther* (New York: W. W. Norton, 1962), p. 67. The quotation has been altered from singular to plural pronouns to avoid gender bias.

17. McLoughlin, *Revivals, Awakenings, and Reform*, p. 20.

18. Washington Gladden, "The Fratricide of the Churches," in *The Church and the City*, ed. Robert D. Cross (Indianapolis: Bobbs-Merrill, 1967), p. 55.

19. Victor Turner, *The Ritual Process* (Ithaca, NY: Cornell University Press, 1977), p. 97.

20. George Beard, *American Nervousness* (New York: G. P. Putnam, 1881).

21. Ibid., p. 99.

22. An overview of Quimby's life and thought appears in my *Mesmerism and the American Cure of Souls* (Philadelphia: University of Pennsylvania Press, 1982), pp. 118–36. Readers who wish to further explore Quimby's thought should be warned that many in the New Thought/Mind Cure tradition present slightly skewed interpretations of Quimby's work, due to their misplaced reliance on Horatio Dresser's editorial commentary in his edition of *The Quimby Manuscripts* (New York: Thomas Crowell, 1921). Dresser was so concerned with exonerating Quimby from Mary Baker Eddy's charge that Quimby had been a "mere mesmerist," that Dresser all but obscures the paramount role that mesmerism had in the early development of Quimby's career. Duly cautioned, readers might refer to Charles Braden's *Spirits in Rebellion* (Dallas: Southern Methodist University Press, 1963) and Horatio Dresser's *Health and the Inner Life: An Account of the Life and Teachings of P. P. Quimby* (New York: G. P. Putnam's Sons, 1906).

23. Quimby, *Manuscripts*, p. 180.

24. Ibid., p. 210.

25. Ibid., p. 227.

26. Ibid., p. 243.

27. Cited in Dresser, *Health*, pp. 47–52.

28. Mary Baker Eddy's indebtedness to Quimby has been the subject of heated debate. There is no disputing the fact that Quimby is responsible for Eddy's introduction to mental healing, that for an extended period after her cure she continued to reside near Quimby to learn his system, and that her first public *address* was entitled "P. P. Quimby's Spiritual Science Healing Disease as Opposed to Deism or Rochester-Rapping Spiritualism." Julius Dresser's *The True History of Mental Science* (Boston: Alfred Budge & Sons, 1887) and his son Horatio Dresser's *The History of New Thought* (New York: Crowell Company, 1919) offer impassioned arguments that Mrs. Eddy's writings borrowed heavily upon Quimby's unpublished manuscripts that she either had direct access to or learned directly from his oral teachings. Mary Baker Eddy's most able apologists who argue for the originality of her ideas are Stephen Gottschalk in his *The Emergence of Christian Science in American Life* (Berkeley: University of California Press, 1973) and Robert Peel in his three-volume biography, the first vol-

ume of which is *Mary Baker Eddy: The Years of Discovery* (New York: Holt, Rinehart & Winston, 1966).

29. In his *A Religious History of the American People* (New Haven, CT: Yale University Press, 1972), Sydney Ahlstrom perceptively identifies the "harmonial piety" underlying the many expressions of metaphysical piety found in nineteenth and twentieth century American religion. Harmony piety, he explains, includes all those beliefs and doctrines predicated upon a view of the world "in which spiritual composure, physical health, and even economic well-being are understood to flow from a person's rapport with the cosmos" (1019).

30. Discussions of the probably psychosomatic nature of many of William James's ailments can be found in such biographies as Gerald Myers, *William James: His Life and Thought* (New Haven, CT: Yale University Press, 1986), and Linda Simon, *Genuine Reality: A Life of William James* (New York: Harcourt, Brace, 1998).

31. These passages come from the thinly disguised autobiographical account included in *Varieties of Religious Experience*, p. 134.

32. Ibid., p. 400, emphasis added.

33. William James, *A Pluralistic Universe* (New York: E. P. Dutton, 1971), p. 267. On the preceding page, James states that "these deeper reaches are familiar to evangelical Christianity and to what is nowadays becoming known as 'mind-cure' religion or 'new thought.' "

34. James, *Varieties of Religious Experience*, p. 66.

35. Ibid., p. 412.

36. See Catherine Albanese, "The Subtle Energies of the Spirit: Explorations in Metaphysical and New Age Spirituality," *Journal of the American Academy of Religion* 67 (1999): 305–26.

37. For a more complete discussion of these metaphysical healing systems, see my *Alternative Medicine and American Religious Life* (New York: Oxford University Press, 1989).

38. See Lakoff and Johnson, *Philosophy in the Flesh*, pp. 49–57 and 60–73.

39. See the discussion of healing in Gerhard Kittle, *Theological Dictionary of the New Testament* (Grand Rapids, MI: Eerdmans, 1978), 3:194–315; William Clebsch and Charles Jaekle, *Pastoral Care in Historical Perspective* (New York: Jason Aronson, 1975); and Martin Marty and Kenneth Vaux, eds., *Health/Medicine and the Faith Traditions* (Philadelphia: Fortress, 1982).

40. Mircea Eliade, *Rites and Symbols of Initiation* (New York: Harper & Row, 1965), p. 3. The pronouns have been changed from singular to plural to avoid gender exclusion.

41. Glucklich, *Sacred Pain*, p. 15.

CHAPTER SEVEN

1. George Lakoff, from an interview reported in the online publication *Edge* 51, March 9, 1999.

2. See, for example, Paula Niedenthal, L. Barsalou, P. Winkielman, S. Krath-Gruber, and F. Rie, "Embodiment in Attitudes, Social Perception, and Emotion," *Personality and Social Psychology Review* 9 (2005): 184–211.

3. See Bruce Lincoln's essay "Beverages" in *Encyclopedia of Religion*, 15 vols. (Farmington Hills, MI: Thomson Gale, 2005), 2:847–50.

4. Lakoff and Johnson, *Philosophy in the Flesh*, p. 4.

5. These examples are taken from George Lakoff and Mark Johnson, *Metaphors We Live By* (Chicago: University of Chicago Press, 1980), pp. 14–21.

6. Quotations are from a documentary titled *Religious America: Lighthouse in Loleta*, produced by Philip Garvin for WCBH, Boston (1972), emphasis added.

7. Freud, *Future of an Illusion*. Freud observed that humans are rendered helpless so long as we think that such natural phenomena as disease, death, natural disaster, or weather are purely impersonal forces. But if we construct imaginative images of the world in which these natural phenomena are controlled by humanlike supernatural agents, we can then believe that we have gained some measure of control over our lives. We can, after all, try to influence these supernatural agents using the same strategies (e.g., flattery, bribery, or appeasement) that we use to manipulate fellow human beings. Freud also argued that religion assuages the insecurities of social existence by reinforcing our commitment to moral conduct. Beliefs concerning final judgment and an afterlife provide powerful incentives to abide by our culture's laws, now understood as universal laws overseen by an omnipotent judge and executioner. The strength of our creatively imagined religious beliefs, Freud concluded, is the strength of the subjective interests they are meant to satisfy.

8. George Lakoff and Mark Johnson suggest that there at least three recurring forms of embodied experience that give rise to the notion of a subjective self: (1) the correlation between body control and the control of physical objects; (2) the correlation between being in one's normal surroundings and being able to readily control the physical objects in one's surroundings; and (3) the correlation between how those around us evaluate our actions (and the actions of others) and how we evaluate our own actions. See *Philosophy in the Flesh*, pp. 561–64.

9. Edward O. Wilson, *Sociobiology*, p. 192.

10. Stewart E. Guthrie, *Faces in the Clouds: A New Theory of Religion* (Oxford: Oxford University Press, 1993); Boyer, *Religion Explained*; Atran, *In Gods We Trust*; and Tremlin, *Minds and Gods*.

11. David Tracy, *Blessed Rage for Order* (New York: Seabury, 1978), p. 105.

12. Alfred North Whitehead, *The Function of Reason* (Boston: Beacon, 1956).

13. Hardin, "Population Skeletons," p. 39.

14. William James developed this point in his famous essay, "The Will to Believe." See *The Will to Believe and Other Essays in Popular Philosophy* (1897; Cambridge, MA: Harvard University Press, 1978). See also my review essay, "The Will to Believe: A Centennial Reflection," *Journal of the American Academy of Religion* 64 (Fall 1996): 633–50.

15. Glucklich, *Sacred Pain*, p. 15.

16. See Paula Cooey, *Religious Imagination and the Body: A Feminist Analysis* (New York: Oxford University Press, 1994); Sallie McFague, *The Body of God* (Minneapolis, MN: Augsburg Fortress, 1993); James Nelson, *Body Theology* (Louisville, KY: Westminster/John Knox, 1992); Lisa Isherwood and Elizabeth Stuart, *Introducing Body Theology* (Sheffield, UK: Sheffield Academic Press, 1998); and Riane Eisler, *Sacred Pleasure*. See also Sarah Coakley, ed., *Religion and the Body* (Cambridge: Cambridge University Press, 1997); and Jane Marie Law, ed., *Religious Reflections on the Human Body* (Bloomington: Indiana University Press, 1995).

17. Peter Berger, *The Sacred Canopy: Elements of a Sociological Theory of Religion* (Garden City, NY: Anchor, 1969), p. 180.

18. Ibid.

19. See both Peter Berger's *A Rumor of Angels: Modern Society and the Rediscovery of the Supernatural* (Garden City, NY: Anchor Books, 1970) and—more important— *The Heretical Imperative: Contemporary Possibilities of Religious Affirmation* (Garden City, NY: Anchor Books, 1979).

20. This definition of the function of religious thought is adapted from Don Browning's *Religious Thought and the Modern Psychologies* (Philadelphia: Fortress, 1987), p. 7.

21. Gordon Kaufman, *Theology for a Nuclear Age* (Philadelphia: Westminster, 1985), p. 43.

22. James Leuba, cited in James, *Varieties of Religious Experience*, p. 399.

23. I have broadly sketched my personal over-beliefs in the fourth chapter of my *Ecology of Care* (Louisville: Westminster/John Knox, 1992). I personally lean to some version of the philosophical position known as "panpsychism." Panpsychism holds that the whole of reality is intrinsically psychical. It believes mind or consciousness is present in various degrees and modes of organization throughout the world of matter. From a panpsychic perspective, there is nothing apart from all experience; all things are self-experiencing. Human brains don't create or generate consciousness, they simply organize it. They give it structure and centeredness. Thus when we identify causal factors that give rise to spirituality in the flesh, we are simultaneously describing how a sacred world becomes self-conscious and self-experiencing. Over-beliefs are by their very nature nothing more than hypotheses drawn from the information we have about humanity's quest for a richer, more satisfying life. Even if my current proclivity for panpsychic constructions of the universe should prove consistent with ongoing personal and scientific experience, there are many competing versions of panpsychism that might nonetheless be embraced. Monistic pantheism is one. So, too, is a modified form of dualism that views spiritual influences continuously flowing into the material universe from other metaphysical dimensions. To this extent, radical versions of the Christian doctrine of the Holy Spirit or a version of Hindu Vedanta such as was articulated by Sri Aurobindo might be viewed as having panpsychic implications. Although I am not a Christian, I might conclude by approvingly citing a passage from theologian Sallie McFague's *The Body of God*. McFague suggests the viewing the world as God's body "makes sacred all

embodiment." She then adds that such a conception "moves us in the direction of contemplation, the glory and grandeur of divine creation, an aesthetic awe at unending galactic wonders, while at another level it moves us in the direction of compassionate identification with and service to the fragile, suffering, oppressed bodies that surround us" (135).

Index